Children as Caregivers

Children as Caregivers

Parental and Parentified Children

Chester A. Winton

San Jose State University

Boston   New York   San Francisco
Mexico City   Montreal   Toronto   London   Madrid   Munich   Paris
Hong Kong   Singapore   Tokyo   Cape Town   Sydney

Editor in Chief, Social Sciences: *Karen Hanson*
Series Editor: *Jeff Lasser*
Editorial Assistant: *Andrea Christie*
Marketing Manager: *Judeth Hall*
Production Coordinator: *Christine Tridente*
Composition Buyer: *Linda Cox*
Editorial Production Service: *Chestnut Hill Enterprises, Inc.*
Electronic Composition: *Peggy Cabot, Cabot Computer Services*
Manufacturing Buyer: *JoAnne Sweeney*
Cover Administrator: *Kristina Mose-Libon*

For related titles and support materials, visit our online catalog at www.ablongman.com.

Library of Congress Cataloging-in-Publication Data

Winton, Chester A.
    Children as caregivers : parental and parentified children / Chester A. Winton.
        p.   cm.
    Includes bibliographical references (p.) and index.
    ISBN 0-205-32702-8
       1. Child caregivers.   2. Parenting.   3. Children—Family relationships.   4. Helping behavior in children.   I. Title.

HQ759.67 .W56 2002
305.23—dc21   2002075799

Printed in the United States of America

10   9   8   7   6   5   4   3   2   1   07   06   05   04   03   02

This book is dedicated to my five grandchildren:

Denae White

Renee White

Jacob Rabin

Eliana Rabin

Jillian Edwards

Contents

Acknowledgments

I was most fortunate to receive guidance and training from some outstanding mentors at the University of California, Berkeley, including Herbert Blumer, John Clausen, and Erving Goffman. Their legacy lives on through the work of their grateful students; I am proud to say that I am one of those grateful students. The use of symbolic interaction theory in this book stems from my experience learning from these outstanding teachers.

The completion of this book was facilitated by a difference in pay leave awarded by San Jose State University in the fall of 2000. Several students including Iben Dyke, Kathy Hille, Andrea Hart, and Bonnie Pearlman assisted in the production of this book by doing literature research. I am grateful to the many undergraduate students who gave permission to reproduce their accounts of growing up as parental or parentified children for this book, providing poignant substance to the ideas presented. This book was supported by Jeff Lasser, an editor at Allyn & Bacon and Andrea Christie, his editorial assistant. Editorial improvements were made by editors Mary Ellen Lepionka and Myrna Breskin, and by the copyeditor Julia Penelope, who wove magic with the manuscript. The following reviewers provided important feedback: Julie Albright, California State University at Los Angeles; Ellen C. Baird, Arizona State University; Eunice Y. Bakanic, College of Charleston; John Bedell, California State University at Fullerton; Adam Shapiro, University of Florida; and the collaboration of David M. Klein and Jessica S. Ziembroski, University of Notre Dame. Thanks also go to Carol Axtell Ray, a colleague whose suggestions and support were helpful. Lastly, I would like to thank my wife, Nancy, whose encouragement, patience, and support made the completion of this book possible.

Introduction

This book is about children who are the caretakers of others. There are two roles that children play as caretakers of family members. In family therapy literature these two roles are called parental children and parentified children. **Parental children** act as parents to their siblings. They may feed, dress, groom, and supervise or monitor their brothers and sisters. They may help their siblings with homework or academically tutor them. They may wash their siblings' clothes or bodies. They may discipline their younger siblings much as a parent would. They protect these siblings, insuring their health, safety, and welfare. In families where there is domestic violence or substance abuse, for instance, children may be parental by keeping siblings from harm's way, protecting them as best they can from the physical, verbal, or emotional abuse of others.

    Parentified children act as caretaking parents to their own parents. According to Boszormenyi-Nagy and Spark (1973, 151), "By definition, parentification implies the subjective distortion of a relationship as if one's partner or even children were his [or her] parent." These children tend to the physical and emotional needs of parents who are fatigued by work. They are caretakers of pained or impaired parents who are chronically ill or mentally ill or chemically dependent. These children care for parents who may be wounded from a divorce or from being widowed or being separated from a spouse because of desertion, incarceration, deployment in the military, or the work demands of a partner who must travel frequently. Adult children, too, become parentified when they care for elderly parents who are impaired, socially isolated, or infirm. In this context, adult children sometimes act as parental figures to their own parents.

Children as Caretakers of Others

The literature on parental and parentified children in contemporary families (Chase, 1999; Jurkovic, 1997; Jurkovic, 1998) indicates that such children are the nurturing caretakers of others in their families. In caring for others, these children frequently sacrifice their own needs, their own goals, and their own autonomy to try to maintain stability in their families. As Chase writes:

> Despite numerous descriptions of theories, concepts, and definitions, it is generally believed that parentification in the family entails a functional and/or emotional role reversal in which the child sacrifices his or her own needs for attention, comfort, and guidance in order to accommodate and care for logistical or emotional needs of the parent (Chase, 1999, 5).

Jurkovic (1997) postulates that parentified children often have difficulty relating to their parents in normative ways. The parent may be self-absorbed or distracted by his or her own problems, whether those problems be physical pain and illness, emotional pain or mental illness, relationship problems, or the demands of employment. The child is ignored and neglected, which is detrimental to the child's image of self. The only way in which these children are recognized by the parent and have a relationship with the parent is when the child adopts a caretaking role relative to the parent. This caretaking by children exists in diverse social contexts that will be explored throughout Part II.

Most of the scholarly literature on parental and parentified children has been written by psychologists and family therapists. Little about children in these roles exists in the literature of other disciplines. One goal of this book is to bring to the attention of sociologists, social workers, and other social scientists an awareness of the literature that exists regarding parental and parentified children. One problem is that the language used by psychologists and family therapists to discuss these roles is often different from the language used by scholars in other disciplines. This book is intended to serve as a pseudo-translation to make the ideas espoused by psychologists and family therapists comprehensible to students and scholars in other disciplines.

Previous literature on parental and parentified children elaborates a narrow range of contexts in which these roles exist. This book will identify a broad spectrum of contexts in which children are caregivers to others. Children may become the caretakers of others when there is domestic violence in the household, whether or not that violence is linked to alcohol or drug abuse. In families where there is alcoholism or chemical dependency, a parental gap or vacuum is generally found in the family. This gap exists because of parental impairment created by the abuse of alcohol or drugs by one parent or because the other parent is so busy caring for the chemically dependent parent that the children are neglected. This parental gap is often filled by an older child who becomes the caretaker of siblings, of the caregiving parent, or of the chemically dependent parent, or caregiver to all these people. As alcohol and many drugs reduce inhibitions and trigger volatile emotional responses to others, one often finds a person who abuses alcohol or drugs exhibiting violent or volatile behavior toward others. This creates a context in which children become caretakers of other family members and try to protect them from the emotional volatility of the abusing family member. Children, sometimes quite small in size, try to protect their younger siblings from violence or anger, and they also try to protect one parent from the violence of the other parent.

This protection can take many forms, from physically stepping in between the perpetrator and victim and offering themselves as targets to subtly distracting the volatile, abusive parent from his or her aggression. This detouring maneuver can involve the distractor as a comic or clown who provides humor in what could become a deadly serious episode to verbally maneuver a change of subject away from the source of anger. The detouring might also involve physical distraction of the abusive parent by exhibiting flamboyant behavior that calls attention to the distracting child rather than the target of aggression.

Children also perform caretaking roles when a family member has a chronic physical or mental illness. A child may become the caretaker of the family member who has the illness or the caretaker of those who are primary caretakers of the ill person when those caretakers are exhausted, frustrated, or stressed from their caretaking responsibilities. A child may also become the caretaker of siblings who are left out of the "ill-person-provider" relationship, who are not adequately nurtured by either the ill or the caretakers of the ill person, or who are forgotten, ignored, or abandoned because other family members have all they can handle with the work they are already doing.

Children often are caretakers of brothers and sisters in households where both parents work because their work schedules rarely are coordinated with the children's school schedules, leaving the children to care for themselves in the afternoon between the time school is out and the parents return from work. This problem is particularly acute for single parents who work full time. Single parents often do not have the financial resources to hire caretakers for their children. When older siblings are available, they are free, and they are apt to care for siblings in much the same way as the parent would because their caretaking reflects the style with which they were raised themselves. Single-parent households are sometimes the result of divorce or widowhood. In either case, the single parent is dealing with loss, whether it is the loss of a marriage or the death of a spouse. If a single-person household is the result of an unplanned non-marital birth, the single parent may also have to cope with the loss of his or her dreams of living with the child and the child's other parent as an intact nuclear family unit.

Children are often caretakers of their parents in families that have recently immigrated to the United States. The children often have better English skills, driving skills, and technology skills than their parents, so they serve as translators, chauffeurs, and liaisons between the parents and the outside world. In this way, they are caretakers of their parents, helping the parents to have their needs met.

When there is forced absence of a parent from a family, such as when a parent is incarcerated or called up for active military duty, a parenting gap or vacuum is created within the family. That vacuum is often filled by a child who performs the tasks that were formerly performed by the parent. This can be caretaking younger siblings (being a parental child) or being a spouse substitute for the parent who remains (being a parentified child). The parentified child acts as companion, friend, confidante, and source of emotional support for the remaining parent. This also occurs in widowhood, when a parent is lost to the family through death.

With adults living longer, the parentification of adult children occurs when adult children become the primary caregivers of their elderly parents, providing their parents with financial, as well as emotional, support. The emotional support exists in the form of visiting these parents, calling them on the phone, chauffeuring them to doctors and other appointments, and being available in times of crisis or stress, when the parents need assurance that people are available as sources of support.

One finds parental and parentified children in large families, where the care of children requires more time and energy than one or both parents can generate. Older children in large families sometimes help the parent financially through their own gainful employment. Older children become parental children when they assist parents in caretaking younger siblings, feeding them, changing diapers, supervising, baby-sitting, or helping younger siblings with their homework. Children become parentified in large families when they serve as friends, confidantes, cheerleaders, or provide emotional support for exhausted, drained parents who are doing as much as they can on a daily basis to feed, clothe, shelter and nurture their many children.

These are some of the many contexts in which children serve as the caretakers of others. This broad array of contexts will be examined throughout *Children as Caregivers,* demonstrating that children are not helpless, dependent people but are important resources in families, acting as caregivers to others. In a world where adults occupy most of their waking hours working outside the family to meet the demands of employers and supervisors, the labor of children as caregivers becomes a critical resource for family survival.

Child Caretaker Roles as Pathology

Psychologists and family therapists tend to write about the roles of parental and parentified children as forms of pathology, labeling them pathological or pathogenic for several reasons. First, the roles are seen as statistically abnormal because the number of children who perform these roles is believed to be on the periphery of a normal curve; few children are seen as playing these roles.

These caretaking roles also are seen as pathological because the consequences of performing them can be detrimental and often play a part in the development of maladaptive personality characteristics. Children who play these roles often grow up to be adults who are serious, competent, compulsive perfectionists, perpetuating their caretaking role as adults. They are attracted to occupations in which they can care for others, just as they cared for others in their families of origin—teaching, social work, psychotherapy, nursing, child care, or geriatric work. Caretaking roles in childhood also may affect the nature of a person's intimate relationships as an adult: caretaker children tend to be attracted to people they can take care of, dependent, needy, perhaps incompetent, people. The caretaking done as a child is thus maintained in the adult lives of many of these children.

Some writers see parental and parentified children as pathological from a developmental perspective (Boszormenyi-Nagy, 1973; Chase, 1999; Jurkovic, 1997). Children may be expected to perform tasks that are beyond their developmental abilities, for example, and meeting unrealistic expectations may be impossible, setting the children up for failure. Keeping an alcoholic parent from drinking or preventing an abusive dad from hitting mom are also examples where children assume responsibilites that are impossible for them to successfully execute. In other cases, the children can successfully complete the tasks, but with such anxiety and stress that they pay a heavy price emotionally. Supervising and protecting the health and safety of younger siblings can be stressful and produce anxiety for adults and can overburden and overwhelm children. Valleau et al. (1995, 158) define excessive responsibilities that are assumed by children when they are destructively parentified. Childhood responsibilities become excessive when: (1) the child is overburdened with them; (2) the child is charged with responsibilities that are beyond his or her developmental competencies; (3) the parents assume complementary, child-like roles in relation to the child; (4) the child's best interests are unnecessarily and excessively neglected in the role assignments; and (5) the child is not explicitly legitimized in his or her parental roles and is, perhaps, even punished for enacting them.

The roles of parental and parentified children also are seen as pathological because they are perceived as constituting the unethical use and treatment of children. This is the perspective taken by two of the major pioneering authors on this subject, Ivan

Boszormenyi-Nagy and Gregory Jurkovic, who believe that children have a right to be supervised, cared for, nurtured, loved, and guided by parents, whose job it is to set developmentally appropriate behavioral expectations for children. When children become destructively parental or parentified, it often is because of neglect, abandonment, or exploitation of these children by parents. The work of these researchers will be explored in the next chapter.

Child Caretaker Roles as Deviance

Sociologists do not generally use the concept "pathology," using instead the concept of "deviance." For sociologists, there are at least two kinds of social norms: statistical norms and ethical norms (Bierstedt, 1957). **Statistical norms** reflect what most people do, how most people behave. **Ethical norms** are "shoulds," rules that prescribe what people should do and how they should behave. Ethical norms range from mores to folkways, depending on the severity of the sanctions imposed for deviance from those norms. Mores, which include laws, can be sanctioned severely with death or imprisonment. Folkways are norms that are weakly sanctioned by verbal rebuke, raised eyebrows, or frowns.

There is no necessary congruence between ethical and statistical norms. Ethical norms prescribe that people should not jaywalk across streets, but rather should cross in crosswalks in conformity with traffic lights (only crossing the street on a green light). Around the campus where this author teaches, jaywalking is commonplace, in part because violations of this norm are rarely sanctioned by authorities. In California, although the speed limit on freeways is 65 miles per hour, most drivers can be observed exceeding the ethical norm, the speed limit, by at least five miles per hour, again because minor violations of the speed limit are rarely sanctioned by police.

In Chapter 1, a norm is explored that reflects a white, European, middle-class expectation that parents in families should be the caretakers of children. This norm is reinforced by television shows that portray a vision of family life, a normative standard of families, in which children lead largely play-filled, carefree lives relatively devoid of work or responsibility. On television, children often exist for comic relief, to be cute or problematic in their juvenile irresponsibility or incompetence. There is a linear view of family life in these shows that parents give and children receive what the parents give, whether that be money, social status, love, attention, affection, food, discipline, or caretaking. When children are caretakers of others in families, this violates a normative standard reflected in these shows and, thus, constitutes deviance.

Child Caretaker Roles as Normative

One purpose of this book is to suggest that the parental or parentified child is neither pathological nor deviant. These roles do not constitute deviance from an expected role relationship between parents and children because not all cultures maintain role expectations of parents and children that are held by the white, middle-class, European families often depicted on television. In many African American families, in many Mexican

American families, in many Chinese and Vietnamese families, in many working-class and poor families, there is an expectation of mutual interdependence among family members. Life is seen as a difficult, sometimes painful, struggle for survival, and this struggle is shared among family members. There is an expectation that family members will help each other and are integrated in a division of labor whereby each member contributes to the family welfare to the best of her or his abilities. We do not see the white, middle-class, European view that only parents are givers and children receivers of what the parents can give. In these other families, all members are expected to work and to care for and assist others when possible.

The caretaking responsibilities of parental children or parentified children in non-white, middle-class, European families do not violate norms. Rather, they conform to norms and expectations that exist in the families of many cultures throughout the world. While parents are struggling at work, older siblings are expected to care for younger siblings, and children are expected to care for their parents in their old age. Thus, the roles of parental children and parentified children do not constitute deviance from norms in these cultures. They may seem like deviance from the norms internalized by white, middle-class, European scholars, but they are not deviance from the expectations of people who live in these families, who are members of these social classes or cultures.

The roles of parental and parentified children may further not be pathological because they might not be detrimental to the mental health of the role occupants. Playing these roles under specific circumstances can be harmful to children, and this will be discussed in the final chapter, but the majority of my respondents did not interpret their experience being parental or parentified children as detrimental to them. Many respondents saw their experience in these roles as strengthening them, as teaching them skills for independence and self-sufficiency. They saw these roles as preparing them for assuming the responsibilities of adult life, and they saw playing these roles as helping them strengthen the bonds they had with the people whom they supported, protected, or helped.

Lastly, this book suggests that the roles of parental or parentified children are a normative part of childhood in most contemporary families in the United States. It is this author's premise that these roles are statistically normative in that most children play these roles to some extent at some time during their childhood. The roles may be performed temporarily, such as when a parent falls ill or has surgery and a child is a temporary caretaker of the parent. This book, however, explores the diverse contexts in which children are more than just temporary caretakers of either their siblings or one or both parents. When the contexts are added together, the number of children who exist within at least one of these contexts constitutes a majority of all children in the United States.

The contexts that are discussed in the coming chapters constitute "opportunity structures" for the development of parental or parentified children (Blau, 1994). In these contexts, there is a need for caretaking in the family or a parenting vacuum has been created by one or two parents who are in some way impaired in their ability to provide the nurturance, guidance, leadership, or protection that is needed by other family members. Children become aware of this and then have a choice to make: whether or not they are going to be the ones to fill that void and assume the parental responsibilities that adults cannot or do not fulfill.

Some of the respondents reported assuming the parental or parentified role as a conscious, deliberate, rational process of thought, whereby they constructed their place in the family as a caretaker of others because they saw the need and realized that, if they didn't perform these roles, nobody was likely to do the work that needed to be done. They perceived the need for help and they volunteered for it. Other respondents saw their caretaking of others as being something they fell into, without reflection on their part.

The Significance of Children's Roles

The study of parental and parentified children is important because the existence of these roles is indicative of the fact that our society is currently grappling with making sense of children and defining what childhood is all about. After a number of school shootings, talk shows on radio and television offered diverse perceptions of children. At one end of the spectrum were opinions that they were monsters, uncivilized, out-of-control threats to order, civility, and respect for law. This perspective saw the unruly behavior of children as indicators that our schools and families were failures at civilizing children and that harsher punitive sanctions were needed to deter further deviance. At the other end of the spectrum, children were defined as innocents, the random victims of violence who needed protection. Within U.S. society, there is a debate going on in which adults are trying to understand and interpret children in order to rationalize what to do with them, how to behave toward them, what social policies to implement in governing them, and what approaches work to socialize them.

Children have long been workers in families; historically they have functioned as "helpmates," a job that often included the caretaking of others. Primarily through studying depictions of children in art, Aries (1962) described children in medieval Europe as being little adults; they worked with adults, interacted with adults, and dressed like adults. Childhood was not seen as a distinct stage of human existence.

In the sixteenth century, the idea that children are distinct beings who are different from adults and have different developmental needs than adults was introduced. This view of children as different from adults led to the separation of children from adults in the world. As children became removed from the fabric of society, they became more socially isolated from the protection of adults, and more easily exploitable by relatives who were protected by an image of family life as private and a man's house was his castle, surrounded by an invisible moat that kept out the external world.

The Progressive Age was a period between 1880 and 1920 that greatly affected the lives of children. In the United States, legislation in the early twentieth century separated children from the mainstream of adult life by mandating schooling for children. This distanced children from adults by segregating them in their own place, schools. Legislation also separated children from adults in the work world through child labor laws. The laws implemented in the Progressive Age were designed to protect children from corporate and domestic abuse. Children were defined as dependent, fragile, and vulnerable and it was society's job to protect them.

Throughout the contemporary world, we are beginning to blur distinctions that exist between children and adults as different kinds of human beings. Increasingly, children are encouraged to behave as adults, so that behavioral expectations for adults and children are less different than they were at the beginning of the twentieth century. In civil wars throughout the world, we see children as warriors, carrying weaponry and participating in warfare. Pictures from the Middle East flash across television screens depicting Palestinian children throwing rocks or explosive devices. Particularly throughout the Far East, children serve as sexual objects, engaging in prostitution at young ages. Sexuality is not confined to adults; it has become a part of children's lives in many parts of the world. They are functioning as sexual beings. International slave trafficking of children exists, where the labor of children is capital that has exchange value, and children are bought and sold as cheap labor, as workers.

In the United States, we are beginning to blur distinctions that formerly existed between childhood and adulthood. In the juvenile justice system, we are trying juveniles as adults such that age has nothing to do with their definition as children; it is the nature of their behavior, the nature of their crime, that defines them as children or adults.

In the United States, sexuality is not limited to the behavior of adults as child pornography rings exploit children as sexual objects for profit. The millions of dollars spent by consumers of child pornography illustrate that children are seen by many as sexual beings. Further evidence of this interpretation of children exists in the number of children who are victims of child sexual abuse in families.

Adults used to be targeted as consumers of commercial products because it was primarily adults who possessed and controlled money. Now children also are perceived in the corporate world as consumers who make and influence purchasing decisions. Children are the targets of advertising for a wide range of products from toys and clothing to food products, cigarettes, or vacation and leisure time activities (let's go to Disneyland!).

When children are sent to school, it is the equivalent of adults going to work. School for children is similar to work for adults, and adults expect children to work at school. Studying and learning is the work of children, and, just as adults often don't enjoy their work, so children often don't enjoy theirs.

Across a wide range of activities, children are increasingly mirroring the behavior of adults. They are being treated within U.S. society as adults, with behaviors and experiences similar to those of adults imposed on them. Children in families often act like adults and assume the responsibilities that are usually thought of as adult responsibilities, particularly in the caretaking they do by maintaining households, parenting siblings, and parenting their own parents. The parentification of children is one part of a societal struggle to define and interpret children and childhood in this society.

Likewise, we are coming to define and interpret the concept of "parent." Who is a parent? Is a parent an adult who gives birth to a child or adopts a child? Many parents who give birth to a child are not adults; they are fourteen- to seventeen-year-old children, children giving birth to children. One way of looking at parenthood has nothing to do with birthing or adopting, nothing to do with age, but involves looking at the *role* of parent, at parenting behavior, defining a parent in terms of what parents do. Parents nurture, parents supervise and monitor, parents protect, parents feed, clothe, and shelter, parents love and comfort, parents transport, chauffeur, or escort, parents play and entertain. What this book suggests is that children also play the role of parent to their siblings and their own parents; adults are not the only people who play the role of parent. Children are parental toward others and act as parents to other family members so that the question of who is a parent and who is a child is often not so easily answered.

Organization of This Book

In the next chapter, the roles of parental and parentified children are presented in a historical perspective. Throughout the history of the United States, children have been workers, helping their families. However, the context in which children worked changed with the nature of technology. The roles of parental and parentified children developed as an adaptation to changes in the roles of parents in U.S. families. As both parents in intact nuclear families increasingly worked outside the home and as single-parent households increased and the single parent had to be gainfully employed, families experienced a parenting crisis: parents were not available to perform parenting functions. How families fill the parenting void is, in part, a function of social class.

Middle-class families often have the resources to hire day-care providers, or they send their children to after-school activities such as sports programs, dance or music lessons, language or culture classes, or recreation or tutoring programs where adult coaches, teachers, or child-care providers supervise, monitor, or instruct children and protect their health, safety, and welfare. In working-class and poor families, the financial resources are often not available to outsource parenting to others, so low-cost or no-cost alternative parental figures must be found within the family. Some families enlist the services of adult relatives who might be available for child care such as grandparents, aunts, uncles, or cousins. In the absence of relatives, older children are enlisted to assume the parental responsibilities of caring for younger siblings.

In Chapter 1, the caretaking roles of children in families are discussed using a sociological framework called "symbolic interaction theory," which shows how children have been defined differently throughout history. For example, farm children were defined as economically productive as they helped their parents to plant and harvest crops. Then, with industrialization, children from working-class and poor families worked in factories, textile mills, and in cities, filling many types of jobs to help their families financially. The paid work of children in families who had recently immigrated to this country was critical in enabling these families to survive, but child labor laws were created in the twentieth century that did not permit children to be significantly employed, and they went from being economic assets to economic liabilities. In the twentieth century, the labor of children did not generate income, but their labor could still be economically advantageous because it could reduce family expenses, enabling families to avoid hiring outside labor to babysit, clean the house, do laundry, or cook food. Using symbolic interaction theory, Chapter 2 describes pioneers who wrote about parental and parentified children, the pioneers who labeled and conceptualized these roles. These pioneers were primarily psychologists and family therapists.

Impaired parenting, discussed in Chapter 3, develops when one or both parents has a substance abuse problem, such as alcoholism, which creates the opportunity for the development of parental and parentified children. In the absence of parental competence, older children become parental when they care for their siblings in a way that a parent usually cares for children: feeding them, bathing them, putting them to bed, taking them to school, or helping them with homework. Chemical dependency in parents often creates danger for children in the form of emotional volatility, anger, or aggression that may be directed toward them. Children become parental when they protect their siblings from potential abusive behavior of a parent.

Children of a chemically dependent parent become parentified when they protect a nonaddicted parent from abuse, anger, or violence from the addicted parent. Sometimes the protection of a parent involves deflecting the aggressive behavior of a parent toward themselves, sacrificing themselves to protect another. Sometimes the protection of a parent involves distracting the abusive parent away from harming others or engaging in management of the abusive parent to "chill them out."

Chapter 4 describes diverse households characterized by impaired parenting. Sometimes one finds impaired parenting in two-worker intact nuclear families, when parents cannot create clear boundaries between work and home. They bring work home or are called in to work overtime at any time of the day or night. These parents are so fatigued by work that they function less than optimally as parents at home. Single parents may be impaired by the same work issues, but their social isolation means that they have a limited external support network. Sometimes impaired parenting occurs when a family member experiences debilitating physical or mental illness, and, as a result, a parent's energy has to be focused on the ill person. Impaired parenting is sometimes found in families that have immigrated recently. Because the children are more fluent in English and more highly acculturated to their new country than are their parents, the parents' skills and competencies may not be perceived as being very useful in the United States. The children of these recent immigrants may act as parentified children, translating for them, chauffeuring them places, and serving as liasions between them and the outside world. These children link the family to government agencies, schools, doctors, or neighbors and thus become family spokespersons, negotiators for the family with representatives of the outside community.

People can also be impaired by the aging process. Parentified children are created when adult children care for elderly parents who cannot care for themselves as a consequence of diminished physical or mental functioning. With life expectancy in the United States at seventy-seven years, people are living longer. The fastest growing cohort group is people aged 80 to 105, which means that adults aged forty-five to sixty-five are likely to be part of what is called the "sandwich generation," because they are sandwiched between two dependent generations. Below them is a generation of adult children, who may still be physically and psychologically dependent on them. Above them is a generation of elderly parents, who also may be physically and psychologically dependent on them. Because they are living longer, elderly parents are increasingly taken care of by their adult children. This is one context in which one finds parentified children who have become caretakers for their elderly parents. When one becomes aware of parentified adult children, one can see how the caretaking functions of children extend throughout life, from the cradle to the grave. Children function as caregivers of others far into their adult lives.

Chapters 5 and 6 explore how parental children arise in families after the loss of a parent. Children often adapt to the loss of a parental figure by taking the role of the absent parent, becoming a parent figure to their siblings and, thereby, reducing the effect of the loss for their brothers and sisters. This kind of parental child is often the result of a divorce, discussed in Chapter 5, particularly when one of the divorced parents disappears.

Chapter 6 explores how parental children are created by the death of a parent. Parental children also exist in military families when a parent is called up for active duty. Parental children also exist in families when one or both parents are incarcerated, leaving one parent or nobody to care for the children.

In Chapter 7, destructive parentification is discussed. At its extreme, fulfilling the role of parental or parentified child can involve sacrificing one's own future, one's own goals, in order to stay home and meet the needs of family members. Playing these roles can adversely affect the ability of a child to leave his or her family of origin. The "caretaker syndrome" focuses on how assuming the roles of parental or parentified child as a child can affect one's life as an adult (Valleau, Bergner, & Horton, 1995). Adults carry legacies from their childhood, even if these adults are not cognizant of them. Parental or parentified children, as adults, tend to carry on their role as caregivers. They may exhibit "codependency" traits that have them take on other peoples' problems as their own (Wells, Glickauf-Hughes, & Jones, 1999). They may have difficulty maintaining boundaries between themselves and others as they seek to block others from experiencing the negative consequences of their negative behavior by covering for another, perhaps lying for them, or performing tasks that should have been performed by another but weren't (such as a parent doing a child's homework or writing a child's school report when the child did not do the work or a student who lends a classmate lecture notes when the classmate regularly fails to attend class). Codependency perpetuates symptoms such as procrastination in children or absenteeism in classmates because the person who manifests the syndrome never pays a price for their behavior and thus has no reason to change. The codependent helps out because he or she wants to be nice, helpful, sympathetic, and understanding. Adults who manifest codependent behavior were often parental or parentified children in their families of origin.

Although assuming the roles of parental and parentified children can be destructive for those children who are overburdened by their responsibilities and unable to find a way of extracating themselves from those responsibilities, destructive parentification is only one of several types of parentification. What is not emphasized in the literature on these roles is that most parental and parentified children handle them and survive them. Most of my respondents saw themselves not as victims of their experiences in these roles, but as survivors who became stronger, more resilient adults as a result of the roles they played in their families of origin.

Voices in This Book

Theoretical frameworks are often linked to a distinctive methodology that is logically consistent with a specific framework's principles. The German sociologist Max Weber once wrote that, ". . . the task of sociology is the interpretative understanding of the subjective states of minds of actors." His statement reflects the symbolic interactionist perspective.

The word "understanding" [*verstehen* in German] involves attempting to take the role of the other, trying to get inside someone else's skin in order to feel what he or she feels, to see the world as he or she does, and to be in his or her shoes, experiencing reality as he or she does. One then takes that understanding of reality and interprets it from a theoretical perspective. What is important is understanding the subjective states of minds of actors—their perceptions, thoughts, and feelings. Only when one grasps the subjective state of an actor is it possible to truly understand why that person behaves as he or she does.

Why does a parent physically or sexually abuse a child? To understand that, a researcher must grasp how the parent perceives children, what he or she perceives as the prerogatives and responsibilities of parents, how he or she thinks about him- or herself and the child, what he or she thought the experience was like for the child, what he or she anticipated would happen to him or her as a parent, how he or she felt about the sexual activity with the child. The answer to such questions can only be obtained through in-depth interviews with respondents. In-depth interviewing is the preferred method of conducting social research for the symbolic interactionist. One cannot grasp the complexity of perceptions and definitions and their link to behavior by administering a questionnaire.

The technique used to collect data for this book is consistent with the methodological writings of Herbert Blumer. Blumer (1969) advocated interviewing informants, who were unusually articulate, verbal, and insightful people, to create hypotheses about the dynamics of social interaction. Once the hypotheses were created, they could be tested by interviewing other, perhaps less articulate and insightful respondents to see if the perceptions and experiences of the informants could be generalized to a larger population.

The eighty-two students who permitted me to use their term papers are my articulate, insightful informants. Instead of conducting personal interviews, I will use their written accounts of what it looked like and felt like to be a parental or parentified child in their family of origin. I have sparingly edited their written accounts and only in order to improve the grammar or revise awkward phrasings. None of my changes have altered the meaning of the students' written words. Their names and the people named in their papers have been changed to protect their confidentiality.

The students' testimony was then combined with the empirical research of other social scientists on children as caregivers. The testimony of the students tends to reinforce and be consistent with the findings of most other researchers who have studied parental and parentified children in diverse contexts.

The students quoted represent diverse racial and ethnic identities, but the numbers for any given racial or ethnic group tend to be small. What needs to be researched more carefully in this field is how some of the propositions in this book relate to specific populations of people using race, ethnicity, social class, and gender as variables.

This book is written by both me and my students as a team project. Students in my undergraduate classes have written papers on parental and parentified children in numerous contexts, and described how they or others they know were parental or parentified children in their families. They have generously granted me permission to quote directly from their papers for this book, with the understanding that their consent or refusal would in no way affect their grade in the class.

Although one may think that quoting a student's paper does not differ from transcribing an audiotape of an interview, the disadvantage of using term paper material is the inability to ask questions or ask for clarification in a give-and-take discussion that would be possible in a semistructured interview. There is no room for dialogue or discussion between interviewer and respondent as there would be in a personal interview. The researcher gets what the student chooses to write with no opportunity for probing further.

I close this introduction with a cautionary tale. I was talking with a secretary who worked at a public elementary school, and she asked me about the book I was writing. I told her it was about children as caregivers. She responded by sharing an observation that she saw two types of children at her school, those who were caregiver children in their families and another type of child who was given no responsibilites at home, who was coddled and treated as a prince or princess by parents. These latter type of children were chauffeured by parents to and from school, and their parents even provided them with hot fast food at lunchtime, which they delivered to their children at the school. These children used cell phones to commandeer their parents to bring them items they forgot. The parents were slaves to their children. This book is not about this latter type of child. The observation of this secretary is that not all children are parental or parentified children, but this book is about the children who do play those roles. From the multiple contexts that are discussed, one might conclude that the number of parental and parentified childen in the United States is sizeable and growing, but to be sure, they are not the only kind of children that exist. With this in mind, we next turn our attention to symbolic interaction theory, the framework that is used to analyze children as caregivers.

Conceptualizing Children as Caregivers

Part I of this book, consisting of Chapters 1 and 2, defines what parental and parentified children are. Chapter 1 focuses on symbolic interaction theory as the analytic framework to be used for interpreting the roles of parental and parentified children. In this chapter, children are analyzed as symbols, capable of assuming multiple meanings. One should not be surprised that children are serving as the caretakers of others in contemporary families in the United States, for a brief history of childhood shows that children have always served as workers in their families. Instead of working in the fields, in textile mills, in factories or stores, contemporary children are working in school and at home. The venue where children work has changed, not their role as workers. Because of child labor laws and mandatory schooling, children are not often gainfully employed today so their work tends to be unrewarded, which can be detrimental to a positive sense of self.

Chapter 2 focuses on the work of three pioneers who have written about parental and parentified children. In this chapter, questions are asked and answered that help to conceptualize the roles of parental and parentified children. Can one be a parental child without being a parentified child? Can one be a parentified child without being a parental child? Can one be a parental and parentified child simultaneously? These questions are addressed in Chapter 2.

1

A Theoretical Perspective for Studying Caregiver Children

The real world is very complex. There is no one theory in sociology that captures all of the diverse aspects of reality, so the discipline of sociology has developed multiple theoretical frameworks and each framework focuses on one element of the real world. One can think of these theoretical frameworks as sets of eyeglasses, each having a different prescription (Winton, 1995). Put on one set of eyeglasses, use one theoretical model, and the viewer sees some aspects of reality clearly while other aspects are blurred. Try on a different set of theoretical eyeglasses and what was formerly clear now is more blurred and what was previously out of focus can clearly be seen. Each theory facilitates perceiving the world differently, with different sets of assumptions and different political biases.

Each of these theoretical frameworks has a distinctive language, a set of concepts that enables the user to talk about reality, to analyze it, describe it, and causally account for why things are as they are. One often selects the theory to be used for analyzing the real world based on how well the theory "fits" that reality, how congruent the theory is with the reality, and how useful the theory is in enabling researchers or writers to comprehend, describe, and account for the reality with which they are confronted.

Symbolic Interaction Theory

Out of many theoretical options available, the roles of parental and parentified children will be analyzed using **symbolic interaction theory,** initiated by George Herbert Mead at the University of Chicago almost one hundred years ago. Mead wrote very little in his lifetime. Most university libraries have a book entitled *Mind, Self and Society,* with Mead as its author, but in fact he did not write that book himself. It was written by his graduate students, who collected their lecture notes and wrote the book under Mead's name, publishing it after his death. They thought it appropriate to list him as the author because the ideas presented in that book were his, as presented in his lectures. The book gets its title from the fact that two of the central concepts of symbolic interaction theory are the "mind" and the "self."

This framework postulates that human behavior is constructed in the mind, through a process of meaningful thought. The framework differs from other sociological perspectives in that it gives the individual significant power to carve out lines of action. The individual is not seen as socially determined by external forces (social class, ethnicity, age, gender, religion) to act in predictable ways or in conformity to social norms. Symbolic interactionists, for instance, diverge from a structural–functional perspective, which views people as constrained by social pressure to conform to social norms. From a symbolic interaction perspective, social norms exist but are taken into account by actors who interpret or give meaning to the norms and decide whether to conform to the norms that exist or violate them. Individuals are seen as having the ability to construct their behavior through cognitive processes that occur in the mind.

Mead's Concept of the Mind

According to Mead, the mind refers to the ability people have to make indications to themselves, their ability to think. In this theory, individuals are seen as constructing their own lines of action based on a rational thought process. How people think and what they think about affects their behavior.

The process by which the behavior of individuals is constructed involves first defining a situation—giving meaning to objects and events in a situation. Next one considers alternatives that are available to deal with or respond to that situation. There may be available alternatives of which a person is not aware. If people are unaware of an option, they cannot choose it. They can only select from the options they know about. This is why it is sometimes helpful to discuss a situation with others: in that discussion, options may come to light that had not previously been considered. One consequence of therapy, for instance, is to expand a client's awareness of options for dealing with difficult situations, options that were not previously considered. Lastly, one anticipates the consequences of the various options. The result of this process is to carve out or construct a line of action relative to a situation. For Mead, these are the three dimensions that comprise the various indications that people make to themselves in constructing their behavior toward others.

The behavior of individuals is affected by how they define a situation. In a classic quote, W. I. and D. S. Thomas (1928) wrote: "if men [and women] define situations as real, they [the definitions] are real in their consequences." How a situation is defined will influence how the individual or group will act in that situation.

Mead's Concept of the Self

Mead defined the self as the ability of people to step outside themselves and relate to themselves as they would relate to any object in their external environment. People can take objects in their external environment and describe their height, weight, shape, or color and they can do this with themselves. They can describe their own height, weight, shape, or color. They can look at other people and describe how they act most of the time, saying that they are happy or energetic, critical or moody, lethargic or depressed. Likewise, people can step outside themselves and describe their own behavior most of the time, their strengths and weaknesses, competencies and incompetencies. How you define yourself can affect how you anticipate consequences of potential lines of action. For example, if you have low self-esteem and underestimate your competencies, you are likely to eliminate many options by anticipating that they will turn out badly for you. Your perception of yourself affects whether you are being an optimist or a pessimist when you anticipate the consequences of alternatives you have available to you.

One can act toward oneself just as one might act toward any object in the external world. You can prod yourself, praise yourself, dress yourself, feed yourself, and talk to yourself, which is thinking.

Mead described two parts of the self, the "I" and the "me." The "I" is the spontaneous self, manifesting behavior that is reflexive and devoid of rational thought. One hears bad news and suddenly bursts into tears without reflecting on what others would think, how the crying might make them feel uncomfortable or at a loss for how to react to the crying, or how he or she might make others sad also. The individual just spontaneously bursts into tears.

The "me" part of the self is a thinking self, a rational self, a reflective self that calculates action rationally. The vast majority of behavior is what Mead called "meaningful behavior," behavior that arises from thought. Mead was only interested in meaningful behavior; he had no interest in "non-meaningful behavior" that was a part of the "I," though he recognized that a minute portion of behavior was spontaneous.

For Mead and for all social interactionists, the self is ultimately a social self. It is social because the self only makes sense in the context of others. People give themselves meaning from what others tell them about themselves. The concept of self arises out of interaction with others. People have meaning in terms of how they are like and how they are different from others.

The identity of a caregiver is also ultimately social. One cannot be a caregiver unless there is an "other" to be cared for. The role of caregiver implies social interaction; it is a concept that makes sense only in a context of interpersonal interaction. It is a concept that assumes complementarity relative to others. The roles of parental and parentified children only exist vis à vis another who is parented by the child.

Sociologists study the behavior of people in groups, such as families. Sociologists study the interaction between an individual and others that exist in that individual's sociocultural environment. By studying children as caretakers, we are at the heart of sociology as a discipline because sociologists study interpersonal interaction. Caregiving involves interpersonal interaction. Such interaction in the context of caretaking requires a look at how the behavior of others creates an opportunity for the development of parental or parentified children and how assuming that role affects others in the family. Sociologists study social processes over time, thus it is appropriate to ask how caretaking by children affects their relationships with others later in their lives.

Cooley's Concept of the Looking-Glass Self

How do we come to know about ourselves? How do we know that we are happy or energetic or moody or critical? Charles Horton Cooley addressed these questions in what he called the "looking-glass self." Cooley believed that we internalize the appraisals of others about us. We hear others talk about us or they tell us what they think of us. Children are told by parents and peers that they are smart or stupid, full of energy or lazy, athletically skilled or incompetent, mechanically talented or incompetent, a whiz at math or a terrible speller. For Cooley, people are like sponges, absorbing the appraisals of others. Our image of ourselves is, thus, a mirror image of what other people tell us about ourselves. Our image of self is a reflection of what we hear from other people.

Mead did not agree with Cooley's notion of the looking-glass self. Mead believed that people do not just soak up appraisals from others; rather, they act as filters, interpreting these appraisals. If someone says something negative or critical of us, we may discount the negativity by defining or interpreting these negative comments as envy or jealousy or by interpreting the critical person as tired or having a bad day. If someone says positive things about us, we may define and interpret the observer as being insightful and astute, thus giving considerable weight to the person's analysis. People analyze, interpret, and give meaning to the appraisals of others in constructing an image of self.

We can act toward oneselves, just as we can act toward any object in the external environment. If I encounter a chair, I can sit on it or lean on it. I can pick it up and throw it, using it as a weapon. I can pick it up to defend myself. I can take an ax to it and chop it up in a fit of anger. Just as one can act toward a chair, so one can act toward oneself. I feed myself, dress myself, bathe myself, praise myself, prod myself, and talk to myself. Thinking is little more than talking to ourselves. How we think and what we can think about is constrained by the language we use to talk to ourselves or to think.

How we defines ourselves, how we perceive our competencies and incompetencies, affects how we will anticipate the consequences of alternatives available to us in dealing with difficult situations. Someone who has a poor self-image is likely to anticipate negative consequences from most alternatives he or she considers as potential lines of action, often feeling stymied by difficult situations. People who have been parental or parentified children can develop a rather weak and ineffectual sense of self when, over and over again, during most of their childhood, they tried and failed to improve situations that were impossible to alter. Such situations exist when children try to stop the drinking of an alcoholic parent and take it as their failure when the parent relapses; when they try to alter the behavior of a parent who is mentally ill and refuses to seek professional help for erratic or irrational behavior; and when they want to but cannot stop a parent's recurrent criminal behavior.

People who spend most of their childhood as caretakers of others develop an identity as a caretaker of others, and that identity may affect the kinds of intimate relationships they develop with others. They may only be attracted to people they can take care of, for example, people who are insecure, needy, incompetent, or in some way impaired. People who spend their childhood as caretakers may also be attracted to occupations that require them to care for others, such as nursing, teaching, therapy, social work, geriatric work, or child care.

Blumer's Concept of Symbolic Interaction

One of the graduate students taught by George Herbert Mead was Herbert Blumer. Herbert Blumer (1908–1987) was a gentle giant, an all-American football player at William and Mary and a professional football player for the Chicago Bears. He was a superb teacher at the University of California, Berkeley, where he was a supportive mentor of many graduate students, and eventually became president of the American Sociological Association, the major professional association of sociologists in the United States.

Blumer gave symbolic interaction theory its name. A symbol is any phenomenon that can have multiple meanings. Words are symbols. The word *stardust,* for instance, can mean the Milky Way, a hotel in Las Vegas, or a song by Hogey Carmichael. One only gets the meaning of a word from the context in which that word exists. When someone says "I love you," the speaker can mean "I like you," "I'm attracted to you," "I like being with you," "I want to own you," "I want to marry you," or "I want to have sex with you." Gestures are also symbols, and the same gesture can have very different meanings in different cultures throughout the world. Behavior or action is a symbol. When someone speaks to you, you have to interpret, give meaning to what he or she has said and decipher whether they are trying to be funny or sarcastic or belittling and disrespecting you, being hostile or sexually coming on to you.

For Blumer (1969), action is constructed in our mind by defining the situation, defining or giving meaning to the behavior of another, to whom we respond, considering alternatives of action that we have available to us in response to the other, and then anticipating the outcome of the various alternatives. We respond and then the other must interpret our response, give meaning to our response. Social interaction thus becomes a circular process whereby two actors are constructing their behavior toward each other by interpreting the action of the other. Behavior is, thus, a symbol, capable of having multiple meanings. The meaning one attaches to the behavior of others will influence the response made to the other.

Goffman's Concept of Behavior as Theatrical Performance

Erving Goffman is thought to have developed what is called the "dramaturgical approach" to sociology. He agreed with Shakespeare that "all the world's a stage" and that all people are actors, playing out a theatrical performance for an audience of others, and the title of his first book, *Presentation of Self in Everyday Life,* reflects his theory of social interaction. Goffman defined human behavior as a theatrical performance designed to manage our identity in the eyes of others, constructing or manufacturing how others perceive us.

When people prepare for a job interview, they go to their closet to select a costume for their theatrical performance. They select clothing that they think will help them create a favorable image of themselves in the mind of the interviewer. They try to present themselves as professional, mature, competent, stable, reliable, and dependable. They try to manufacture an image in the interviewer's mind such that the interviewer will be so impressed that he or she will offer the candidate a job. Conversely, the interviewer tries to convey an image of the company such that, if a job is offered, the applicant will accept it.

During the process of interaction, our image of another is constructed by that other; we are consumers of the theatrical performance of others. If that person succeeds in "selling" us that image, we will see the individual as he or she wants to be perceived, just as we are constructing an image for that person. Social interaction, for Goffman, is a mutual process of impression management in which each person is trying to manage his or her identity in the eyes of others.

Goffman was interested in con-men and their ability to construct an image in our minds of who they are so that they can exploit us. A robber, for example, can gain access to our residence by dressing as a utility or phone repairperson dressed in a uniform because we tend to assume that people who are in uniform are who they appear to be; the uniform constitutes a badge of legitimacy and reassures us of our perception of reality. Let's say that it is November or December and this person rings the doorbell and announces that the utility company has noticed that our usage has increased signficantly (information that would only be known by an employee, assuring us further of the person's legitimacy, but everybody's utility bill goes up during the winter because it is colder and we use more heat) and has sent this person to look for potential gas leaks. We give this person access to the inside of the house, because, if leaks are found, he or she will save us money so is of potential benefit to us. The person goes through the house, surreptitiously pocketing valuables he or she finds in various rooms. The person has successfully constructed in our minds an image of who he or she claims to be—a repairperson—and uses this image to exploit us.

The movie *The Sting* nicely illustrates how realities can be constructed. People tend to assume that settings with lots of noisy equipment running is what it appears to be. So, if a bookmaking operation is installed behind a Western Union telegraph office or a bank, it would function as a front for what is actually a gambling establishment. Because the noise of the machines would assure us, we would never question whether the telegraph office or bank is what it appears to be. The con-men successfully constructed a reality that others consumed.

George Herbert Mead, long deceased before Goffman's writing, would probably have thought that Goffman presents people as too passive. For Mead, people would not just passively consume others' performances, but would define, interpret, and analyze their performance and give meaning to that performance. People can see through fronts and interpret someone as phony or contrived, as not what he or she appears to be.

Fronts are not only constructed by individuals but by organizations. This is what advertising does; it creates an idealized image of an organization, whether that be a corporation or a branch of the armed forces, to construct in the mind of the viewer an image that works as a corporate identity.

Goffman's work on life as drama, as a theatrical performance, focuses on the nature of social roles. When an actor is in rehearsal for a performance, the actor practices taking on the role of another, acting as someone who is not really them, but they project themselves onto the character they are enacting. This metaphor of actors, playing out roles, is relevant to children playing the role of parental or parentified children. In acting out a performance, the actor behaves "as if" they were the character being played. Parental and parentified children behave "as if" they were adults, even though they are really children. They execute adult-like responsibilities, playing the role that adults generally play in families, performing tasks that adults normally perform. Parental children behave "as if" they were the parents of younger siblings, even though they really are an older brother or sister. They act the part of a parent. Parentified children play the role of parent to one or both of their own parents, being a nurturant caregiver that in some way eases the pain or lightens the emotional load of those parents. These children develop "lines" or scripts that work for them in getting siblings to do what they need the siblings to do or in comforting parents. In being parental or parentified, these children play out a role in a family drama.

Some children play parental and parentified roles in a family as a hero. When children play the role of family hero, they are strong, reassuring, in-charge, competent, responsible, dependable, and mature. They take their work seriously and they usually come through with flying colors. They are stars academically, in sports, and in most activities they attempt. They are social and are popular, well-liked and respected by peers. Most parental and parentified children perform as heroes.

Other children perform the role of parental or parentified children as villains. They have academic difficulties in school, where they also may exhibit deviant behavior. They may be in trouble with the law. They may abuse alcohol or illegal drugs. As deviants, they caretake other family members by distracting parents from parental pain, depression, or boredom. They mask the pain and suffering that is created by the deviant behavior of other family members, such as a parent's alcohol or drug abuse or parental abuse or neglect, by calling attention to themselves, thereby detouring negative attention that might otherwise be directed at some other family member by focusing negative attention to themselves. In being the center of negative attention, they protect other family members from being sanctioned for their own deficiencies. As this book unfolds, readers will encounter both heroes and villains who serve to protect other family members.

Goffman's Concept of Stigma

Goffman's second book was entitled Sti*gma: Notes of Management of Spoiled Identities*. A stigma is something about us that has the potential of damaging our identity in the eyes of others. Everyone has one or more stigmas, things about us that we have to manage, because, if others knew about it, it could be detrimental to our image in their eyes. A stigma could be a chronic illness, the fact that one has impaired visual or auditory acuity or once had an abortion, or that one has had cancer or has tested positive for HIV. A stigma could be that one has a parent who has an arrest record or is addicted to alcohol or prescription drugs or illegal drugs, or that one's parents are divorced. A stigma could be that a person is a member of a minority religious or ethnic group or is a homosexual. A stigma could involve being held back to retake the first grade. Stigmas can be big or small, and whether they are perceived as big or small is determined by the person who has the stigma. What might seem small to someone else might be big to the person who has the stigma. The problem for the person who has the stigma is to manage the stigma in a way that minimizes its damage to how others perceive that individual.

Many of the respondents interviewed for this book have stigmas related to their childhood. Some students had alcoholic parents, while others had parents who were chronically physically or mentally ill; some had parents who had been incarcerated, widowed, or divorced. For some students, the fact that their parents are recent immigrants to the United States was perceived as a stigma. By writing about these issues, these students revealed a part of their lives that they perceived as stigmas.

In trying to manage these stigmas, one can try to "pass," withholding or hiding information about the stigma. Passing, pretending that the stigma does not exist, is a theatrical performance. This strategy is detrimental to the development of intimacy in relationships. Intimacy involves a mutual sharing of self, sharing information with others about who you are, what you think, how you feel, where you have been, and what you have done throughout your life. The development of intimacy requires mutual self-disclosure. Hiding stigmas, keeping secrets, is a failure to fully self-disclose. When the stigma is eventually discovered, it undermines the other person's trust in the relationship because the partner feels he or she cannot fully trust in the honesty and forthrightness of the other.

Another way of dealing with stigmas is to reveal their existence. People spend hours rehearsing scripts for revealing their stigmas to others, altering wordings and practicing voice inflections so as to minimize the damage that may result from the revelation. Generally, if one conveys to others that he or she feels OK about the stigma, others will pick up on this and it will also be OK with them. The way one conveys one's own cognitive and emotional stance relative to the stigma is critical in constructing how others respond to it.

Theatrical performances are played out in what Goffman calls "front regions," places in which the performance is played out for an audience. In homes, living rooms and dining rooms tend to be front regions. Back regions are where actors prepare for the performance. Bedrooms, kitchens, and bathrooms are often back regions where costumes are donned or makeup applied. What are usually back regions, however, can become front regions, for example, when company watches dinner prepared in the kitchen. In this case, the kitchen becomes part of the performance and is a front region.

The childhood of many respondents in this book reflects a duality of performances. On the one hand, there is the back region of family life that may involve alcohol abuse, domestic violence, mental illness, or parental crime. On the other hand, this reality must be hidden from the outside world, so they gave outsiders a theatrical performance in an effort to convince them that nothing was wrong. Secrets must be kept; family members must be protected from the shame that would come if the reality of their family life was discovered by others. However, feelings of shame also exist when the outside world does not know the family secret. Out of this shame, parentification is constructed and children protect their parents by playing performances to others that convey a functional family life. The child may be competent, mature, bright, and responsible, but it is all a front to guard against others suspecting that any problems exist.

Theatrical performances are also played out within the family. Constructed diversions are enacted to distract an alcoholic from another drink or an abusive spouse from lashing out and hurting someone. Theatrical performances are enacted for siblings to convey to them a sense of security, a sense that everything is under control when sometimes, inside, the parental child is feeling highly anxious about his or her tasks and far from secure about his or her ability to function as a parent. The protective and caretaking roles of parental and parentified children create an image of self in which identity is linked to the caretaking and they identify themselves as the person who holds everything together, the person who is the rock, the source of stability or sanity or survival on which all others depend. It is this image of self that makes it so difficult for these children to ever leave the family. They fear that, if they left, everything and everyone left would fall apart. If they do manage to leave, they leave with enormous ambivalence and guilt.

Using Symbolic Interactionism: Giving Meaning to Children

How a parent defines children influences how he or she raises and disciplines those children. In this section, we explore two contexts in which children have been defined and interpreted. Children, as symbols, are capable of being defined in multiple ways. The first context in which they are defined deals with the essential nature of infants. Newborn infants have been defined by social scientists as being innately good, evil, or neutral.

Innately Good, Bad, or Neutral?

One can define children as angelic, innately and intrinsically good. This is a position that can be found in the writings of the Enlightenment French philosopher, Jean Jacques Rousseau (1762/1993), who advised parents to back off and give their children the space to allow their innate, natural goodness to develop. This view of children as basically good is congruent with a permissive orientation in raising children.

Rousseau interpreted human beings as being essentially good, however they could be corrupted by the institutions of a civilized society. For instance, he perceived that children were innately good, but he defined teachers in schools as being corrupted, so he advised that schools should be child-centered and not teacher-centered or content-centered. Like Enlightenment philosopher John Locke, he defined children as being naturally cooperative, but they could be corrupted and made competitive and aggressive by external forces. Rousseau's writings are relevant to this book because he saw childhood as not like adulthood and children not like adults. He believed that children had different and special needs. He wrote that children should not be expected to take on adult responsibilities or be forced to live by adult standards. Rousseau would have been disturbed by the widespread development of parental and parentified children in society.

Children have also been defined as inherently neutral, a blank slate to be written on by others. Karl Marx (1906) saw that children could be trained to manifest behaviors congruent with the economic system in which they lived. If children live in a capitalist system of economic competition, they will be trained to be aggressive and competitive and acquisitive. An illustration is the phenomenon of youth sports in our contemporary U.S. society.

Youth sports programs play an important role in training children to be competitive and aggressive; they are a training ground for life in a capitalist business environment. Sports teams symbolically represent corporations that are out to beat the competition.

When the team wins, there is no compassion for the losers and no taking the role of the other or commiserating over how the losers feel. What is learned is to vanquish the competition, a metaphor for corporate warfare. Marx believed that children raised in a socialist society will be trained to be cooperative and to integrate harmoniously into social groups rather than pursue individualistic activity. They will be encouraged to share rather than to individually own toys or other objects. For Marx, children are trained to be what they will have to be given the economic system in which they are raised.

Children also can be defined as inherently evil. Thomas Hobbes was an Enlightenment philosopher who saw children as innately evil. In the writings of Sigmund Freud (1961), children are seen as being capable of considerable evil because Freud believed that children were born with a libido, the sex drive. In his discussion of the Oedipal and Electra complexes, Freud believed that children lust after the parent of their opposite gender and become sexual rivals with the parent of the same gender. The libido has the potential of great destruction if it is unchanneled and uncontrolled by social norms that regulate sex. These norms are needed to prevent incest, rape, and sexual assault and to protect people from each other, for if the sex drive of people is uncontrolled by society, there will be a junglelike existence of "might makes right," a sexual war of all against all.

Children, as symbols, can be defined and interpreted in multiple ways. They can be perceived as being basically good or evil or they can be seen as innately neutral but capable of being made good or evil, depending on the economic system in which they are raised. How children are defined by adults will influence how children are treated by those adults.

Most social scientists believe that children, at birth, are innately either good or neutral because if one believes that children are innately evil, one might as well pack their tent and go home if one aspires to implement social change to improve society. If one believes that people are innately evil, then one will always have an evil society because it is people that make up a society. No matter how much change one seeks, that society will be composed of innately evil people. To avoid this pessimism, most social scientists see children as being inherently good or neutral.

Socially Constructed, Collective Definitions

Symbolic interaction theory is often seen as explaining the behavior of an individual actor, but this theory can also be applied in describing and accounting for the behavior of people in social groups. Mead defined a social group as a collectivity of people who share common definitions of objects (such as children) and events in their environment. Definitions of objects, events, or people are socially constructed through interpersonal interactions between people. Their shared definitions lead them to act toward those objects, events, or people in similar ways. Social groups can share common definitions of children, religion, politics, or specific social causes, wherein they manifest a kind of collective mind. An example of a social group sharing a common definition of children is provided by some Puritan groups in Colonial America.

Many Puritans saw children as being born with the original sin of Adam and Eve (Corsaro, 1997; Kenkel, 1977). Children were defined as inclined to deviance and mayhem, and their misbehavior was evidence of their innate evilness. Parents were encouraged to treat children harshly, to beat the sin out of them, because it was believed that, if the deviance of children was not severely sanctioned, they would bring chaos and grief to all members of the family. Parental hierarchy and discipline were critical to maintaining order and structure in the household. There is some debate among social historians about how severely, in fact, children were disciplined by parents in the early New England Colonies (Pollock, 1983). Those parents who did engage in harsh discipline, because they defined children as inherently evil, illustrate Thomas and Thomas' belief that "if men [and women] define situations as real [children are evil], they [the definitions] are real in their consequences" (1928, p. 572).

Economic Assets or Economic Liabilities?

Children have been collectively defined throughout history as being either economic assets—productive workers expected to be "helpmates" in a family's struggle for survival—or as economic liabilities who are not expected to be gainfully employed or economically productive. The ways in which children are defined in a society affects the ways in which they are treated within that society, whether they are exploited as free labor or coddled as helpless dependents.

The discussion of children as symbols will be structured using Alvin Toffler's (1970, 1984) discussions of three waves of technology. Toffler discusses preindustrial, industrialized, and post-industrial societies as exhibiting three different types of labor. In the first wave, in preindustrial societies, most gainful employment exists in occupations that involve the harvesting of raw materials: fishing, lumbering, mining, and agriculture.

Children in a Preindustrial Society

In ancient times, the Egyptians, Greeks, and Romans all seemed to value children for their labor, for the services they could provide adults. In agriculture, the unpaid labor of children was important. Children were also expected to care for their parents in their old age.

Children in the Middle Ages in Europe had few rights. They were seen as the personal property of their parents, who could submit them for conscription into the military, marry them into another family as a means of enhancing the family's wealth, or they could be offered to a monastery or convent. According to Greenleaf (1978), children in medieval Europe actually spent relatively little of their life at home with their parents. They were often "bound out" to other families between the ages of seven to nine to serve as apprentices for artists, blacksmiths, carpenters, or farmers. Greenleaf quotes an Italian visitor to England, writing in the fifteen century:

> The want of affection in the English is strongly manifested towards their children; for after having kept them at home till they arrive at the age of seven or nine years at the utmost, they put them out, both males and females, to hard service in the houses of other people, binding them generally for another seven or nine years. And these are called apprentices, and during that time they perform all the most menial offices; and few are born who are exempted from this fate, for everyone, however rich he may be, sends away his children into the house of others, whilst he, in return, receives those of strangers into his own. And on inquiring their reason for this severity, they answered that they did it in order that their

children might learn better manners. But I for my part, believe that they do it because they like to enjoy all their comforts themselves, and that they are better served by strangers than they would be by their own children (p. 36).

The practice of "binding out" children was practiced primarily among poor families in the New England Colonies in America (Kenkel, 1977). When these families could not afford to feed, clothe, and shelter their children, they would bind them out to middle-class tradesmen or farmers. The contractual arrangement gave the family who was receiving the child the opportunity to extract whatever labor they could from the child in exchange for feeding, clothing, and sheltering him or her. In addition, if it was a male child, the new father of the child was expected to teach the child the skills of his profession: carpentry, blacksmithing, printing, shopkeeping, or farming. If it was a girl child, the new family was expected to teach the child the skills needed by women: how to cook, sew, care for children, maintain a garden, or can fruits and vegetables.

In the plantation South, slave children were not expected to work full-time in the fields until they were around thirteen. It was thought that this practice of giving children reduced work until then maximized the ability of the landowner to extract a relatively long lifetime of work from the slave. If one worked young children too hard, it was felt that this would impair their ability to mature to fully productive adulthood (Alston, 1992, p. 360). Still, slave children under the age of thirteen were expected to haul water, fetch wood, tend gardens, clean yards, and feed livestock. They were also expected to care for and supervise younger children in the slave community, which functioned as an extended family system in which children were raised by the entire "village" (Wiggins, 1985).

West and Petrick (1992) describe the work of children on farms in the Midwest at the end of the nineteenth century. Boys and girls as young as eight plowed fields in the spring and worked to chase away birds, cattle, or horses that might threaten to destroy crops. When a parent could not find relatives or neighbors to care for children, the children would accompany parents when they worked in the fields. Both boys and girls planted and maintained gardens. While boys mainly helped with farm chores, such as tending cattle and horses and harvesting hay, girls helped with household chores such as cooking, cleaning, and canning.

> Children supplemented the family food supply by gathering fruits and berries, hunting, and fishing. Children as young as seven or eight hunted antelopes, raccoons, ducks, geese, deer, prairie chickens, bison, wild hogs, and above all, rabbits (West & Petrick, 1992, p. 30).

When the United States was a preindustrial society, prior to approximately 1820, women and children were defined as "helpmates" to the male head of household. Women and children played important economic roles in producing family income from making products in cottage industries to helping sow, tend, and harvest crops on farms. The children of farmers were seen as valuable unpaid sources of labor. Children often did not go to school during planting time or harvesting time to help their families with these tasks. Children were so important as free labor that families often had many children. In Colonial America, women sometimes had twenty children in their lifetimes; the job of women was to bear, tend for, and bury children, and they did a great deal of all three (Kenkel, 1977).

Demos (1986, p. 6) writes that, in the New England colonies in the seventeenth century, married couples generally had eight to ten completed pregnancies. Death rates of both parents and children were high, making families as unstable in this country three hundred years ago as they are today (Demos, 1986). The vehicle that created that instability, however, has changed over time from death to divorce. When parents were widowed, they remarried, usually rather quickly, thus the existence of single parent households and stepfamilies is as old as this country itself. Children in colonial America consistently encountered change in their lives with new siblings being born, siblings dying, parents dying and surviving spouses remarrying, and new siblings being acquired through the remarriage of a parent, creating stepfamilies.

Children in an Industrial Society

The second wave of technology produced jobs in manufacturing, whereby raw materials were converted to manufactured goods in urban factories. The United States became an industrial and urbanized society as people moved from rural areas to cities for jobs in manufacturing and in offices. Working conditions in factories were dangerous and harsh and the working hours were long. The work was seen as inappropriate for middle-class women, so men were employed. In 1890, only 5 percent of married women were gainfully employed, and the number of mothers with young children working for wages was even lower (Hoffman and Nye, 1974, p. 3). Middle-class women, in particular, were expected to stay out of the commercial world of men and to be the domestic guardians of religious and ethical values. The lower the social class, the more frequently children worked in cities to supplement the family income by scavenging or through part-time employment.

David Nasaw (1985) describes how urban children, mostly working- and lower-class immigrant children at the beginning of the twentieth century, helped their families survive. They scavenged yards, alleyways, construction sites, and city garbage dumps looking for anything of value that they could haul back to their family to be used or sold. The garbage dumps of major cities were playgrounds for youth, who congregated in them (Nasaw, 1985, p. 93).

Girls helped their mothers in many capacities. It was common for families to contract piecework, and the home became a factory producing products. All family members participated in making the family a unit of production. Grandparents, parents, and children all helped out, as is illustrated by a 1913 account of a tenement family (grandmother, father, mother, and four children, aged four, three, two, and one month) in New York City who engaged in the cottage industry of making artificial flowers:

> All except the father and the two babies make violets. The three year old girl picks apart the petals; her sister, aged four years, separates the stems, dipping an end of each into paste spread on a piece of board on the kitchen table and the mother and grandmother slip the petals up the stems. . . . 'We must all work if we want to earn anything,' the mother said (Van Kleeck, 1913).

Lower-income urban families often took in boarders to supplement their income. Children were enlisted in these homes to do the work it took to care for these boarders and family members, from cleaning to shopping, doing laundry, and cooking and doing dishes.

Because technology was so primitive or nonexistent, household chores took extensive time and preparation.

> The laundry had to be done by hand from beginning to end: sorted, soaked, rubbed against the washboard, rinsed, boiled, rinsed again, wrung out, starched, hung to dry, ironed with irons heated on the stove, folded and put away. Cooking involved not only preparing the food and cooking it but hauling coal for the fire, dumping the ashes afterwards, and keeping the cast-iron stove cleaned, blacked, and rust-free. Housecleaning was complicated by the soot, grime, and ashes released by coal-burning stoves and kerosene and gas lamps. Shopping had to be done daily and in several different shops; there were no refrigerators to store food purchased earlier in the week and no supermarkets for one-stop shopping (Nasaw, 1985, p. 105).

In addition to this housework, girls as young as seven or eight were responsible for supervising and attending to the needs of their younger siblings. According to Nasaw, "In many working-class families the babies and small children were effectively raised by their older sisters" (1985, p. 107). This sometimes was in addition to any baby-sitting jobs that might be obtained and girls tended the children in other families who could afford to pay for surrogate parenting.

The urban environment created many jobs for children. Some worked part-time in stores stocking shelves, cleaning, running errands, or delivering goods. Others functioned as independent entrepreneurs selling candy, gum, flowers, or fruit. A popular urban job for children was as "newsies," selling morning and evening newspapers. Other children, as young as four years old because they were small enough to fit in chimneys, were chimney sweeps, and these children often died of lung cancer or respiratory illnesses contracted in their work.

Between 1880 and 1920, in the United States, children worked long hours in factories, mines, or textile mills under difficult conditions. The 1880 U.S. census showed one million children between the ages of ten and fifteen holding down jobs, while the 1890 census showed 1,750,000 children between the ages of ten and fifteen gainfully employed (Greenleaf, 1978). Children often worked in coal mines in West Virginia and Pennsylvania. Twenty percent of coal miners were children.

Children frequently worked in textile mills in the South, where they would operate dangerous machinery that sometimes severed hands or fingers. They had no medical coverage. They would be housed in collective dormitories that were filthy and unhealthy and many died. By the late 1800s, children as young as four could be found working in textile mills beside their older brothers and sisters. In southern mills, a full 30 percent of the employees were children (Sugar, 1994, p. 26). One can find accounts such as the following from the Massachusetts Bureau of Labor Statistics on "The Working Girls of Boston" that document the use of children as laborers.

> One of the most frightful features of the 'sweating' system is the unchecked employment of very young children. In these districts it is no unusual sight to see children of five, six, or even four years, employed all day sewing on buttons, pulling out bastings, or carrying huge piles of work to and from the 'sweater's' shop (Cott, 1972, p. 328).

From Economic Assets to Economic Liabilities

The first two decades of the twentieth century were critical in changing the definition of children from being economic assets to economic liabilities. Social reformers were critical of the family as a viable social institution. Divorce rates, for example, between 1870 and 1920 increased fifteen times over what they been previously. By 1924, one in seven marriages were ending in divorce (Lasch, 1995). Furthermore, rates of juvenile crime and delinquency were rising, apparent evidence of the fact that the family was not doing a competent job of socializing and supervising children.

There was a perception that working-class and poor children particularly were being exploited both inside and outside the family system. Children needed to be protected against the abuses of child labor in factories and textile mills, and legislation was enacted in 1912 that paved the way for the abolition of child labor (Sugar, 1994, p. 26). These child labor laws went far in changing the definition of children from economic assets to economic liabilities. Now children could not be gainfully employed and, with urbanization, they increasingly became an economic burden. They took up space and, in a city, space was scarce and therefore expensive. They also represented an extra mouth to feed, an extra body to clothe, an extra body to shelter. The expense of raising children in cities motivated parents to reduce the size of their families, particularly in the middle class.

Because middle-class families were having fewer children, some social conservatives feared that immigrant families, who had many children, would come to populate the country, and eventually make white "Americans" a minority population. These conservatives further saw immigrant families as undermining the social integration of U.S. society because, in these immigrant families, people continued speaking the language, cooking the foods, practicing the customs, and celebrating the holidays of their homeland (Lasch, 1995). To integrate society, children had to be pulled out of their families and collectively get socialized in schools. Schools would further impose discipline on youth and reduce juvenile crime in the society. Compulsory school for children became law and, over time, the number of years children were expected to go to school was extended so that they spent more time in school.

The phenomenon of "high school" was initiated, which separated younger children from older children. This facilitated the definition of adolescence as a separate and distinct stage in the life course. Adolescents were segregated from both younger children and adults to lead their lives together. Their independence was hampered by their inability to work, making them financially dependent on their parents. It was not until automobiles were mass-produced in the 1920s that adolescents began to gain some freedom from their parents. It was not economic autonomy, but the automobile went a long way to reduce parental supervision and control of the lives of their adolescent children. Cars and high schools also enhanced the power of peer groups in the lives of adolescents.

Social reformers were not only interested in protecting children from exploitation by external forces, but also interested in protecting children from abuses within families, from economic exploitation to protection from physical and sexual abuse. Social workers and child protective services began the child welfare movement because they believed that children constituted a class of persons unto themselves who needed to be protected from society. Prior to the twentieth century, children were viewed as the possessions of their parents, who could do as they wished to them. In the eyes of social reformers, this entitlement led to tyranny and abuse.

Protecting Children.   The definition of children as vulnerable to victimization and exploitation is a theme that continues today. Media coverage of rare events, such as Susan Smith putting her two children in the family car and driving them into a lake, drowning them, or Andrea Yates, who drowned her five children in a bathtub, suggests to the public that some children are at risk within their families. Laws that require school teachers, physicians, therapists, and day-care providers to report suspected child abuse or neglect are designed to protect children from abuse within their homes. These laws change the family from a private to a public domain, allowing "outsiders" to intrude to protect the health, safety, and welfare of children. Children become not just the concern of parents and siblings, but, rather, the responsibility of an entire community, which has to protect them from whomever might threaten them.

The threats to children do not just exist within the family, however. Media coverage of school shootings at Columbine and Santee reminds the public that schools can also be unsafe places for children. The McMartin case caused the public to question the safety of children in day-care centers. The occasional random abduction and killing of children such as Kevin Collins or Xiana Fairchild reminds the public that children are not safe anywhere in the "outside world," and that, perhaps, the family is the only safe place in a potentially hostile and dangerous world.

The perceived need for children to be supervised, monitored, and protected puts contemporary families in a bind. Parents today are out working; they are not at home and available to supervise and monitor their children. The options for parents are to place children in child-care facilities that are often expensive, afterschool recreation and educational programs where they are taught and supervised by adults, but which can also be expensive, or having older children stay at home to be child-care providers who will protect the health, safety, and welfare of their younger siblings. This latter alternative can result in the creation of parental children in families, where they act as parents to their younger brothers and sisters.

Children in a Post-Industrial Society

How did American families get to the point where parents are not home and available to nurture and protect their children? This is a post-World War II phenomenon that was triggered by another change in the nature of labor in the economy and a change in the way technology is used in our society.

At the end of World War II, a third wave of technology began in which products were manufactured by robots, computers, and machines, which increasingly replaced people in the production of goods. By the early 1970s, jobs decreased in the industrial North in companies that employed hundreds of thousands of people in industries such as the manufacture of steel or automobiles. The growing sector of the economy was in service-related jobs, where, rather than a product being produced, a service was rendered. The growing part of the economy was in teaching, social work, recreation, and leisure (diverse aspects of the hospitality management industry—resorts, hotels, restaurants, cruise ships, travel agents), law, medicine, real estate, and the information management, computer, and telecommunications industries at the high end of the economy, and in fast-food services and retail sales at the lower end of the economy, where one finds hamburger makers, sandwich makers, pizza makers, delivery personnel, and sales clerks. Physical strength is not required in any of these service-sector jobs; success is based on being able to get along with people, giving women an advantage.

The Gainful Employment of Women.   The problem with high-end service-sector jobs for women is that they often require a college education. Until World War II, colleges and universities had quotas for the admission of women. At just the time the sectors of the labor force were expanding in areas where women could work productively, the quotas for admission of women into colleges and universities were abolished, and women were free to seek higher education so that they could get the training necessary to gain access to these new jobs.

The number of married women with children who were gainfully employed steadily rose during the latter half of the twentieth century. In 1940, the U.S. Department of Labor estimated that 8.6 percent of married women with children under the age of seventeen were gainfully employed (Sugar, 1994, p. 27). By 1948, 26 percent of mothers with children under the age of eighteen worked outside the home. By 1991, 66.8 percent of married women with children under the age of eighteen worked in the labor force, with approximately 60 percent of those women working full-time (Sugar, 1994, p. 27).

The cost of living in most urban areas created the need for both parents to work. It is virtually impossible for families to maintain middle-class status today without both parents working full-time. One reason for this is inflated real estate prices. Whereas fifty years ago it was common for mortgage payments to represent 20 to 25 percent of a family's income, today mortgage payments in many metropolitan areas represent 40 to 60 percent of a family's income, making it increasingly difficult for families to be homeowners. Often, one way of attaining the American dream of home ownership is to buy a home on the outer fringes of an urban community, resulting in commutes of sometimes two or more hours each way to and from work. This is time spent in frustrating, exhausting creep and crawl commute traffic that leaves the parent very little energy or tolerance for family members. Economics in our society takes its toll on the quality of life in contemporary families.

With both parents in an intact nuclear family working, a parenting gap is created at home. There is no longer a parent home to care for and nurture the children. In the absence of both a homemaker husband and father as well as a homemaker wife and mother, a vacuum exists in families that has to be filled.

The vacuum is frequently filled by children. In contemporary post-industrial societies, children often perform the domestic chores that parents used to do. Fathers can no longer provide for the family's physical needs of food, clothing, and shelter by themselves so their wives help them perform this instrumental role. The children then shift their role to accommodate to the loss of a parent's labor and supervision at home; usually an older child takes on a parental role relative to their younger brothers and sisters. National census statistics from 1995 reveal that 18 percent of children aged five to fourteen years, representing approximately 6.9 million children, cared for themselves on a regular basis when not in school (Smith, 2000). Chase (1999) writes of the stresses and strains for families in a post-industrial society that are conducive to the creation of parental and parentified children:

> Many believe that greater prevalence of certain social conditions such as one-parent families, financial stress, social isolation, and disintegration of community result in greater demands on children to raise themselves, to become parentified in response to overtaxed adults who are unavailable, or at best are 'doing the best they can' in a depleting and confusing postmodern society (p. 4).

In filling the role that was formerly filled by homemaker wives and mothers, children in today's families face the same problems that homemaker mothers faced earlier in the twentieth century when the labor of women in families was largely unacknowledged, unappreciated, and certainly unpaid. In today's families, the labor of children goes largely unacknowledged, unappreciated, and unpaid. Their contributions to the family system are taken for granted by others, just as the labor of women was taken for granted by others. This basic unfairness, making significant contributions to family welfare that others fail to see, drove many housewives to experience anger, depression, and low self-esteem. It led them to seek psychotherapists and take psychotherapeutic drugs (Coontz, 1992). Likewise, the unrecognized contributions of children can lead to psychological stress, anger, and depression among parental and parentified children (Jurkovic, 1997).

The Process of Socialization.   In the discipline of sociology, the concept socialization does not mean "socializing" or interacting with others. From a symbolic interactionist perspective, socialization is a lifelong process, taking place from the cradle to the grave, that teaches people how to define, interpret, and give meaning to objects, events, and people. Children learn to give meaning to family members and themselves; they learn what it means to go to school or church. They learn to give meaning to police or firefighters. Adults learn what it means to be gainfully employed or to be a college student or a spouse or a parent. Older adults learn what retirement or widowhood or old age means. We may have images of these phenomena, but how we define and interpret them constantly changes as a result of experience.

Television is an important instrument of socialization. From watching it, viewers learn to buy lots of things, an important lesson in a capitalist society that requires a consumer-based economy. The major message delivered on television is *buy,* though what it is that we are supposed to buy changes every fifteen to thirty seconds. Viewers learn that buying the right liquor or driving the right car is a symbol of success, that using the right deodorant will bring social popularity, that buying jewelry will bring happiness, that buying the right shoes will bring victory, that using the right stock brokerage house or insurance company will bring wealth and a comfortable retirement, that consuming the right vitamins or taking the right medicines will bring health. Clearly, what is portrayed on television is not always an accurate portrayal of reality. Television is a transmitter of images, a programmed controller of definitions and interpretations that the viewer is to consume and internalize. Many of these images constitute exaggerations or distortions of reality; sometimes they are just lies.

Distorted Images of Children in the Media.   Television is an enormously powerful medium for constructing images of reality in the minds of viewers. The perception that children are to be cared for by parents, that childhood should be a play-filled, carefree, and workfree stage of life is, in part, a function of family life as it is portrayed in television sitcoms. Many family life shows produced in the 1950s, such as *Ozzie and Harriet, Leave It to Beaver, Father Knows Best,* and the *Donna Reed Show,* are still aired on many television channels today. The families in these shows have a wage-earning husband who leaves home every weekday to work and a homemaker wife, whose job is to manage the home, cook, clean, and be a primary parent always available to attend to the physical and emotional needs of the children.

As Stephanie Coontz states in *The Way We Never Were: American Families and the Nostalgia Trap* (1992), the families portrayed on television shows produced in the 1950s were illusions, myths. Very few real families in the 1950s could maintain the lifestyle portrayed on these shows. The images reflected more of a fantasy, the manufacturing of a dream (or, for feminists, a nightmare) that appealed to the millions of working-class and poor families who could not afford that lifestyle. These shows presented a social ideal of middle-class family life in which children enjoyed a carefree life, free from the anxieties and work of everyday life. Before they went to school, they had a breakfast prepared by their mother. They were sent off to school with a goodbye kiss. They had a lunch packed for them by mom. When they came home from school, mom was home waiting for them; milk and cookies were available as a treat. Afternoons, after school, were spent playing with friends. There seemed to be relatively little homework that needed to be done. In the evenings, the children interacted with their parents, who both seemed to be available to them and both had energy for them. Weekends were often spent as a family playing ball or picnicking at a park. Nuclear families were intact, with little conflict or concern for divorce.

To whatever extent these shows portrayed the reality of middle-class life in post-war America, there were sides of it that were not portrayed. Not all was well in paradise. Housewife mothers flocked to the offices of psychotherapists, complaining of boredom and depression, and they were frequently given tranquilizers. There were 462,000 pounds of tranquilizers consumed in the United States in 1958 and 1.15 million pounds in 1959 (Coontz, 1992, p. 36). Alcoholism, particularly among women, also rose dramatically in the late 1950s (Lisansky, 1958). Partly as a function of increased use of alcohol and drugs, physical abuse of children was a "hidden" phenomenon of the 1950s (Crawford, 1978). Mirra Komarovsky researched marital happiness in working-class families of the 1950s and found that "slightly less than one-third [were] happily or very happily married (Komarovsky, 1962).

Although homemaker mothers generally were home to supervise children, the use of automobiles by teens enabled them to escape adult supervision. Petting in cars on dates was common and the back seats of cars sometimes replaced bedrooms for sex. The effect was high rates of teen pregnancy in the 1950s, and out-of-wedlock babies placed for adoption between 1944 and 1955 increased 80 percent (Vinovskis, 1988). Age at first marriage dropped in the decade of the 1950s, in part because of pressure placed on young female teens to marry when they became pregnant.

As portrayed on television, the family consisting of a wage-earning husband and homemaker wife in middle-class families further diverged from the real world in the latter part of the 1950s as more and more wives and mothers either went to work or went to school to prepare for work. When these women returned to school, a vacuum was created at home, a parenting vacuum, that came to be filled by older children who often functioned as parents to their younger siblings. These older siblings took the role of parental children, children who became parent figures to their younger siblings.

After World War II, the United States government offered service personnel the opportunity to go to colleges and universities on the GI Bill and paid their tuition, so many servicemen took advantage of this opportunity for upward social mobility. When they did, their wives often worked to cover family living expenses. The reality of the male college student father and the gainfully employed wife stands in stark contrast to the TV families of the 1950s.

If the reality of life in middle-class families in America did not match the portrayals of family life on television programs, the real lives of working-class and poor families did not match those portrayals either. In working-class families, wives could not afford to be homemaker wives. But their husbands, who spent a great deal of their leisure time watching television, internalized the ideal of the middle-class family structure of wage-earning husband and homemaker wife, and that became what he wanted for his family. So his wife's working symbolized his own failure to earn enough money to enable the structural ideal to become a reality, and he came to resent the fact that his wife had to work. His wife's working outside the home was seen as a "necessary evil" (Komarovsky, 1962; Rubin, 1992, 1995). Because he didn't really want his wife to work, he saw little need to help her out when she came home from work, so she often put in what came to be known as a "second shift" (Hochschild, 1980), creating a gendered division of labor in families. The wife was expected to do as much domestic labor in the household—cooking, cleaning, laundry—as if she were not working at all.

The middle-class family of the 1950s in the United States usually did not reflect the TV portrayals of these families. Of course, television executives would argue that they never intended to capture the reality of peoples' lives. After all, television is entertainment, and entertainment, to be entertaining, must distort reality to be interesting. In the 1950s, the distortion was to create a dream, a fictional "utopia" of family, that all too often was used as a yardstick by which one's own family was measured or was used to create a goal of family life. The reality of working-class and poor families differed from the TV portrayals of family life. What further diverged from such TV portrayals were the everyday lives of children, who were often ignored or abused or exploited for their labor.

It is my impression that much of what was true of television in the 1950s continues to be true today. Most television shows today seem to portray childhood as a play-filled, carefree stage of life, relatively devoid of work or responsibility. This imagery, when absorbed by viewers, assumes the status of reality. In the minds of viewers, the images manufactured by television executives becomes more real than what exists in the real world. In this book, we will be confronted by accounts of childhood that are discrepant from the images of childhood one sees on television. These accounts portray children assuming very adult responsibilities as the caretakers of others in their families. These accounts do not depict trivial problems that can be solved in thirty minutes. The adults who write of their childhood encountered problems from which they saw no escape, problems that threatened their life, health, and welfare as well as the well-being of other family members. In such stories, one encounters a vision of childhood that may not be entertaining but is a more accurate image of reality for children than one finds portrayed by the entertainment industry.

Summary

Symbolic interaction theorists perceive children as symbols capable of assuming multiple meanings in different societies or within one society at different times. In the United States, children in the seventeenth, eighteenth, and nineteenth centuries were defined as workers, helpmates whose labor was essential for a family's survival. In the twentieth century, the definition of children changed. Child labor laws and the mandatory schooling of children changed the perception of children as economic assets to economic liabilities. Both parents in a family left the household to be gainfully employed, leaving a parenting gap in contemporary families, a gap sometimes filled by professionals, sometimes by relatives, and sometimes by children. The labor of children in families is usually unpaid and often underappreciated or unrecognized. This can have detrimental effects on the self-image of children who often work very hard and are not acknowledged for their labor. This lack of recognition is one component that can lead to detrimental, destructive consequences for parental and parentified children.

2

Exploring the Minds of Pioneers

Having discussed the framework of symbolic interaction theory, the time has come to apply this theory by examining the thoughts of pioneers who have written about parental and parentified children. I do this by examining their writings, much as was done in examining the writings of my students about these roles. How did these pioneers define and interpret these roles, what meaning did they attach to these roles, how did they theoretically interpret the subjective states of minds of the respondents or clients they served who experienced being parental or parentified children? Their writings are akin to talking with us in an interview, for through their writings, they share their thoughts and feelings about this subject.

Salvador Minuchin

One of the first authors to write about parental children was family therapist Salvador Minuchin. Minuchin was a psychiatrist (a physician with a specialization in psychiatry) who came to the United States from Argentina. His first job in the United States was at the Wyltwyck School for Boys in New York state. At what was basically a reform school for delinquent youth, Minuchin treated children with a wide range of problems including poor grades in school, truancy, delinquency, and psychosomatic illnesses. At Wyltwyck, Minuchin began to formulate an idea that, regardless of the problem, these children were coming from families that, in Minuchin's mind, had a pathological structure.

These pathological family structures were the "real" problem. The structural problem in these families was manifest in the behavior of the children, so it looked like the problem was the child. If you were a clinical psychologist, you would likely attempt to change the behavior of the child by doing individual psychotherapy with the child, trying to change the child's thoughts and feelings in order to change the child's behavior. However, Minuchin saw that the behavior of the child was linked to structural disorders in the child's family, so he sought to conduct what came to be called "structural family therapy," in which he attempted to change the structure of the family system to change the behavior of the child.

Minuchin saw the social structure of the families of these children as pathological because they differed from what he thought of as functional family structures. Minuchin had a clear idea of what functional families ought to look like, and viewed families as social systems. A system is a boundary-maintained unit composed of interrelated and interdependent parts. A society can be seen as a system. A family can be seen as a system.

Systems in Families

The concept of a system comes out of the biological sciences in which the prototype system is the human body. The boundary of the body is the skin. Within the body system are subsystems: the digestive system, circulatory system, reproductive system, endocrine system, skeletal system, and so forth. Within the circulatory system are subsystems called "organs." Organs of the circulatory system are interrelated and interdependent in a specialized division of labor. The heart pumps blood, the lungs oxygenate blood, the kidneys filter blood. A change in one of these organs affects all other organs as well as organs in other systems. If the heart stops pumping blood, for instance, the whole system can collapse and the person can die.

Outside our body lie other bodies, systems that are external to us, inasmuch as they lie outside the boundary of our skin. These external systems can affect us. If somebody gets angry at us and yells at us or calls us a bad name, it can sadden us, anger us, or result in a rise of blood pressure within us. These external others can hit or stab or shoot us, causing great bodily harm or death. Likewise, in the process of social interaction, what we do or say affects others in our environment, so we also have the ability to sadden, insult, hurt or praise, inflate, or make others happy. At a biological level, we can contaminate others with our germs or diseases just as they can contaminate us.

A society can be seen as a social system and, within that societal system, is a political system, an economic system, a military system, a religious system, and an educational system. Within each of these subsystems lie other subsystems, so within the political subsystem are the Democratic, Republican, Libertarian, American Independent, and Green national political party systems; within the military subsystem are the subsystems of the Army, Navy, Air Force, Marines, and Coast Guard. Within the economic subsystem are corporations and within the religious subsystem are Catholics, Protestants, Jews, Buddhists, Muslims, or Hindus. All subsystems are interrelated and interdependent on one another so an economic recession affects the political, educational, and military systems. Similarly, a change of the dominant political party in Congress or in the presidency affects the economic, military, and educational subsystems.

Systems that are external to any society are other societies, and, particularly, in an era of globalization, all societies are interrelated and interdependent. A change in any one society affects changes in other societies, so a recession in Japan or Europe affects the economy of the United States; an invasion of one country by another or a civil war in one society may cause military deployments by other countries.

Families can be seen as systems. Within families are subsystems: the grandparent system, the spousal subsystem, the parental subsystem, and the sibling subsystem. With increased longevity, it is common for family systems to contain at least three generations.

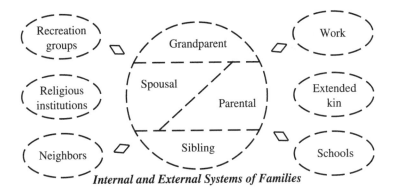

Internal and External Systems of Families

In the grandparent subsystem are each child's grandparents, or the parents' parents. In the spousal subsystem, the spouses relate to each other in the roles of husband and wife. What they talk about in these roles are marital or spousal issues. In the **parental subsystem,** parents relate to each other in the roles of mother and father. What they talk about in these roles are parenting issues related to their interaction with their children. In the **sibling subsystem,** siblings relate to each other in the roles of brother and sister.

Boundaries

Boundaries exist between the subsystems of a family and also between the family and the outside world. Boundaries between the family and the outside world distinguish who is in a family system and who is outside a family system. Minuchin described three kinds of boundaries: diffuse boundaries, clear boundaries, and rigid boundaries. Diffuse and rigid boundaries are often dysfunctional (detrimental to a system), while clear boundaries are ideal and functional (beneficial for a system). **Diffuse boundaries** are like having no boundaries at all. Diffuse boundaries are associated with what Minuchin calls **enmeshment** or overinvolvement. For a family, the work setting for parents is part of the family's external environment. If a parent is tethered to work by E-mail or a cell phone and those items of technology are permitted to intrude into the family home at all times of the day or night, for example, if the parent is available at the whim of an employer, there is a diffuse boundary between work and home. When there are clear boundaries between work and the home, a person can say "no." For example, when an employer or supervisor calls and asks an employee to come in to work off schedule and the employee says, "No, this is family time and you can't intrude on that. This is your problem, your crisis, don't make it mine. Find somebody else," a clear boundary exists.

Minuchin developed a system of charting the nature of relationships in a family system by drawing what he called "family maps." In a family map, diffuse boundaries are signified by a dotted line, clear boundaries are identified by a broken line, and rigid boundaries by a solid line.

RIGID BOUNDARIES	CLEAR BOUNDARIES	DIFFUSE BOUNDARIES
(People are disengaged)	(Normal range)	(People are enmeshed)

A functional family should appear as follows, with clear boundaries connecting the family to the outside world and clear boundaries between people of different generations. The reason that clear boundaries are signified by a broken line is that, in the spaces, family members are free to leave the family system to get their needs met. The outside world can also have access to family members such that people outside the family system can provide support to its members.

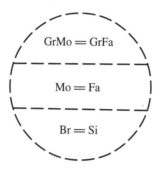

Map of a Functional Family

Legend: GrMo = grandmother;
GrFa = grandfather; Mo =
mother; Fa = father; Br = brother;
Si = Sister; — is an alliance.

If a family goes to a family therapist to help them resolve problems they are having, this signifies clear boundaries. They allow nonfamily members in the outside world to assist them in dealing with problems, and they can use resources from the outside world to help them or to enhance the quality of their lives. Families with clear boundaries are free to consult with clergy, attend bible-study classes, or take classes at a college or university or community center. Family members are free to leave the family to participate in sports activities or to join cooking, gardening, bicycling, or other special interest groups.

In a postindustrial society, middle- and upper-middle-class families are increasingly opening the boundaries of their system by outsourcing labor. Just as corporations "outsource" labor, by using cheap labor in less developed countries to manufacture or assemble products, families are outsourcing labor by hiring gardeners, housecleaners, car wash centers, laundries, handymen, dog-walkers, and nannies to perform tasks that make a household operate smoothly when the parents are too busy working to do these tasks themselves. This opens the boundaries of the family to the outside world using resources in the outside world to meet family needs.

In contrast, a family that has rigid boundaries does not permit family members to go outside the family system to get their needs met and does not allow the outside world into the family system to provide resources. Families that have stigmas tend to exhibit rigid boundaries between the family and the outside world. Families that feature chemically dependent persons, such as alcoholics, tend to exhibit rigid boundaries. Children are not permitted to invite friends over to play for fear that the alcoholism will be discovered, and the family secret will be revealed to the outside world. Families that have domestic violence or physical or sexual abuse of children often exhibit rigid boundaries because the family has a secret to be kept from the outside world. In attempting to keep the secret, the family closes itself off from the outside world. Families with rigid boundaries would not share problems with a family therapist, and children in these families would not reveal their pain to teachers or friends. These families are highly privatized, as if the home is their castle and the castle is surrounded by a very wide and deep moat that keeps the outside world at a distance.

Jealousy can create rigid boundaries. I have seen jealous spouses prevent their partner from enrolling in college classes because the partner thinks, "How do I know what you're doing when you say you're studying in the library?" Such people are afraid that their partner will meet somebody, fall in the love and leave, so they close the boundaries of their system by not allowing partners outside to get their needs met.

For Minuchin, clear boundaries should exist between people of different generations in families. For him, the major organizational variable structuring families is age. The closest bonds in a family should be between people of the same generation. This is illustrated in the previous illustration in which double lines connecting members of the same generation signify an alliance between these people who support one another. When generational boundaries get crossed, problems in families arise. When a wife is closer to her mother than she is to her husband, for instance, the husband is likely to perceive that he has mother-in-law problems. When a parent is closer to a child than to a spouse, anger and resentment toward the parent who is enmeshed with a child can arise, creating marital problems. This can also result in the enmeshed child experiencing problems leaving the family of origin.

Crossing Generational Boundaries

When one finds parental children, generational boundaries have been crossed. The child leaves the sibling subsystem to become a parent figure to their brothers and sisters. The child crosses a generational boundary to play the role of parent (hence the label, *parental child*), to become part of the parental subsystem. The child, although biologically a brother or sister, acts like a parent, assuming adult responsiblities and making family decisions with very little guidance from the parent. Jay Haley (1976), who worked for fifteen years with Minuchin at Philadelphia Child Guidance Clinic, sees the existence of parental children as constituting a confusion in the generational hierarchy of families. Haley writes:

> In some families, particularly one-parent families with many children, there is a third generation that is not clearly a "generation." There is a mother and her children, but in between there is an older child who functions as a parent for the younger child. He or she is not of the adult generation but is a child, and yet the child functions as an adult insofar as he or she is taking care of the younger children (p. 113).

The parental child is elevated into the parental subsystem because of the parent's absence and the need for guidance and control of the siblings. The child, in assuming adult responsibilities, manifests the executive authority of a parent. Minuchin writes:

The allocation of parental power to a child is a natural arrangement in large families, in single parent families, or in families where both parents work. The system can function well. The younger children are cared for, and the parental child can develop responsibility, competence, and autonomy beyond his years. A family with a parental child may run into difficulty, however, if a delegation of authority is not explicit or if the parents abdicate, leaving the child to become the main source of guidance, control and decisions. In such a case, the demands on the parental child can clash with his own childhood and exceed his ability to cope with them (Minuchin, 1974, pp. 97–98).

When one finds parentified children, generational boundaries have also been crossed. They leave the sibling subsystem to become parent figures to their own parent. Sometimes the parent, although chronologically an adult, acts like a needy, dependent child and the child assumes the role of caretaker.

It is often difficult for parental and parentified children to leave their families of origin to become autonomous, independent adults because there is nobody else in the family system who will or can assume the caretaking functions. These children often feel as if their siblings will never survive without them, so parental children may give up their future as college students, for instance, to stay home and care for their brothers and sisters. Or, the parentified child feels that the needy parent who is being cared for cannot survive if he or she goes off to attend a college or university and so stays home to care for the parent.

In playing these roles, children become engulfed within their family systems, and the boundaries appear to be rigid around the family. Such children also find it difficult to get their needs met by age-appropriate peers. When it is time to leave the family of origin, it becomes difficult to leave without considerable anxiety and guilt. As a result, some parental and parentified children never make it out of their families of origin. The roles become dysfunctional when they become so rigid that one cannot leave the role, even though one may want to.

For Minuchin, the roles of parental and parentified children are pathological because the child is not functioning within the boundaries of its generation. The crossing of generational boundaries constitutes a structural pathology of the family. These roles are also pathological because the children often assume adult responsibilities beyond their developmental abilities, or the roles interfere with the leaving process. Minuchin sees that a normative developmental task of families is to allow children to leave and become independent adults.

Impaired Executive Systems

How do children become parental or parentified children, according to Minuchin? It is to this question that we now turn. After leaving the Wyltwick School for Boys, Minuchin was director of the Philadelphia Child Guidance Clinic, where he treated children of primarily poor African American and Puerto Rican families. These children had been referred for a variety of problems, ranging from poor grades in school or delinquency or truancy to psychosomatic illnesses. Minuchin linked the problems of these children to the social structure of the families in which they lived. The families, according to Minuchin, exhibited a weak, ineffectual executive parental system, a "relinquishment of executive functions," whereby the parents' competence was diminished. The parents were heavily burdened and overwhelmed by an absence of resources, from financial resources to support and help from within as well as outside the family system. Sometimes the parents exhibited absolute, autocratic power and control, while at other times they felt totally helpless. According to Minuchin,

> Our conception of the parental response and the relinquishment of the executive role was that it pushed the child to look to his siblings in search of guidance, control, and direction as to how to cope with the familial and outside world. The "parental children" to whom authority was allocated by the parents and/or siblings became the source of reference for executive guidance and control (Minuchin et al., 1967, p. 11).

Minuchin saw impaired competence particularly in mothers who were single parents (for which he has been severely criticized for "mother bashing"). He discussed the ineffectual power of parents as their own personal incompetence, rather than focusing on how poverty impaired their ability to parent. He saw impaired parenting as constituting an impaired ability to establish rules and to sanction violations of those rules. Parents were often unaware of the activities of the children outside the family system, and they exhibited limited ability to control those activities. There was a parenting vacuum in the family system, a vacuum that was filled by the parental child as an adaptive response to impaired parenting.

Throughout this book, I expand on Minuchin's ideas, as a variety of contexts are examined that reduce the competence of parents. Parental vacuums can be created by alcoholism and other chemical dependencies. Parental gaps can result from chronic physical or mental illness of a parent, by the stresses and fatigue from gainful employment, or by the pain of divorce or widowhood. A parent can also become more dependent on others through the infirmities of old age. All these factors can result in parents being less available to children and less nurturing, protective, and supportive of them than they might be without these stressors in their lives. Salvador Minuchin interpreted families structurally, in terms of how people organized themselves relative to one another. Parental and parentified children, from this perspective, develop as adaptive responses to a weakened executive subsystem. Minuchin interpreted the problems of children as arising from problems in the parental system.

Some sociologists may question why the work of Salvador Minuchin, a structuralist, would be covered in a symbolic interactionist book. First, Minuchin was a pioneer in writing about parental children. Second, it is consistent with symbolic interaction theory to examine the minds of actors. What I have done, as a symbolic interactionist, is to examine how Minuchin defined and interpreted the development of parental children in families. Minuchin interpreted parental children as an adaptive response to an impaired executive parental system.

Ivan Boszormenyi-Nagy

Ivan Nagy's writings are a combination of psychodynamic thinking coupled with an analysis of interpersonal relationships in families. Nagy was the creator of what was called "contextual family therapy." The context in which interpersonal relationships are viewed in Nagy's writings is the concept of fairness. Fairness involves a reciprocal give-and-take in relationships. When a family member consistently, over a significant period, gives as well as receives, and demonstrates an ability to take into account the welfare of others, he or she is seen as trustworthy. Mutuality of trustworthiness is a fundamental building block for family and social relationships and must exist for a relationship to be defined as fair. Nagy's work is based on a principle of ethics: it is unethical when relationships are not fair.

Parentification as Unfair

The concept of fairness is a subjective process of defining a relational situation as being a balance of give-and-take (Boszormenyi-Nagy & Ulrich, 1981, p. 164). Nagy's work is consistent with symbolic interaction theory because fairness is an interpretation between the two actors in a relationship as to whether or not there is a balanced ledger of fairness. The way two actors give meaning to their relationship in terms of fairness will affect how they will relate to each other. Neither another family member's assessment of fairness nor the appraisal of an outside observer will weigh heavily in determining the quality of that relationship. The external assessments may be taken into account, interpreted, and defined by the actors, but ultimately their own judgments affect their relationship.

According to Nagy, we all carry within our minds a ledger or balance sheet of entitlements and indebtedness from our families of origin. We are entitled based on the contributions (labor, care, or kindness) we have made to another; we are indebted based on the contributions others have made to us. The ledger of entitlements and indebtedness constitutes invisible loyalties that exist within our families of origin and affect our relationships in our families of procreation. The relationships we had with our parents affect the feelings we may have about our relationships with our children.

When parents received little nurturance, time, attention, or affection from their own parents, they may resent having to give these qualities to their own children. They may resent their own children if they perceive that children are granted a right in our society to receive time, attention, affection, money, and the material goods that money buys in exchange for nothing. Thus, parents may see families as inherently unfair because they give and the children receive without reciprocation until they are at least school age. Boszormenyi and Spark maintain that, when parents feel exploited in this way, they can unconsciously cover their feelings through overprotectiveness, overpermissiveness, martyrlike devotion, or other defensive behaviors (1973, p. 83).

Boszormenyi and Spark (1973) see overburdened parents as failing to provide children with limits and sanctions for crossing boundaries or acceptable behavior (absence of discipline). They see this permissiveness as bordering on parental neglect.

> Parental emotional depletion and lethargy tend to drive an increasing number of modern parents to the parentification of their children through overpermissiveness. Technical progress tends to further magnify the effects of a no-constraints attitude. The vast freedom of mobility and communication made possible through the automobile and television are not balanced by an increased competence of human authorities. The abandonment and

subsequent alienation of youth is expected to continue to rise in most sections of society (83).

Parental Permissiveness

These authors see permissiveness as a form of parentification, because, without the parents raising their children, the children are left to raise themselves, to create their own sense of right and wrong, their own morality, their own order and structure. Children have to become parents to themselves.

> Overpermissiveness as a form of parental abandonment of children, aside from bordering on neglect, is probably one of the most widespread forms of exploitative parentification. It constitutes a true double bind, since it appears to be giving something (freedom of actions) when its essence is in the nature of unilateral taking (nongiving of concern or limits, and expectations of spontaneous self-propulsion from the child) (83).

The neglectful, disengaged parent is only one way in which parents parentify children. The overindulgent, ever-present, and giving parent creates another form of parentification, because this parent invokes guilt in the child if the child does not repay the "sacrifices" made by the indulgent parent. This child is ever-indebted to his or her parents for the rest of his or her life. This kind of parentified child has great difficulty gaining autonomy from the family of origin because attempts at gaining autonomy and independence are interpreted as ingratitude. This kind of parentification adversely affects the ability of the child to leave the family of origin as an autonomous adult and, thus, is pathological inasmuch as it interferes with normative developmental processes. For Boszormenyi-Nagy and Spark (1973),

> As a birthright, children deserve to be reared responsibly; rearing is not a reward for their earned merit. Paradoxically, however, the child's privileged position, if carried to an extreme, may lead to his exploitation through his becoming permanently, symbiotically dependent on the parents. The secured possession of an obligated partner, especially if the latter is an overavailable parent, may lead to an insuperable wish never to relinquish the relationship. In addition, a guilt-laden obligation to the overdevoted parent might make every consideration of change and growth difficult. Excess indulgence thus can lead to as much exploitation as overt child abuse (87).

The gainfully employed single parent and dual worker parents in intact nuclear families may tend to overindulge their children out of guilt they feel for leaving their children alone as much as they do. These parents may have the money to overindulge their children with material possessions. The children then feel obligated to pay back their parents by being competent in some way, either through academic excellence, sports, music, or as family caretakers. This creates a circular process of guilt-evoking activity between parents and children, in which each engages in behavior out of their feelings of guilt.

Only children are often lavished with material possessions and are overindulged by parents. As the only child, they are the exclusive focus of parental love. This sometimes gives them the reputation of being "spoiled brats." However, what often fails to be realized is that great pressure is placed on only children to be successful in their lives, because the only child represents the only chance parents have to demonstrate to the world that they are successful parents. Although these children may be showered with material possessions, the other side of the coin is that great pressure is placed on them to be shining stars. In many Asian cultures, furthermore, these only children are expected to be the source of financial and emotional support for the parents in their old age. Overindulgence of children thus carries with it expectations that can burden these children throughout their lives.

The Rights of Children

Bosmormenyi-Nagy and Spark (1973) articulate seven items that constitute what they perceive to be a child's inherent rights. The rights of children constitute obligations for parents to provide children with implementation of these rights. These basic rights are as follows:

1. No one should produce a human life without a commitment to raising the child to maturity. Abortion of the unwanted fetus can be a much kinder fate than being born unwanted.

2. The child has a right to be brought up in an atmosphere in which he will be imprinted with the value of parental responsibility as a value of high priority. Consequently, he has the right not to be instilled with distorted ethical priorities, such as an undue emphasis on the absolute value of the suppression or denial of sexual urges, or of loyalty in a sexual partnership—especially if these values are divorced from the much more fundamental obligation to the life interests of one's children.

3. The child is entitled to be parented in a way which does not constitute overprotection, overpermissiveness, and overparentification. As a sign of subtle decay in any human group, psychological exploitation of children can be masked by permissive, protective, or martyr-like pseudogiving attitudes, which can amount to an abandonment of the child. Covert parentification of the child may take the appearance of an overdose of caring. In other words, it is the child's right and need not to be overindulged.

4. It is the child's right to be raised by adults who assert themselves in their own rights and who know what they should demand of the child, thus providing him with a structured outlook on society.

5. The child has the right not to be exploited through overt cruelty or scapegoated in displaced retributive revenge on the parent's family of origin. This type of exploitation is rarely intended consciously by the parents, except in cases of gross child abuse.

6. The child should be able to count on being loved and accepted by the family regardless of his earned merit. Yet, at the same time, a capacity for meaningful contribution should be expected of every child.

7. It is the right of the child to be taught to deal with his siblings justly, to learn to respect the incest taboo, and to be available as a continuing resource to other members in their struggle for survival (89).

The ledger of entitlements and indebtedness between parents and children within a nuclear family system is often asymmetrical at any given point in time, usually running a developmental course based on the age of the child. During the child's infancy, the child is seen as entitled to care, nurturance, attention, and affection, and the child is seen as having little indebtedness to the parent at this point. The parent is gaining "merit" without repayment by the child during the child's early years. Nagy believes that, if the parents seek repayment for their earlier child care during the child's adolescence or young adulthood, this is unfair because the adolescent may lack the maturity or developmental ability for acceptable repayment. It is problematic for adolescents and young adults to be encumbered by debt before they are developmentally ready to assume the responsibilities of debt repayment.

When debt repayment is expected by parents too early, it can adversely affect the perceived level of trustworthiness in the parent–child relationship because the trustworthiness of a parent is linked to the child's perception of the parent's consideration for his or her welfare. If the parent demands repayment too early, the child may perceive that the parent is selfish and oblivious to his or her needs. If the child is expected to do more than he or she can developmentally deliver, this creates environmental stress for the child that can result in symptomatic behavior (pathology).

When the parent is old and the child is an adult, the ledger of entitlement and indebtedness may again become skewed, with the elderly parent perceiving his or her entitlement to care and nurturance given past caregiving and the adult child perceiving indebtedness to the parent. Sometimes the intergenerational process of reciprocity plays out with an adult child neglecting the needs of his or her elderly parents. This is apt to occur if the adult child feels he or she got very little from a parent during childhood and thus feels no obligation to give more than he or she received earlier in life.

Multigenerational Processes

An important part of Nagy's work is that processes of reciprocity in family systems are multigenerational, often extending over three generations. The kind of parenting a person gets from his or her own parents affects the parenting that person gives to his or her children in return. Nagy writes about a **revolving slate** in which "patterns shall be repeated, against unavailing struggle, from one generation to the next" (Boszormenyi-Nagy & Ulrich, 1981, p. 166). What Nagy postulates is that, if children get nurturant, attentive parenting from their own parents, they feel indebted to their parents, even though sometimes they cannot compensate their parents in kind. A parent may die or may not need financial or psychological help. If their own parents cannot be repaid in kind, the adult children can repay the family ledger for what they got by giving to the next generation, their children. If the parents feel obligated to repay their parents by being attentive to their own children, this could result in the parents renouncing support that could be given by extended family members, because the parents feel they have to parent their children all by themselves.

The parentification of children arises as a form of reciprocity, a payback, that entails invisible loyalties. Loyalty may involve a ledger of entitlement or indebtedness of parents to their own parents or loyalty of children to their parents for services received. The parentification of children is unfair and unethical, because in the process of parentification children are giving to their parents more than they received from them. It is unethical when adolescents are parentified because parents are imposing expectations on children who are often unable developmentally to deliver what are unreasonable parental expectations.

Complementary Roles

Nagy, as a family therapist, focused on interpersonal relationships between people. When he writes about parentified children, there is always an element of complementarity implied. People often take **reciprocal roles** toward one another, such as one person being dominant and the other submissive, one person being a giver and the other a taker, a caregiver and a person cared for. Parentified children often assume a reciprocal role to a parent. The child becomes the responsible, caretaking "parent" to a parent who is functioning as a needy, dependent "child." The child gives nurturance and support that the parent receives.

> children attempt to be parentlike substitutes to their own parents. They assume roles which are inappropriate in terms of age and sexuality, in attempting to fulfill the parental vacuum. Family therapists see the effects of being a parentified or scapegoated child: depression, learning and behavioral difficulties, psychosomatic illnesses, accident-proneness, suicide, and battering (Boszormenyi-Nagy & Spark, 1973, p. 273).

Parentification does not only exist between parents and children. It can also exist between adults, such as lovers, when one partner assumes the role of a needy child and the other takes care of them as a responsible adult, or parent. Parentification is not just intergenerational but can exist as a process of assuming reciprocal roles among age cohorts.

The existence of reciprocal or complementary roles are not intrinsically problematic. However, these roles can become problematic when they become rigid. They become troublesome when the role cannot be altered, when, for instance, the people being taken care of do not want to be dependent anymore, but the caretaker will not stop caretaking or allow them to fend for themselves or become independent.

Roles Restrict Experience

Playing any role in a rigid, inflexible way becomes problematic inasmuch as it imposes limits on the experiences people are allowed to have. The role of the hero in a family, for instance, does not allow this very successful, popular, "perfect child" to experience failure, just as the role of "scapegoat" in a family (troublemaker, deviant, the person responsible for all the family's problems) does not allow the person playing this role to experience success. Whenever one plays a role, there are limits to the patterned behavior outside of which the role occupant is not allowed to go.

> When children are not permitted to be children, to pursue and gain mastery over their interests and work (school), then they feel overresponsible and attempt to carry parentlike

functions. These are overburdening roles for children. If children are emotionally needed, then out of deep loyalty to their parents, they accept such inappropriate roles as the parentified child, the scapegoat, or the sexual partner (Boszormenyi-Nagy & Spark, 1973, p. 272).

From a symbolic interactionist perspective, the accepting of caretaking roles occurs as a rational process in the mind. Children are aware of their loyalty and sense of obligation to one or both parents and they indicate this to themselves. Parental children often believe they must stay in the role of caretaker, of responsible, dependable, mature parent figure. They believe they should not play as a child, or be irresponsible or undependable. Thus, they deprive themselves of a full range of experiences that are available to them. The role confines and restricts them like a straightjacket.

Gregory Jurkovic

Ivan Boszormenyi-Nagy was a mentor to Gregory Jurkovic, who, in turn, became a mentor to graduate students at Georgia State University, several of whom wrote significant works about parentification—Goglia, Jurkovic, Burt, and Burge-Callaway (1992); M. A. Karpel (1976); Sessions and Jurkovic (1986). Jurkovic focuses on parentified children, and does little to distinguish parental from parentified children in part because his mentor did not make such distinctions. But Jurkovic (1997) builds on his mentor's work by creating a continuum of caretaking roles that children play in families. Readers are advised to pay close attention to this continuum and grasp the difference between the four types of parentification because the continuum provides a context for interpreting the process of parentification.

Destructive	Adaptive	Healthy	Infantilization
Parentification	Parentification	Non-parentification	

- -

Jurkovic's Model of Parentification

Destructive Parentification. At one end of the continuum is "destructive parentification," which involves overt extreme caretaking of one or both parents over an extended period of time when expectations for the child are not age-appropriate. Between parent and child, caretaking tends to be unilateral (by child toward parent) rather than being reciprocal. The role of caretaker tends to be internalized as part of the child's identity, and it is difficult for the child to identify him- or herself as an individual outside the interpersonal context of caregiver to another.

With destructive parentification, the child receives no credit or appreciation for performing the caretaking function, which is detrimental to the child's image of self. If the child's caretaking efforts are not acknowledged by others, then the subtle message sent to the child is that his or her labor is so insignificant that it is not worth mentioning, and the child comes to internalize that his or her work is worthless, that, perhaps, he or she is worthless.

The tasks that are assigned to these children often are developmentally inappropriate given the child's age. Therefore, these children are apt to have difficulty fulfilling these inappropriate expectations of them and their failures are internalized, which is also detrimental to the development of a positive image of self. When they attempt to care for others in a situation that they are powerless to fix, these children feel worthless and powerless, which undermines their sense of competence. This is apt to occur when children take on the unreasonable task of preventing an alcoholic parent from drinking or a heroin- or cocaine-addicted parent from using drugs or when they attempt to make a schizophrenic, bipolar, or borderline personality disordered parent display predictable, stable, responsible behavior. Taking on such responsibilities undermines the development of a positive sense of self.

Adaptive Parentification.   The next role in Jurkovic's model is "adaptive parentification," in which caretaking responsibilities often exist as a consequence of family crisis or acute stress. Although these responsibilities may exist long-term and may be excessive, the child's contributions are recognized and appreciated by family members and by the community. The difference between destructive parentification and adaptive parentification is an issue of fairness. In destructive parentification, the child is performing vital tasks but is not getting much in return for his or her efforts; at least in adaptive parentification there is acknowledgment of the child's contributions, even though he or she may still be overburdened by responsibilities.

In the coming chapters, adaptive parentification will be identified in a variety of familial situations: when children become caretakers of parents who are wounded or pained as a result of a divorce or widowhood; when children assume responsibilities in military families when one or both parents have been deployed into active duty; when children become parental figures to siblings as a result of parental incarceration; when a child fills in for a parent who becomes either physically or mentally ill; and in families of recent immigrants, when the child adapts by providing the parents with linguistic help in the new culture and serving as a liaison between the parents and the outside world. In adaptive parentification, the child perceives a hole or vacuum that exists within the parental system and fills that hole, for however long is necessary. Adaptive parentification is central to this book as the experiences of many respondents qualify as adaptive parentification, not destructive parentification.

Healthy Nonparentification.   "Healthy nonparentification" involves children being assigned tasks that are age-appropriate. In this situation, children are expected to be integrated into a family's division of labor; they are contributing members of the family system; they do work. They are often assigned to do some caretaking of themselves, such as cleaning their room and putting dirty clothes in the laundry, but their tasks are age-appropriate and their work is often supervised by adults. Their contributions are acknowledged and appreciated. There is role flexibility: these children not only work but they also play. Their identities are not shaped by the work they do or by their caretaking responsibilities. Their work is only one part of their lives.

Infantilization.   At an extreme end of the continuum is "infantilization," in which children are very egocentric, underfunctioning, and dependent and do virtually no caretaking of others. Their needs are sometimes excessively attended to by parents, and they are not challenged developmentally to grow and assume responsibility and fulfill commitments. These children appear to be immature because they are "babied" or coddled by their parents. This style of parenting is conducive to the development of narcissistic tendencies as these infantilized children become adolescents and adults because they believe that the world revolves around them, and they act as if others exist to meet their needs. Family princes and princesses, discussed in the introduction of this book, illustrate infantilization.

Infantilization relates to Nagy's discussion of overindulged children who are not permitted to repay their parents, generating guilt in the child. This guilt is a barrier to leaving the family of origin because if the child leaves the parents, they may appear to be unappreciative, ungrateful for all the parents did for them. The guilt keeps them as children who cannot "grow up" to lead independent lives.

As a therapist, Jurkovic (1997, 1998), tends to focus on destructive parentification in his writings, probably because the clients he sees are those who are most severely affected by parentification, those who have experienced destructive parentification. He is less likely to have clients who manifested healthy or adaptive parentification in their families of origin because many of them benefited from being parental or parentified children. These are the people who, through performing these roles as children, learned how to be more independent, autonomous, self-sufficient adults.

Although this book utilizes Jurkovic's schema, most of the respondents who provided data constitute a nonclinical population, so healthy nonparentification and adaptive parentification come into sharper focus than in Jurkovic's writings. Nevertheless, the identification of different types of caretaking, as posed by Jurkovic, constitutes a significant contribution that builds on the more general portrayal of parentification by Nagy because it establishes that parentification is not a singular phenomenon but exists in different contexts with different levels of severity. By focusing on the full spectrum of parentification, we can ask two related questions: Under what conditions is the development of parental and parentified children most likely to be harmful to these children? Under what conditions is the development of parental and parentified children most likely to have constructive consequences? By focusing on the full spectrum that Jurkovic presents, we can identify the differences between destructive parentification and its more healthy forms. Jurkovic finds that parentification is most likely to be destructive when the role is filled by children over a long time and when children receive little positive reinforcement for their caregiving—less recognition, less acknowledgment, and fewer compliments—from others, the more destructive this role is apt to be.

Instrumental and Expressive Caretaking

Following from the work of Parsons and Bales (1955), Jurkovic and colleagues distinguish between instrumental and expressive caretaking (Jurkovic, Jessee, & Goglia, 1991). Parsons and Bales originally described instrumental and expressive roles as reflecting a gendered division of labor within industrial age families living in the United States in the 1940s and 1950s, families that featured a wage-earning husband and a homemaker wife.

The wage-earning husband performed the **instrumental function** of providing for the family's physical needs for food, clothing, and shelter. In performing this role through his gainful employment, the husband connected the family to the outside world (he also

was apt to take out the garbage and do the yard work, which also linked the family to the "outside world").

The wife in an industrial age family (as portrayed in *Ozzie and Harriet* and *Father Knows Best*) was apt to be a homemaker who performed the **expressive role** in the family. Her job was to provide for the family's emotional needs, to make sure everyone was happy, and to ensure that everyone got along. She connected family members to each other. Children can perform both instrumental and expressive roles simultaneously; these roles are not mutually exclusive.

Parental children perform instrumental caretaking when they provide for the physical needs of siblings, when they cook dinner, bathe siblings, do grocery shopping, and do laundry.

> I cooked, cleaned, bought groceries, wrote checks, did laundry, ironed clothes, cared for my sister, went to my sister's school functions, bought school clothes, etc. I raised my sister as if she were my child. . . . I really did not have time to be a child; I was overburdened.

There are two kinds of instrumental caretaking. The first kind, illustrated by the previous respondent, involves physical caretaking of a household and its members. This meeting of physical needs includes grocery shopping and cooking because family members need to eat. Family members need clothes to wear and, for clothes to be available, they may need to be washed and dried. The second kind of instrumental caretaking involves providing money for the purchase of things like food or clothing or heat in the winter by providing money through gainful employment. Adolescents often provide this second form of instrumental caregiving by working after school and giving their earnings to their parents.

This second type of instrumental caregiving is often found in single-parent households and in families of recent immigrants. Single-parent households often experience a shortage of money because only one adult provides financial resources to support a household. Single parents, as well as their children, worry about how they are going to manage financially, particularly in dealing with unusual crises such as a roof leaking or a furnace or car breaking down. Adolescents in these households sometimes recognize the need to pitch in and help financially, so they get after-school jobs in retail stores or provide child care, yard care, or pet care to neighbors.

Because of their limited English skills, adults in immigrant families often work for low wages, making family survival difficult, so adolescents in these families may work after school to help their parents meet the financial needs of the household. Parents are often torn between having their children gainfully employed and economically productive or not working and doing schoolwork and achieving scholastically, sacrificing short-term rewards for what may be long-term gains in the future. The following account illustrates instrumental caregiving, as a child provides for his family rather than going to school.

> Father became a migrant worker when he was very young. He lost his father at the age of thirteen. At that particular moment, he became the caregiver to his siblings, mother, and grandmother financially and emotionally. My father never had the opportunity to attend school because working and earning money always took priority over school. In his case, my grandmother could not afford to send my father to school. Instead, they sent my father

to work in the fields, working long hours harvesting peppers, berries and other agricultural products. My father had to choose between going to school and feeding his family. Of course, feeding his family was more important.

Parental children exhibit expressive caretaking when they comfort, provide security, love, companionship, and support for their siblings. As parentified children, they exhibit expressive caretaking when they do "emotion work" for their parent(s). The following description illustrates how a child becomes a confidante to her divorcing mother.

> My mother began to confide in me the details of why the divorce was taking place and not long after that I knew the whole story. My mother needed me as a friend. She needed me to tell her that her decision was the right one, and she needed someone she could cry on. She needed someone who could cry with her. My mother also confided in her sisters, but I think she was ashamed to tell them everything.

The following respondent provided emotional support for her mother, who was trying to cope with an alcoholic spouse. She performed expressive caretaking by being available to her mother so that her mother would have somebody with whom she could share her burden. This respondent provided a shoulder on which her mother could cry.

> While my father was still drinking and even after he stopped, I was my mother's emotional support. Even though I was very young and did not quite understand why she was always mad at daddy, she talked to me a lot. I remember times when she would not say a word but lay in bed with me and cry. I always tried to make her feel better, but I did not understand what was wrong.

This respondent illustrates that expressive caregiving does not require the caregiver to cognitively comprehend the problem. It does not require that the caregiver have the right words or say the right thing. Rather, caregiving can consist of just "being there," being available to a pained or wounded parent so that the parent can release his or her emotional stress.

When adult children become parentified in caring for elderly parents, adult male children are apt to engage in instrumental caretaking, helping their parents financially, while female children are more apt to take on an expressive role by visiting, calling by phone, and providing companionship to keep the parent happy (Houser, Berkman, & Bardsley, 1985; Seelbach, 1997). Often male children of elderly parents will ask their sisters or their wives to do the emotional work, the visiting and phone calling (Matthews, 1995; Silverstein, Parrott, & Bengtson, 1995).

As Jurkovic points out (1997), parentified children can perform in a number of roles. Heroes are competent, reliable, dependable, outstanding, and popular. Scapegoats or rebels may be truants or delinquents, chemically addicted, sexually promiscuous, fail in school, or manifest physical or psychological illnesses or disabilities. Both extremes constitute styles of emotional caretaking of parents, distracting parents from their own problems or supplying them with excitement or adventure. It is tempting to think of parentified children only as heroes, but some children are parentified through their deviance. This will be elaborated on in the next chapter on chemical dependency.

The distinction between instrumental and expressive caretaking at first blush seems straightforward, but distinguishing between instrumental and expressive caretaking can be quite complex. If a male adolescent becomes gainfully employed and contributes his earnings to help his single mother financially, it looks as if the child is providing for the physical needs of family members through his employment and is thus performing instrumental caretaking. However, what if the primary motivation of the working child is to lessen his mother's worry and concern about a shortage of money? What if his motivation is to enable his mother to feel more secure financially? Is his working then expressive caretaking, inasmuch as he is trying to make his mother feel less worried and more secure?

A symbolic interactionist would likely explore the motivation of the child, the decisions that the child made in his mind prior to his action that would enable an observer to understand why he acted as he did. If the motivation was emotional caretaking of a parent, then his behavior would be described as expressive caretaking. If the motivation was to provide for the physical needs of family members, then the behavior would be described as instrumental caretaking. Distinguishing between these two styles of caretaking is not an easy task when respondents are unclear or their motivation is fused with elements of both instrumental and expressive caregiving. This fusion would exist if a respondent told a researcher that he was working to help the family pay bills and buy food and also to help his mother feel less burdened and worried financially.

Gender and Social Class

Jurkovic writes of gender differences relative to whether a child will be parentified overtly as a hero or as a deviant. According to Jurkovic, "females typically report greater caretaking responsibilities in their families of origin than males," while males are more likely to exhibit parentified behavior through deviance, "such as distracting misbehavior, reflecting their status as a loyal object rather than an overt parentification process" (1997, p. 44).

Goglia (1982) found parentification to be more prevalent in females than in males. Among adolescents and young adults, females, who at this stage in their lives should be focused on differentiating from their families of origin and spending more time on self-development and peers, were unable to differentiate from their families of origin and remained enmeshed in family problems and responsibilities. Particularly for females, assuming the roles of parental or parentified children adversely affected the ability of these children to leave their families of origin to become autonomous adults.

Jurkovic, following Minuchin, links parentification to poverty. According to Jurkovic (1997, p. 39), "Joblessness, a correlate of child abuse and neglect is often in the family backgrounds of parentified children whom we and others (e.g., Minuchin, Montalvo, Guerney, Cosman, & Schumer, 1967) have seen." He goes on to say that "The 'working poor,' whose jobs often require odd hours and yield limited income, may rely heavily on their children to help manage the household."

I would add that social class constitutes an opportunity to influence the style in which children perform the roles of parental or parentified children. Middle- and upper-middle-class children have a greater opportunity to play the role of hero in an expressive way, regulating their parents' emotional states via extracurricular activities, because the instrumental functions of the family are provided for. There is money to pay nannies, baby-sitters, launderers, gardeners, maids, or take-out restaurants. There is less apt to be a vacuum of instrumental caretakers as there is in working-class or poor families, who cannot afford to outsource their labor to meet family needs.

Middle-class families have the money to create opportunities for their children to be parentified in an expressive way as musicians, athletes, or dancers because they have the money to pay for sports lessons and activity programs (from summer camps to competitive sports leagues), music or dance lessons, language or culture classes, art, reading, or tutoring programs. These parents have the financial resources to outfit their children with the finest equipment and clothing so that they can excel in their area of expertise. As these children become stars in their activity, they provide parents with an area for recreation and diversion from depression, stress, fatigue, or the grind of their everyday lives; they provide the parents with the excitement of their child's competition as well as a social arena in which the parents interact with one another and form a community of support for a team or group. They provide parents with a sense of pride and success as they perform with competence and skill. These middle-class children are doing "emotion work" for their parents and are parentified children in an expressive modality.

Working-class and poor children tend to be parentified in a more instrumental modality, perhaps being gainfully employed as adolescents to ease their parents' financial burdens. They also are parental when they care for younger siblings so that their parents have the assurance and peace of mind (parentification, caring for parents emotionally) that the children are safe, protected and supervised by a family member. Their caretaking is instrumental if the motivation for caretaking younger siblings is to help their parents financially, so that the parents do not have to pay external caretakers for supervision, thereby enabling them to save money. Social class, then, appears to influence the style in which children play the roles of parental and parentified children.

A Parentification Scale

Any science must develop propositions that are empirically verifiable through research, and the concepts used in those propositions must be measurable. Toward this end, Jurvokic and Sessions (1986) helped to develop a parentification scale whereby the existence of parentification could be measured. The parentification scale is a 42-item true/false questionnaire with items such as "In my family I often felt called upon to do more than my share," "In my mind, the welfare of my family was my first priority," and "Members of my family rarely needed me to take care of them." Higher scores on the scale indicate parentification while lower scores on the scale indicate infantilization. Moderate scores indicate either healthy nonparentification or adaptive parentification. The scale gives equal weight to instrumental and expressive caretaking styles as well. The scale is somewhat limited in that it is a self-report questionnaire that measures the subjective perceptions of only one member of a family. Other family members might perceive the role of the child in the family very differently, and there is no mechanism for assessing this. Yet the Sessions/Jurkovic parentification scale has been used in an intergenerational study of adult children who grew up with alcoholic parents (Goglia et al., 1992) and a study of personality development in parentified children (Jones & Wells, 1996).

Conceptualizing Caretaking Roles

Family therapist Salvador Minuchin used the concept of the parental child to refer to children who were parent figures to their siblings. He wrote about parental children existing primarily in poor families with a single female head of household. He wrote virtually nothing about parentified children.

Boszormenyi-Nagy and Jurkovic wrote about parentified children when children were parent figures to their own parents, providing physical and/or emotional caretaking to them. These authors wrote only of parentification and abandoned distinctions between parental and parentified children, lumping both concepts together under the label "parentified child." This generic use of "parentified child" seemed appropriate because both parental and parentified children function as parent figures. Both are caretakers of others.

What gets lost in the generic use of "parentified child" for both the roles of parental and parentified children is the object of the parentification. Does it make any difference whether it is a parent or a sibling who is the object of the caretaking? Because I think it does, I have attempted to differentiate these roles precisely in this book, using the concepts of parental child and parentified child in their appropriate contexts.

Some children, of course, are both parental children and parentified children simultaneously. These children are caretaking both their siblings and their parents. An example of this would be a parental child in a single-parent household, where the mother works and the child helps her out by caretaking siblings. By caretaking the siblings, the adolescent is a parental child. But if the motivation for supervising and nurturing siblings is to help the mother out, by easing the mother's burden of finding external child care services both financially and to ease her anxiety or worry about the safety and welfare of the children, then the caretaking of siblings also constitutes parentification. This adolescent is taking care of the mother, serving the mother's need to have the children cared for, supervised, protected, and, perhaps, fed and bathed.

However, other children, such as "only children" in a family, have no siblings to parent. They may be parentified children, but they do not experience the role of a parental child. When there is an only child, it is only the parents who are around to be cared for. This child may be parentified in maintaining the parents' fragile marriage by giving them a common source of pride or a shared interest in his or her activities, the only thing they might have in common that keeps them together. Or this child might be parentified by engaging in deviant behavior, which brings parents together in their shared concern over the child. This child might be parentified in protecting the mother from abuse by the father or by taking charge of trying to reduce a parent's use of alcohol or drugs. This child might be a companion and source of emotional support to a single parent who is left by a deployed military spouse or one that has been incarcerated. With families in the United States having fewer and fewer children, one-child families represent a sizable and increasing percentage of families in this country.

Parental children can exist without being parentified. Siblings of children who are chronically ill, either physically or mentally, protect and assist their ill sibling, not to be of assistance to the parent but to assist and support their brother or sister. One can have totally competent parents who are ably caretaking their child and still siblings might participate in caretaking functions. This is not to fill any parental vacuum, but is, rather, an altruistic act. That this assistance is not parentification in disguise is an issue of the *motivation* of the parental child (Karpel, 1976). Is the parental child's motivation to relieve parents, in which case parentification exists, or is it only to come to the aid of the brother or sister? If the latter, the child is a parental child but not a parentified child.

Psychoanalytically-oriented therapists may respond to this by invoking the issue of unconscious motivation; that is, are there motivations that lie outside the conscious awareness of actors that are motivating forces nevertheless? The writings of Boszormenyi-Nagy and Jurkovic are riddled with references to the unconscious, a legacy of their psychoanalytic training. From their perspective, parental children can be seen as always, unconsciously, caretaking one or both parents when they care for siblings. One problem with this interpretation is that the unconscious usually cannot be retrieved, made conscious, so the unconscious cannot be tested or measured because it lies outside the parameters of science as we know it. The unconscious can only be inferred, guessed at, or interpreted without verification.

The issue of the unconscious is addressed in this book by virtue of the fact that symbolic interaction theory frames the analysis of parental and parentified children. If one employs symbolic interaction theory, the unconscious, if it exists at all, is irrelevant because behavior is carved out by indications people make to themselves in their minds. Such indications only exist at a conscious level and any issue of an unconscious is moot. People carve out lines of action in a process of rational thought; behavior is constructed through cognition.

George Herbert Mead distinguished between meaningful and nonmeaningful behavior. Meaningful behavior is behavior constructed through a process of rational thought. Nonmeaningful behavior is reflexive, automatic behavior that is not preceded by thought, such as uncontrollably crying when hearing tragic news without thought of what others might think or how they might feel about one's crying. Mead did not deny the existence of nonmeaningful behavior—behavior that might be constructed in the unconscious—but such behavior was of no interest to him. The only behavior of interest to him was "meaningful behavior." In this regard, a symbolic interactionist would not deny that some children may assume caretaking roles by default, without that caretaking being preceded by a process of rational thought. They would further not deny that some people may have forgotten the process of rational thought in which they engaged prior to assuming caretaking roles. Many prospective respondents cannot retrieve the cognitive process that existed in constructing their behavior. They "don't remember" the thoughts they had in the past. When we are asking people to retrieve thoughts that led to caregiving in childhood, we are asking them to retrieve thoughts they had long ago. The symbolic interactionist is interested in the few insightful, articulate respondents that do recall their thoughts that led to caregiving behavior in childhood. Those respondents are called "informants." It is reasonable to seek out these informants in a college population, because it is here that one is apt to find reflective, insightful, introspective, and articulate people who can serve as informants.

To understand whether the caretaking of a child constitutes parental or parentified behavior requires a researcher to assess the motivation of the child. Whom does the child perceive he or she is helping? If the motivation of the child is to help or care for a sibling, then the child is parental. If the intent of the child is to help or care for a parent, then the child is parentified. If the intent of the child is to help or care for both siblings and parents, then the child is both parental and parentified simultaneously. The assessment of motivation is congruent with the methodology of symbolic interactionism because retrieving motivation requires in-depth interviewing, probing the indications respondents make to themselves in their minds. The researcher is trying to grasp the child's interpretation of the situation. Such inquiry is congruent with Weber's discussion of *verstehen,* understanding, for the research is trying to take the place of the other and grasp why the child behaved as he or she did in terms of the cognitive processes that preceded his or her behavior. How did the child define the parent and the siblings in terms of their needs, impairments, limitations? How did the child define him- or herself in terms of his or her ability to offer assistance? What indications did the child make to him- or herself in terms of alternatives? Could others perform these functions? Would others perform them, and what did the child perceive as the consequences if others attempted to serve as caretakers? These are exactly the kinds of questions symbolic interactionists are good at asking through in-depth interviewing of respondents. These are the kinds of questions my respondents attempt to answer throughout the remainder of this book. Their written accounts constitute the equivalent of transcribed interviews. In their accounts they share their experiences as parental and parentified children as well as the process by which they came to assume these roles in diverse contexts.

Summary

Salvador Minuchin is a family therapist who described parental children as caretakers of their siblings. These children filled a need that existed in their families by virtue of an impaired executive subsystem that failed to provide the family with the leadership and caretaking that the children needed. The writings of Boszormenyi-Nagy and Jurkovic describe parentified children as caretakers of their parents. Destructive parentification overburdens children because the caretaking functions tend to be long-term, beyond the ability of children developmentally, and are taken for granted (unacknowledged and unappreciated) by family members. These children get their identity from their caretaking and, thus, they are undifferentiated from those they care for; they fail to establish a sense of self apart from others. These authors see destructive parentification as inherently unfair because these children give to their parents more than they get from them. It is also unfair because expectations are placed on these children that are difficult or impossible to meet, setting them up for experiences of failure, frustration, and fatigue, which undermine a positive image of self.

Part II

Contexts for the Development of Parental and Parentified Children

Sociologists often write about the effects of social structure on the behavior of individuals. In analyzing social structure, they focus on how society is organized by social class, ethnicity, race, and gender. Symbolic interactionists recognize the existence of social structure and its influence on behavior. They realize, however, that social structure does not determine behavior; rather, social structure is taken into account in the minds of actors who may either overcome the obstacles of social structure or take advantage of unique opportunities that social structure provides them. Norms or rules, for instance, exist in social structures, but people may consider the norms and opt to either conform to them or violate them.

This part of the book suggests that the ways in which certain families are organized presents increased or decreased opportunities for children to become parental or parentified children. Dual-worker households, single-parent households, military families, families of chemically dependent persons, families of recent immigrants, families who experienced divorce or widowhood, families in which a member is chronically physically or mentally ill, very large families, families in which there is an elderly parent, and families having an incarcerated parent all present greater opportunities for children to become either parental or parentified. The social structures in these families, which often feature some kind of parental gap or vacuum, will not determine the existence of parental or parentified children. They only present an opportunity for children to take these roles. Hence, those families that exhibit parenting gaps or vacuums are referred to as "opportunity structures." Although these families present children with the opportunity to be parental or parentified, not all children take that opportunity.

Whether or not children take the opportunity is determined by cognitive processes in the minds of parents, children, and other relatives. The children in these families become caregivers by acknowledging that (1) there is a problem, (2) something must be done to address and reduce the impact of the problem, and (3) I can help.

3

Chemical Dependency and Alcoholism

A person has a problem with drugs or alcohol when his or her use of drugs or alcohol, no matter what the amount or frequency of consumption, impairs interpersonal relationships. If use of drugs or alcohol impairs the quality of the marital relationship, then a drug or alcohol problem exists. If the partner perceives that there is a drug or alcohol problem, there is, because the usage is adversely affecting the relationship.

If the use of drugs or alcohol is adversely affecting one's relationship with a boss, supervisor, or coworkers, the user of that drug or alcohol has a drug or alcohol problem inasmuch as the usage is adversely affecting the relationship with coworkers. If supervisors and coworkers believe that the use of drugs or alcohol is adversely affecting one's job performance, then alcoholic consumption is problematic. If alcohol consumption results in chronic lateness or absence, or if alcohol consumption adversely affects competence, accuracy, or efficiency on the job, then the worker has a drug or alcohol problem. The user may deny the deterioration of work performance, but if supervisors say such deterioration exists, it does. If the boss says there is a problem, there is. This reasoning is consistent with symbolic interaction theory in which "reality" is subjective, perceived reality. If colleagues or family members interpret a problem as existing, the problem exists and colleagues or family members will orient their behavior in line with their perception and definition of the situation.

If the use of drugs or alcohol is adversely affecting relationships with friends, neighbors, or congregants, the user has a drug or alcohol problem. It is a common denial response (Black, 1981; Woititz, 1983) for a user to respond to accusations that "you have a problem" or "there is a problem here" with "you're the one with the problem, not me" or "it is your problem, not mine." Problems are shared by people, problems exist in relationships, between people, so if one person has a problem with another's behavior, the problem is shared by both parties.

When a person is an alcoholic, there are usually at least six other people affected by the alcoholic's drinking, including family members, coworkers, neighbors, and friends.

This is one way in which an individual's alcohol abuse is a system problem, affecting that person's interpersonal relationships.

Alcoholism has also been described as a system problem, not the problem of an individual, inasmuch as people in families with an alcoholic member play roles that unwittingly contribute to the maintenance of the alcoholic's drinking. Much as members resent the alcoholic's drinking and wish for change, they subtly act in ways that maintain the alcoholic's abusive consumption. Families of chemically dependent people tend to be rigid and resistant to change.

This chapter will examine how chemical dependency in one or more members of a family is perceived to affect other family members. Alcoholism is one form of chemical dependency. Dependency on foods (candy or sugar, for instance), prescription drugs, or illegal drugs constitute other forms of chemical dependency. The literature on family dependency tends to portray a consensus view of how chemical dependency affects family life. The authors writing on this subject constitute a social group that seem to share a collective perception of how alcohol and other drugs become like a member of the family, such that the bottle (of pills or alcohol) becomes to family members like a competitor for money, attention, affection, time. The substance creating the dependency, alcohol or drugs, is like a lover in an extramarital relationship, drawing one partner away from the family by focusing his or her interests, energy, and attention outside the family. It is to the shared perception of scholars studying the effects of drugs and alcohol on family life that we now turn. In effect, we are exploring the minds of these scholars, much as we explored the minds of authors doing pioneering work on parental and parentified children in Chapter 2.

Boundaries in Families of Alcoholics

I previously described Salvador Minuchin as the creator of "structural family therapy." Though a psychiatrist, he is more interested in analyzing how the structure of a system affects the behavior of individuals living within that system than studying individuals in a vacuum, isolated from their psychosocial environment. Rather than focusing on how thoughts and feelings within an individual affect his or her behavior, Minuchin sees the behavior of children as a consequence of interpersonal dynamics that exist in their families and their behavior is a response to the behavior of others, a response to how parents relate to the child and, more importantly, the ways in which parents relate to each other. Children usually get too powerful and out of control because there is a fragmented parental system: parents subtly sabotage each other, canceling out each other's power and giving the child more power than either parent has.

Minuchin (1974) created "family maps" that portray relationships in family systems. In these maps, Minuchin identifies three kinds of boundaries: diffuse boundaries, clear boundaries, and rigid boundaries.

RIGID BOUNDARIES	CLEAR BOUNDARIES	DIFFUSE BOUNDARIES
(People are disengaged)	(Normal range)	(People are enmeshed)

Boundaries Used by Minuchin for Family Maps

When Minuchin constructed family maps, he signified diffuse boundaries with a dotted line, clear boundaries with a broken line, and rigid boundaries with a solid line. The broken line has spaces through which family members can leave the system to get their needs met and through which the outside world can enter the family to support its members. The illustrations of families used in Chapter 2 showed clear boundaries by using a broken line separating generations within a family as well as separating the family from the outside world. The solid line of rigid boundaries blocks family members from leaving the system and prevents the outside world from entering the family.

Diffuse boundaries are pathological inasmuch as they are blurred, shadowy, almost nonexistent boundaries; they are open to a fault. Diffuse boundaries exist when people are **enmeshed,** when they are overinvolved with one another. This exists in families that have an anorexic daughter, for instance. Anorexia nervosa (Minuchin et al., 1978) is a syndrome in which a person, usually an adolescent girl, starves herself. This can be fatal if unattended; an anorexic can starve to death seeking skinniness. Minuchin was an expert, recognized in the 1960s for his understanding and treatment of anorexia nervosa.

Enmeshment.　In an effort to keep their anorexic child alive, one parent, usually the mother, immerses herself in the eating disorder of the child. This involves a blurring of personal boundaries so that two people function as one. Mother devotes her life to keeping her daughter alive, getting her daughter to eat anything. As she becomes enmeshed with her daughter, the mother becomes disengaged from the father, who will not help the mother nor support her in her parenting. Father distances himself from the mother because he resents the attention mother is giving to the daughter and not to him.

Enmeshment often exists between people in chemically dependent families when the parentified child can become enmeshed with the alcoholic or drug-dependent parent. The child takes it as his or her mission to keep the parent sober or nonabusing. These two people function as one, becoming tangled together like strands of spaghetti. When the parent drinks, it is the parentified child's failure to keep the parent sober. If the child cannot maintain sobriety in the parent, the child cleans up the mess that the parent creates by drinking. When the parent excessively drinks, the child feels guilty, as if he or she is a failure for not being able to maintain the parent's sobriety. There is a lack of individuation, a blurring of personal boundaries; one does not know where one person ends and another begins. In many ways, the child is feeling what the parent should be feeling but is not feeling—embarrassed—so the child carries these feelings for the parent.

The problem with diffuse boundaries is that those involved give up some of their own personhood. They sacrifice some of their own individuality and uniqueness to fuse with the other. Murray Bowen (1978), a family therapist, in fact calls the existence of diffuse boundaries "fusion" between people.

If a parent is depressed, parentified children will see the parent's depression as their problem, which they must solve or cure, often either with humor or distraction. The child only feels OK if the parent feels OK—the feelings of parent and child are intertwined—so the child works to make life acceptable for both of them. Where one finds parentified children, one usually sees diffuse boundaries between the parentified child and the parent being cared for; in symbolic interaction terms, the child's sense of self is inextricably linked to one or both parents. Where one finds parental children, one usually finds diffuse boundaries between the parental child and the siblings for whom that child is responsible.

Disengagement. The opposite of enmeshment is disengagement. People are disengaged as a result of rigid boundaries between people. Disengagement occurs when people are emotionally, physically, or cognitively unaffected by the behavior of others. When father comes home from work and plants his nose in a newspaper or the television and the children are fighting with each other in the room and he is oblivious to their conflict, a rigid boundary exists between the children and their father. He is emotionally and cognitively unaffected by their fighting.

The boundaries between people in families containing an alcoholic, however, tend to be enmeshed. People in this system take on the alcoholic's problem as their own. They take responsibility for solving the alcoholic's problem either by trying to get the alcoholic to stop drinking or by covering for the alcoholic, doing the tasks that the alcoholic should be doing but is not doing, so that the family does not experience negative consequences from the alcoholic's incompetence.

Norms in Families of Alcoholics

The authors who write about alcoholism in families perceive these families as exhibiting norms that maintain the alcoholic's drinking behavior (Kritsberg, 1985), norms of isolation. Such families tend to have closed boundaries that isolate the family from the outside world. The parent's drinking and everything else that goes on in the house is a secret to be kept from the outside world. The following respondent, who had an alcoholic father, learned norms of silence at age six. Note that the motivation this respondent articulates is the desire to please her parents. This is "emotion work," managing the emotional state of parents so that they are happy. This is what parentified children do; they take care of the emotional well-being of parents by engaging in behavior that keeps the parents happy.

> It was important to please my parents, and I learned quickly that the way to please was to remain silent. One of the most important norms was of silence, which included the idea that what goes on in our house will remain in this house. I can remember when I was six and my sister was seven years old. We were told to make our parents' bed after the sheets were dry. As we were making the bed, my sister found a gun under their mattresses and showed me. I remember us contemplating who my father was going to shoot with it. My sister thought that she was going to be shot because my dad liked me better. The next day at school, I told my first grade teacher what had happened. When I got home from school that day, I guess that my teacher called my mom and told her what I said. My sister and I were in trouble and my mom told us, 'What goes on under this roof stays in this house and nothing is to go outside of this house.' We were told that our father could be taken away to jail for us telling. We also received a spanking with a belt for this incident. From an early age, I learned the code of secrecy and fear for disclosing information within an alcoholic family.

Using Goffman's work, one can interpret alcoholism in this family as a stigma. The way of dealing with this stigma was to conceal it. Family members hid the alcohol abuse by keeping it a secret from the outside world, trying to "pass" as if the alcoholism did not exist. Secrets are the enemy of change. When families have secrets to keep, such as in child physical abuse or sexual abuse, spousal domestic violence or drug or alcohol abuse, they close their boundaries to the outside world. This means that children cannot invite friends over to the house for fear that the friend will see someone inebriated. It means that adults cannot have friends over for fear that the family secret will be discovered.

The consequence of maintaining closed boundaries is that family members have limited access to resources outside the family system to bring about change or get support. This means that family members tend to deal with their fears, feelings of powerlessness, and anxieties alone, weakening their power to affect change.

The feeling that family members are alone in dealing with a member's drinking is exacerbated by the existence of a norm of silence. The norm of silence prescribes that family members not share with others their perceptions of what is happening. Members do not talk to others about what they see (mom is drunk or dad is hung over), which functions to reduce the likelihood of coalitions being formed that would enhance any individual's power to deal with the situation. One does not share with others how he or she feels about the drinking and what it does to him or her internally.

Internalized Legacies

There are legacies that children of alcoholics carry with them (Jones & Wells, 1996; Prinz & West, 1987; Sher, 1997). One of those legacies is that adult children of alcoholics often have problems entering into and maintaining intimate relationships in their adult lives (Martin, 1995; Newcomb, Stollman, & Vargas, 1995). Intimacy involves sharing one's thoughts and feelings. It requires self-disclosure, sharing with another information about oneself. This self-disclosure is very difficult and seems strange for a person who was born into and raised by a family with norms of silence. This person has little experience sharing thoughts and feelings with others (Arbetter, 1990); in fact, he or she has spent years living in an environment where sharing and talking was discouraged.

There are organizations for Adult Children of Alcoholics (ACAs) that enable people who were raised in alcoholic families to recognize the legacies that become part of them and to overcome these legacies. Many people who were reared in these families are unaware of the impact the alcoholism of a parent has had on them.

Should children state what they are observing in a family with an alcoholic, norms of denial are implemented to counter the expressed observation. If a child, for instance, should say that dad looks "hung over," a family member may counter with denial, saying "no, he's got the flu" or "no, he's getting a cold." The consequence of being exposed to habitual denial is that children come not to trust their own observations or feelings, their own perceptions of their situation. They become insecure about their own interpretations of reality, and this affects their self-esteem, for they begin to question their own competence in making sense of the world, which further reinforces silence. If one is consistently told that his or her observations are inaccurate or wrong, soon one learns to hold his or her tongue because he or she will always be made to be wrong. Not sharing one's observations or interpretations will then adversely affect one's ability to build intimate relationships.

Norms of denial quickly lead a person to distort the truth and tell lies. Children are sometimes encouraged to lie in order to maintain the secret of alcoholism from the outside world. When children lie for an alcoholic parent, they act as parentified children. The lying is a means of protecting the parent and the parent's image in the eyes of others.

> Many times I have lied for my dad. I even lied to law enforcement several times when my dad would get in an accident while driving drunk. One time my dad was driving home from the bars and mistakenly pulled into the neighbors' driveway and hit a utility pole. The neighbors saw this and called the police. The police came to my dad's house and pounded on the doors in the middle of the night. I was awake . . . we were instructed not to open the door and pretend we were sleeping. As the police were about to break down the door, my dad opened it. He said he had been sleeping. The police were on to him but played along. . . . When they asked me, I said he had been home all night.

If lying becomes a habit, this can adversely affect one's relationships with others as an adult because intimacy is based on trust; trust is impaired when people are not honest.

Roles in Families of Alcoholics

The literature on alcoholism pays considerable attention to roles people play in families exhibiting alcoholism. These roles are interrelated and interdependent, creating a system that unwittingly maintains the alcoholic's drinking pattern. In highlighting the interrelated character of these roles, alcoholism is seen as a system problem, not the problem of an individual. It affects multiple others and is maintained by multiple others.

The Dependent

The alcoholic plays the role of the dependent, the person who is physically and/or psychologically dependent on alcohol or drugs. Particularly in the early stages of alcoholism, such people vehemently deny that they have an addiction problem. Denial, in symbolic interactionist terms, constitutes a definition of alcoholism by the alcoholic as "no problem." However, when one deals with the issue of "denial," one sees the existence of discrepant definitions of a situation in which others, family members, coworkers, and, perhaps, a therapeutic community, see the alcoholic as having a problem but not realizing it or denying the problem. These others, who see the alcoholic as "out of control" or abusing alcohol, define the alcoholic's definition of their situation as "denial," failing to define their own situation as problematic when, in the eyes of others, it is problematic. The people affected by the drinker's alcoholism see their task as getting the alcoholic to accept their definition of the situation—a problem that requires the alcoholic to change.

Denial results in the dependent people being very sensitive to comments made by others about their drinking. They become touchy, taking offense easily. They manifest defensive behavior around talk of alcohol consumption. They make comments like, "Why don't you leave me alone?" "Why are you always on my case about this?" "You just don't understand." "Why do you make so many demands?" Such comments are often accompanied by displays of anger.

The anger exhibited by the alcoholic is often accompanied by domestic violence or threats of violence. Children adapt to this violence by taking on the responsibility of protecting family members against it. In protecting a parent against violence, they are parentified children; when they protect siblings, they are parental children. It is the job of parents to protect, and, in assuming a parental role, they protect others either by being violent themselves, taking action against the alcoholic, or, more commonly, by distracting the alcoholic. Note how, in the following account, the respondent defines members of his family; his father is a "bad man" and his brother is a "guardian angel." The descriptions indicate how the respondent perceived other family members and the interactional dynamics among them. He presents his family as engaging an almost epic battle between good and evil. By protecting this respondent from danger, the brother served as a caregiver by being a parental child. In consoling his mother at night, the brother was a parentified child to the mother.

> My father was an abusive alcoholic and an all but worthless father. I remember when he would hurt my mom and my older brother and I would try to console her. I always wished that I was more powerful and that I could do something to make the 'bad man' go away forever. That's the way my brother and I would refer to him, as a 'bad man.' He completely destroyed our household and left a twelve year old little boy to pick up the pieces. My brother used to cook for my dad and, of course, bring him his beer. He would put him to bed when he would pass out drunk, and he would console my mom late at night when she would cry. My brother was also my guardian angel. I remember he would hide me in the closet when my dad would come home madder than hell and when my dad would come after me, my brother would try and block his path. There were a lot of times when my brother would tell my dad that he did whatever it was my dad was mad about, just so my dad would ease up on my mom and me.

In the next account, one sees how children not only have to adapt to violence within the home but violence outside the home also. Children often have to adapt to frequent moves because of the parental unemployment that results from alcoholism. Males particularly are apt to assume the role of family protector.

> There were six children all together, with my uncle being the oldest. Both their parents were severe alcoholics, which left all responsibility on Tony [name changed to protect confidentiality]. The family moved constantly because of evictions and loss of work. 'Each time we moved,' explained Tony, 'the neighborhood got worse. We mainly moved around the San Francisco area, Mission District, where fights and stabbings were an everyday occurrence. Being the only male in the family, I took it upon myself to take care of my younger sisters. They were so young and witnessed such terrible things in their little lives. My parents drank constantly and were very violent when drunk. My stepfather constantly beat the hell out of me, my mom, my sisters, and for what reason, I still don't know. The heart-wrenching part was seeing my one sister, Lilly [name changed], being beaten so severely that neighbors had to rush her to the hospital. She was so young, maybe eight, damn they were all young. No matter how good a kid you were, in my stepfather's eyes, you were bad. We would go to school all beat up, and kids would tease us, causing us to fight with them as well. It was not uncommon to have to fight your way into a new neighborhood, you had to be tough. And taking care of younger sisters isn't an easy task. We were taken away by Child Protective Services countless times, and foster homes became like vacation homes. One day I remember clearly is the time our mother dropped us off at a

babysitter's house for the night. Only the night turned into weeks and then into months. The babysitter couldn't take us and we were once again taken to the shelter. Hearing my little sisters cry for their mother was the most heartbreaking sound in the world and all I could tell them was that "She'll come back." And one day she did—six months later and drunk as ever. It got so bad one night that I finally had enough and I stood up to my father and told him never to touch one of us again. He looked at me crazy and started calling me names, but he stopped and went out to the local bar. It was that night that I knew I had to leave. I was twelve years old and felt like a thirty year old man. I told my mom I was moving out, kissed my sisters, and was on my way. I worried about them constantly and felt extreme guilt for leaving, but I knew I had to leave for all of our sakes. I truly wanted to kill him and was afraid that I might. I rented a slum apartment for $8.00 a week and worked at the local chicken joint. I bought myself a beat up car and gave any extra money I could to my mom and sisters. I did the best I could with them and today, despite the hell we had to go through, we all turned out okay.'

This respondent's conclusion, that "we all turned out okay" is a theme that will be discussed in the concluding chapter of this book because it is a statement made by a majority of the respondents. Although their childhood may have been painful and difficult, they believe that their experiences neither destroyed them nor did they result in irreparable damage to them. They saw themselves as surviving their experiences intact.

The ability of this child to leave is unusual. The last chapter of this book describes how difficult it is for parental and parentified children to leave nuclear families in order to lead independent lives. The guilt that the respondent reported feeling on leaving keeps many parental and parentified children from leaving their families of origin. Note that leaving the family was an act that came with considerable "soul searching," which, in symbolic interaction terms, involved defining his situation, as well as the situation of his sisters and mother, considering alternatives, and anticipating consequences. For instance, he anticipated that, if he stayed, he might wind up killing his father.

Children raised in families with an alcoholic learn to be placaters; they learn to please others, to make others happy to avoid inciting the parent to anger. They become hypervigilant to the emotional state of others and learn to look for signs of anger and an impending explosion. These children watch for gestures and give meaning to certain parental gestures as signifying anger or imminent danger. In this way, they act as parentified children because they seek to manage or regulate the emotional state of the alcoholic. They perform parentification in an expressive way, keeping the parent happy so that anger will not become manifest. Note how the next respondent indicated to himself that it was his "responsibility" to please his father. This was a child that was clearly burdened, if not frightened, by that responsibility.

Due to my father's weekend drinking binges and unpredictable behavior, I would be his helper since my other sisters did not want to be around him when he was drinking. I would do anything my dad needed when it came to helping in the yard or getting him another beer. I felt it was my responsibility to please him so that he would not get angry or violent.

In the next poignant description, we get a child's glimpse of an alcoholic's anger. Several themes are illustrated in this account. One can see that the child of an alcoholic has an unpredictable life, in which violence cannot be controlled and in which the child feels powerless. We see that the child often blames herself for this anger, that she experiences self-blame and guilt when anger arises, particularly when she believes that she is the cause of the parent's anger. We see how protection becomes a critical theme in families with violent alcoholics and the goal becomes merely survival in a dangerous and chaotic world. Note that, as a previous respondent interpreted protection as his "responsibility," this respondent assumes that she has an "obligation" to clean up before mom comes home. This is how she defined her situation. In protecting her mother, she assumed the role of a parentified child.

> I laid stiff with my blanket pulled up to my eyes that widened and winced with every slurred, muttered word that would spill out of his mouth accompanied by the impact of bottles, dishes, and furniture breaking. My father's nightly bout of intoxication was like a hurricane that instantly appeared with an unforgiving fierceness, demolishing everything in its way. The process of destruction would begin around five o'clock every evening when my father wheeled his Ford into the parking lot to pick my brother and I up from school. I can still remember the haunting murmur of his truck, the way the thick tires hummed against the pavement as he rolled with bitterness into the school yard. We made the usual stop at the liquor store to load up on supplies for the evening. With an icy Coors between his legs, and the familiar yet restless silence, we made our way home.
>
> My brother and I would rush to clean up the mess that Dad had made before Mom came home from work. We knew how it hurt her to see this every day so we adopted it as an obligation to our family. Re-hanging pictures, picking glass, and plant soil out of the carpet, and struggling to put the lawn furniture back in place after it was thrown against the house was our daily routine. Our small frames grappled to clean up as quickly as we could while he changed out of his work clothes so we wouldn't make him angry. After all, we 'learned' we were the cause of his unhappiness, therefore believed it was our responsibility to clean up after him.
>
> How I would have done anything to make my father happy. To make him proud of me, smile at me, talk to me, to know me. Instead the only attention I received from him was in the form of a stern glare, or an unpredictable physical scolding. I couldn't do anything right. The tension in our house was so great that anything would send this man into a rage, and the consequence would be another long night of battle filled with physical and verbal abuse, accompanied by endless tears. Despairing, I thought it was my fault that he got so angry and drunk. I tried everything I could to get his attention and love, but somehow it was never enough.
>
> When I was nine years old, I remember counseling this drunk stranger in the backyard, sitting on a stack of wood in the middle of the night. Between my tears and trembling, I can recall pleading with him that he must stop drinking, yet still naive of the impossibility to reason with a drunk man. Talking to him during the day was out of the question; he was hung-over, sober and mean. He was a different person. Sometimes when my mom would go out of town for the weekend he would make me sleep with him and tried to cuddle with me. This made me very uncomfortable, and I knew then it wasn't normal. However, if I angered or deceived him, the consequences would be devastating not only for me but for the rest of my family. As a child in my family of origin, it was my job, my role, to take care of my drunk father and my helpless mother. . . .
>
> The goal of our family was to survive. We were dreadfully aware of the long night we had in front of us. Country music wailed throughout the house while dad repeated his

> favorite phrase, 'I work all day and have to come home to this shit.' We considered it a good night if he didn't come into our rooms and hurt us or our dog, who would bark at the noise and chaos that he would produce. I begged my mom to sleep in my room every night so she wouldn't have to be near this sick man. Occasionally she took me up on my offer; this made me very happy. Yes, I did want to die. I wanted him to die. I believed there was no end or solution to this abuse and destruction within my family.

This respondent is aware that her father exhibits two very different personalities, one when drunk and one when sober. This is part of the uncertainty to which the child must accommodate. This respondent had a sense of what was normal and what was not, and she clearly indicated to herself that her situation was not normal, that there was a problem here; she just couldn't construct a long-term solution to the problem, as much as she wanted to.

Later Stages of Alcoholism.   As alcoholism progresses, the alcoholic becomes socially isolated from family, friends, coworkers, and neighbors, and may turn to increased contact with drinking companions to counter the increasing isolation from nondrinking people. This may be accompanied with comments that drinking buddies "are the only ones who appreciate me; they don't complain, they don't hassle me."

The progression of alcoholism is associated with deteriorating health and personal appearance. The dependent experiences deteriorating sexual drive and interest, deteriorating job competence, deteriorating satisfaction with life—with work, family life, and friends.

Alcoholics experience increased fear: fear that they will be discovered as an alcoholic and fear that they couldn't stop drinking if they wanted to. Alcoholics also fear that they will lose their jobs as their job competence deteriorates, and they sometimes do lose their jobs. When this happens, it usually falls to their spouses to assume the instrumental function and provide for the family's physical needs through their work and the spouse becomes the sole source of the family's financial support. This creates a parenting gap and the children are frequently left to care for themselves. Children often are forced into the labor market at young ages to supplement family income as well. This event presents an opportunity structure for the creation of parental and parentified children.

> I remember growing up with an alcoholic father. My mother had to go to work since my dad was fired over and over again from jobs. Being raised in the Mexican culture, I had to take the role of the mother while my older brother took the role of the 'man of the house.' I was expected to feed my brother and sister and nurture them when they needed. My mom taught me to cook when I was nine years old. . . . My brother had to take care of us and protect us. He often implemented rules and curfews that my sister and I had to follow. He helped my mom with decision making. At the age of fifteen he was helping an uncle with side jobs so he could earn money for the house. He got a job in a construction site with the permission of my mom. We couldn't play after school sports because my mom had to work and wanted us home right after school. Having us home gave her a peace of mind and that's the way she was able to take care of us from her job.

Alcoholics fear that they will lose their family if spouse and children leave the household. Having family members leave is often a critical component to breaking the denial process. It is only when family members leave, or force the alcoholic to leave, that alcoholics must confront the realization that maybe they do have a problem. The family leaves only when all alternatives have been exhausted, when they admit that they are powerless to effect change and that they have reached their limit in accepting life as it is. They are frustrated, fed up, and distraught with the prospect of continuing the status quo; yet, they see that, if they do not leave, life will only continue as it is. The decision to leave or have the alcoholic forcibly removed from the family residence through a court order is extremely difficult and only comes with considerable support from family, friends, therapists, and others in the world outside the boundaries of the family.

The removal of the alcoholic from the family creates a single-parent household. The remaining parent usually works full-time to help support the household, leaving a parenting gap that tends to get filled by an older child who becomes a parental child, caretaking younger siblings while the parent is working.

The Codependent or Enabler

The spouses or partners of the dependent are called the "codependent" or "enabler." They are very competent, very responsible and reliable, so competent and responsible that they perform the work that the alcoholic should perform but cannot. This attempt to be helpful enables the alcoholic to deny that there is any problem. The alcoholic feels there is no problem because all the work that needs to get done gets done—by the enabler.

Over time, the enabler gets exhausted performing the work of two people. The enablers are often so busy caring for their incompetent spouse that they cannot care for the children as much as they would like. A parental child often helps the enabler with parenting duties or a parentified child supports the fatigued and frustrated enabler, serving as the enabler's confidante, cheerleader, and friend.

Enablers are caretakers who are very nice, sympathetic, and understanding. They are compliant placaters who do not want to rock the boat. They want everybody to be happy. Enablers do not complain. They silently endure the pain and embarrassment of living with an alcoholic. Wells, Glickauf-Hughes, and Jones (1999) suggest that codependent behavior is developed in childhood through the process of parentification. Parentified children learn how to become adaptive caregivers in their families of origin and then replicate those behaviors in their own families.

The following is the experience of a nice, understanding enabling child who recounts her experience with her divorced, alcoholic father and never complains despite her hunger. As a child, she "practiced" codependent behavior, which may well become a life script that she carries to adulthood.

> He went out so often and was always at a loss for money that I would rarely eat when I was with him because there was never any food at his house and he was always broke or on his way out. I remember staying up until 2 or 3 o'clock in the morning waiting for my dad to bring me back a slice of pizza from the gas station on his way home from the bars. I never complained. I just waited until he got home to eat.

The following respondent was born and raised in a Mexican family. He describes his father as an alcoholic and his mother as an enabler who insisted that the children show their father love and respect, despite his frequent absence from the family.

I got my first job cleaning rain gutters in town for fifty cents apiece. It was not much, but I felt it helped and that was all I wanted. My mother appreciated this and told me to save it so I could buy something nice for my father. No matter how much I loved my mother, I never truly understood her. I could not understand how come she wanted me to be nice to dad when dad was never even with us. In any event, I saved my money like I was told and I gave it to my father on my birthday when he came to visit me. I did not see my father again for a while and to this day I am afraid to know how he spent the money I gave him. . . . No matter how I felt about my father, I was always told to be 'nice to him and show him that you love him.' Yet I never felt loved by him, and I always felt alone when I most needed someone like him to be there.

The boundary between the alcoholic and enabler is often diffuse, as if there were no boundary at all. These are two people who function as one. When they go to a party together, the alcoholic drinks more than he or she should and acts inappropriately. The alcoholic is oblivious to the response of others to his or her behavior. The enabler feels embarrassed for the alcoholic, a feeling the alcoholic does not experience.

When the alcoholic cannot perform well on the job, the enabler feels embarrassed. The enabler worries for the alcoholic and covers for the alcoholic. The enabler may well call the alcoholic's place of employment and report that his or her spouse is sick with the flu, not hung over. This is called "codependent behavior" because it protects the dependent individual from experiencing the negative consequences of his or her behavior. Codependent behavior unwittingly contributes to the maintenance of alcoholism because, when the dependent person does not experience the negative consequences of his or her behavior, there is no reason for him or her to change.

Codependents are usually seen as having low self-esteem, which is bolstered by solving the problems of the dependent and relieving the dependent's pain. The enablers' values, hobbies, and interests are put aside to spend time with the dependent, engaging in the dependent's hobbies and interests. The enablers' friends diminish as they become increasingly involved with the dependent. This results in greater and greater social isolation for the enablers, reducing their external resources of support and their power to effect change.

The enablers' feelings about how they are doing in their own lives reflects the dependent's feelings about how he or she is doing. The enablers feel they are only doing as well their spouse is doing and only feel good about themselves if they win approval from the dependent. They are only OK if the dependent says they are OK, internalizing how their spouse appraises them.

In families of alcoholics, the person who plays the role of enabler might change over time. When one person who played the role for some time refuses to continue, somebody else may assume the role, thereby maintaining balance in the family. The stability that is maintained is that there continues to be an alcoholic whose drinking is maintained by an enabler. The person who plays the role of enabler may change, but the structure of the family remains unchanged.

In the following illustration of such a situation, the respondent's mother divorces her alcoholic husband, the respondent's father, and the respondent assumes responsibilities that are not age-appropriate. Because of the burden of responsibility and obligation felt by such children, authors who write about parental and parentified children give their books bleak titles such as *Burdened Children* (Chase, 1999) and *Lost Childhoods: The Plight of the Parentified Child* (Jurkovic, 1997).

> My parents divorced when I was very young. I spent every other weekend at my dad's house. I felt that since he didn't get to see me that much that he would look forward to our visit and stay home with my brother and me. Instead he went out drinking. When I was very young he would go to a party and bring me along. During the day he would take me with him to happy hour at the bar. At night I would sit out in the car as he ran in for what he promised would be 'just one drink.' Once I got to be about ten years old, he would leave me at home when he went out. A few years later he would have me baby-sit for his girlfriend's kids while they went out to the bars. I was rarely paid as my dad offered my services without asking me first. The time he spent at the bar I spent taking care of kids and cleaning his house because I knew he never would.

In the next passage, the respondent's grandmother left an alcoholic grandfather and the respondent's mother (the alcoholic's daughter) assumed the grandmother's role.

> When my grandmother finally left my grandfather, he suddenly needed someone to help him with his physical needs. He was used to living a life that was filled with days of insobriety, and he never had to do things such as clean, cook, or shop. My mother was very loyal to her father like many children of alcoholics tend to be. She took care of his physical needs when he was not able to do so for himself. Even though she had been damaged by many years of hurt and shame caused by her father's drinking, she was willing to take responsibility for him when she knew that he could not survive on his own. His drinking was very serious, and after many years of alcohol abuse, my mother realized that if she did not take care of her father, he would drink to his death. Eventually, that is what happened. But, my mother did everything she could to try and help him fight his disease. She cared for him by providing physical care. . . . She did not provide him with money, but rather helped him with cooking, cleaning, and shopping for both food and clothes. My mother said that it was very hard for her to see the effects of her many hours spent with her father actually helping him. She said, 'I felt like I was constantly doing things to help him, but when I looked at my father, I could see that his drinking problem never improved. It only got worse as the years went on.' After many years of being a parentified child, my mother watched her father until his last days of life were spent battling cirrhosis of the liver. My mother never stopped supporting her father and took responsibility over the things that he was not capable of doing in his state of intoxication.

We will return to the parentification of adult children who care for elderly parents in a later chapter for, with increased longevity in U.S. society, many adult children become the caretakers of elderly parents who are not necessarily alcoholics. Children who become parentified caretakers of their parents arise when the parents divorce, as in the above case, or when a parent dies, as we will explore when we discuss parentification as a consequence of widowhood in Chapter 6.

The Hero

When there are one or more alcoholic parents in a family, the children adopt adaptive roles that may involve some form of parentification. For instance, the oldest child may come to adopt the role of **hero** (Brown, 1985). This is the super-responsible, super-dependable child who is an excellent student academically, often a superb athlete, popular among peers, and often a parental and parentified child in his or her family.

The hero is a caretaker of the alcoholic inasmuch as heroes help the alcoholic deny that there is any problem in the family. If there were a problem, how could the family produce such a model citizen? The hero is sometimes called a "little enabler" because he or she does a considerable amount of domestic work in order to hide the incompetencies of the alcoholic. The hero, like the enabler, is competent, responsible, and dependable. Like enablers, they unwittingly contribute to the alcoholic's denial that there is any problem.

In performing an instrumental function, the hero cleans house, does grocery shopping, cooks, does laundry, and sometimes cleans messed up bedding or carpeting after an alcoholic vomits. In performing an expressive function, he or she often serves as a distraction from the family problems created by the alcoholic's drinking. If the hero is a musician, he or she provides the family with recreation and entertainment when they go to concerts in which the hero performs. The family members experience pride and accomplishment when they can vicariously rejoice at the success of the child, it gives the parents an opportunity for social interaction with other adults, particularly adults of other student musicians, when they would otherwise be socially isolated.

If the student stars in theater or in dance, performances again provide a temporary reprieve from the rigors of everyday life, particularly for the spouse of the alcoholic. The performance is a source of pride for the family, showing the outside world that the family has no problem. If the child is a star athlete, competitive games provide family members with recreation and entertainment, a focus of attention outside the family and a reprieve from the stresses and anxiety of everyday life at home. Athletic competition opens up the boundaries of the family system when members venture out to the athletic field to interact with the parents of other athletes. During a season, parents often form a temporary social system, engaging in pizza nights where they interact with one another.

One of my respondents saw her mother as playing the role of hero to get adulation from others in order to fill the void created by the absence of love and attention from her parents, who were alcoholics.

> In high school, my mom distracted the public eye from her parents' drinking to her extracurricular accomplishments. My mom went to high school in a small town and lived on the Air Force base where my Grandpa was stationed. I always remember my mom sharing stories of her dinner parties, of how she was captain of the cheerleading squad, Homecoming Queen, voted most popular and most friendly, and I was genuinely curious as to why she talked about something that happened a while ago. But now I understand these were her glory days. She was loved and respected by her peers in her community which helped but never completely filled the void of her parents' absence of love.

Heroes, as competent, reliable, dependable people, are well suited to play the role of a parental child. When both parents are consuming alcohol or other drugs, the hero may be the only person who holds things together in the family. The hero defines the family as problematic, indicates that something must be done to ameliorate the effects of the problem, and does something about the situation by caretaking others. If one parent is addicted, the enabler may be so consumed by the needs of the addict, so exhausted by trying to please and appease the addict, that his or her parenting competencies deteriorate. The hero picks up the pieces and fills the parenting void. Heroes often function as parentified children, helping the enabler deal with the alcoholic and being a confidant, supporter, and friend to the enabler, helping the parent to maintain his or her role in the face of frustration and powerlessness to successfully reduce the behavioral manifestations of substance abuse.

When heroes marry, they often marry a chemically dependent person, and they become enablers or codependents in their own families. They have been socialized into caretaker roles and so maintain the roles in their family of procreation.

The Scapegoat or Rebel

If the role of hero is taken by the oldest child in the family, the next child often cannot compete successfully for this position and so becomes a parentified child by playing the role of the **scapegoat** or **rebel.** These are children who distract from the parents' alcohol and drug use by calling attention to themselves as troublemakers. Their families can identity the scapegoats as "the problem" in the family, taking heat off the dependent and distracting from the often troubled, stressed marriage of the parents. By detouring attention away from the chemically dependent parent and focusing attention on themselves, these children are caretakers of the chemically dependent parent, protecting him or her from being discovered or hassled for drug abuse.

These are also children who get poor grades in school. They are often truant from school and may be in trouble with the law. They may use alcohol or drugs or be sexually promiscuous. One of my respondents was a juvenile rebel in an alcoholic family, which led him to a life of crime.

> I learned how to be a clocker and to watch for the v-8 squad cars that patrolled the area. I guess my playing the role of the scapegoat with the law, and more importantly my mom, had its benefits, though. For not only did it bring in more money, but it also allowed for us not to concentrate on my dad's problem and it led my brother to take on the hero role.

But this respondent writes that assuming the role of scapegoat carried certain costs for him.

> We would never talk about what went on at home, however, and we certainly did not talk about school because I did not stay at school very long. First chance I would get, I would jump the fence with my associates and leave. I guess my brother stayed and liked it because before I knew it, my mother was talking about him to her friends. She told them all about him and talked of him in a way I still wish she would talk of me. I guess that is not to be, though.

One unrecognized consequence of the scapegoat's deviant behavior is to link the family to outside resources. Through the acting out of the child, the family may come to the attention of social workers, law enforcement personnel, counselors, and community programs through court orders, and the child may be ordered to counseling, which might involve the entire family. This brings the family one step closer to external resources that are available to support change.

The deviant behavior of the scapegoat is similar to the deviant behavior of the dependent alcoholic and so they may become aligned in the family. The hero is more likely to align with the enabler because both are competent caregivers.

Boys are more likely than are girls to become the scapegoats in their families (Black, 1981). Deviant behavior in boys is somewhat more expected, accepted, and tolerated in U.S. society as a function of the expectations for sex-specific behaviors in the culture. "Boys will be boys" expresses the tolerance and expectation that boys more than girls will misbehave. Girls are expected to be more compliant and obedient. Symbolic interactionists tells us that, if people define situations as real, the definitions are real in their consequences; that is, people will behaviorally comply with the expectations that others have of them. This is certainly a contention of labeling theory, an offshoot of symbolic interaction theory, which states that, if a person is labeled or defined in a certain way, e.g., a troublemaker, he or she will tend to exhibit behavior congruent with the label. Stierlin (1974) notes that the scapegoat role may be constructive for families as a distracting, detouring behavior that constitutes a form of caretaking because it facilitates denial or avoidance of the alcohol problem.

Some family therapists, such as Jay Haley (1976) and Cloe Madanes (1980, 1981), interpret deviant behavior in children as a protective mechanism, as attempts by the children to protect one or more family members. Perhaps the children are trying to divert attention away from an alcoholic parent. Perhaps they are trying to distract family members with their deviant behavior or to protect the parents' marriage by unifying them with a common concern, a common goal, perhaps extricating the children from the trouble. Without the deviance, the parents might have little in common and might drift apart. Perhaps the children's deviance creates an external enemy for the family to rally against, uniting family members against a perceived external threat, for example, a teacher who is unfairly accusing the deviant child or a school principal who is unfairly disciplining the child. Such an external enemy might be an unfair police officer or probation officer or social worker that the family rallies against. Without the perceived enemy, the family might fall apart, but the enemy integrates the family unit, providing it with energy and purpose. When family therapists define deviance as protection, they must ask, "Who in the family is being protected by this deviance?" The children are not defined as bad or wrong, but as protective and caring of others in the only way they have discovered to help another family member, by stirring up trouble, by creating excitement and energy, by calling attention to themselves and away from others.

The Lost Child

If the roles of the hero and the scapegoat have been taken, the next child may assume the role of the **lost child.** The primary job of lost children is to stay out of the fray. These are the children who retreat to their bedroom or escape to a computer or book. They generally withdraw from social interaction with others and become loners, socially isolated from other family members and from age-appropriate peers at school. They escape negative attention, but, by socially withdrawing, they also lose out on receiving positive attention. Often, they get no attention at all, and usually have little interaction with their parents. This can be interpreted as a way of caretaking the enabling parent in the family, who has his or her hands full covering for and dealing with the chemically dependent spouse. Lost children do not add to the enabler's burdens inasmuch as they ask for nothing and do not demand attention or energy from anyone, a tactic that can be helpful to the already over-burdened codependent parent. It can also be helpful to older siblings, who do not have to expend much energy in caretaking such children. They quietly and unobtrusively take care of themselves. Note that, in the next example, the child's withdrawal to his own world came through a process of rational calculation, a process of making indications to himself in his mind. He opted to protect himself from his parents by taking care of himself, but, in the process, he took care of his parents by not imposing any parenting responsibilities on them. This child would not be acknowledged or appreciated by his parents for staying out of their way.

> One aspect of my childhood that I think I should mention is the fact that I was an only child and that I spent a lot of time alone. I felt that it was better to be alone and away from my parents than to be subjected to the ritual abuse that accompanied their drinking epi-sodes. I usually took care of myself for most of my psychological needs as my parents' priority was getting inebriated . . . I was parenting myself.

With limited experience in socially interacting with others, lost children are apt to be shy and socially awkward. They may experience loneliness and a sense of worthless-ness, as they are rarely noticed or acknowledged for doing anything worthy of praise. With no vehicle for expressing negative feelings, these children may experience physical ailments, which can be psychosomatic illnesses. By becoming sick, they can legitimately ask for attention or affection, that they might otherwise not get. With their social awk-wardness (Segrin & Menees, 1996), they are apt to have few, if any, intimate relationships with others, are apt to marry very late in life or not at all.

To some extent, the social isolation of lost children was experienced by many of my respondents, regardless of which role they played in their alcoholic family. The existence of closed boundaries around the family system, coupled with rules of silence and denial, had made the children feel socially isolated generally. These who played the role of hero, who cared for everyone's needs in the family system, often felt socially isolated from peers because they were so busy caring for family members, particularly siblings, that they had no time to maintain friendships with friends.

> After school, my brother and I would take the school bus home and then go inside and do our homework and watch TV until my mom came home from work. We would tidy up the house, and my brother would make something for dinner so that when my mom got home, she could just relax. Amazingly, my brother never complained about the responsibilities that he took on, although I know he sometimes resented them. My brother was never al-lowed to go over to his friends' houses after school or go outside and play because he had to watch me. Sometimes his friends would come over and play, but not very often. I re-member feeling very isolated, like we were not a part of the outside world.

The next respondent writes about her mother, who, after her parents' divorce, decided to live with and care for her alcoholic father.

> Her parents divorced when she was 12 years old, and it was at that time that she made the decision to live with her dad. I remember one occasion I had asked my mother, 'If grandpa was an alcoholic, why did you ever choose to live with him and not your mom?' 'Because if I left him, there would be nobody to take care of him, and I would feel so guilty.' From cooking meals, cleaning house, and doing laundry, to calling my grandfather's place of employment when he was 'too sick' to go into work, my mother was the ultimate 'parent' to her father. My mother had a very limited social life. She was so busy taking care of her father that she had no time to spend with friends, and hardly any quality time for herself. Because of this, her grades suffered in school and invitations to any type of social event(s) were out of the question.

Scapegoats felt socially isolated in being cut off from anyone who was not generally perceived in their school as a "loser" because the role severely limited the kind of people who would be receptive to engaging in social interaction with them. Although all children tend to feel cut off from the outside world, lost children were cut off the most. The emergence of the Internet as a vehicle for communication with the outside world has reduced the isolation of lost children, who often go into cyberspace to play games or enter chat rooms, but this is not face-to-face interaction with other human beings.

The Mascot or Clown

It is usually the youngest child in the family who plays the role of **mascot** or **clown.** These are children who are cute, funny, and always on stage stand-up comics, who provide the family with comic relief.

Children who adopt this role are immature, the "babies." They have a hard time "growing up" because it means being responsible, dependable, and serious, all qualities uncharacteristic of mascots or clowns, so they have trouble getting others to take them seriously. They also have trouble getting others to treat them as genuine and authentic, because they are perceived by others as always joking, always funny, and never really "themselves." The mascot or clown is constrained to exhibit a narrow range of behavior—be happy, be funny, be cute, so these children have difficulty showing sadness or anger, being serious or intellectual, or insightful or analytic.

Children who play this role are caregivers. They protect the chemically dependent parent by calling attention to themselves and away from the parent. By protecting a parent, they become parentified children. They are also providing comic relief to the burdened enabling parent. The child shows this parent that there is humor in the world and provides this parent an opportunity to laugh when most of the time this parent wants to cry. The mascot or clown provides this parent with energy to keep going.

Roles as Restrictive.   One reason all the above roles are problematic is that they restrict the role occupant from manifesting behavior that lies outside the role. The hero cannot experience failure and has a hard time playing or having fun. Play is usually competitive play where skill level affects winning or losing. The scapegoat cannot experience success or competence, except for competence in getting into trouble. Scapegoats are noticed, but in a negative way. They are not recognized for positive qualities they may have and are discouraged from enhancing positive qualities because they would be deviating from their "image." Lost children do not experience positive or intimate social interaction with others or bond with them, even in friendship. They have no vehicle for getting support, encouragement, or validation of themselves because they are so socially isolated, nor do they really know their parents or siblings because of their restricted interaction with them.

These roles, however, are not the exclusive property of families with an alcoholic. One will find them in families without alcoholism or drug dependency. The roles are more detrimental the more rigidified they become, when people cannot break out of them to exhibit a range of diverse behaviors.

People do not necessarily play the same role during the course of their life, and roles in families can change over time. When the hero leaves and goes away to college, for instance, some other child in the family may suddenly blossom to assume the vacated role. When a scapegoat leaves the family because of incarceration or hospitalization or is expelled from the family, another child may start to exhibit deviant behavior and assume the vacated scapegoat role to serve as a distracter for others.

The roles discussed in this section—dependent, enabler, hero, scapegoat, lost child, and mascot or clown—are the roles used in the work of Stephanie Brown (1985; Brown, Beletsis, & Cermak, 1989), but hers is not the only presentation of roles in families of alcoholics. Claudia Black (1990), for instance, uses different role labels to describe children in alcoholic families. What we have described as the "hero" she calls "the responsible child," which she refers to as "the little adult" or the "household top sargeant" (Black, 1990, p. 13). The scapegoat or rebel in Brown's portrayal is called the "acting out child" by Black, who writes that "in reality, acting out children tend to suffer from less denial than the others in the chemically dependent family. They are closer to knowing the truth and are acting out the dysfunction of the family" (Black, 1990, p. 16). Black calls the lost child the "adjuster." I see some problem with this label because, in many ways, all the roles involve children who are adjusters. What we have are different styles of adjusting to parents who are impaired as a consequence of one or more members being abusers of alcohol or drugs. The responsible child and the acting-out child are both adjusters in their own way. Black calls the mascot or clown a "placater," a person who is nice, understanding, and sympathetic, who doesn't want to rock the boat and exists only to make others happy, and describes this role as the "household social worker."

Goglia et al. (1992) write of the role of "child as parent," when children act as either parent to their siblings (a parental child) and/or parent to their own parents (a parentified child). In many ways all child roles, whether hero, scapegoat, lost child, or mascot, involve parentification as they are styles of taking care of either the dependent or the enabler or both.

These authors also write of the "child as mate," children who become spouse substitutes. We will be exploring many contexts in which one spouse becomes absent in a family—when there is a divorce, when a parent in the military is deployed to active service, or when a parent is incarcerated. In such contexts, an older child may rise to fill the void left by the absent parent and act as a mate to the remaining parent. This may involve parenting the children as parental children do or it may involve serving as a confidant, companion, friend, support system, or financial provider to the adult who remains.

The "child as mate" role can also arise when both parents are physically present in a system but one parent is so incapacitated as to adversely affect his or her ability to function as a competent parent or spouse. We find this situation with drug dependency or when one parent suffers from chronic illness or from mental illness. In these contexts, a child may rise out of the sibling subsystem to enter the spousal subsystem functioning as a substitute spouse (without necessarily performing the sexual functions of a spouse).

Consequences for the Future

The literature on alcoholism suggests that assuming the role of hero in a family affects the development of personality of these children as they become adults (Goglia, Jurkovic, Burt, & Burge-Callaway, 1992; Newcomb, Stollman, & Vargas, 1995). Children who performed as heroes become serious, competent, dependable, responsible people in their adult lives (Chase, Deming, & Wells, 1998). They have trouble having fun and playing and cannot act spontaneously or dive into activities that are unplanned or unscheduled. They also have difficulty accepting any failure, and are very critical of themselves should they achieve anything less than competence or outstanding success. They expect a lot from themselves and establish lofty goals, which puts them under considerable pressure and stress.

Valleau et al. (1995, p. 159) find that assuming excessive childhood responsibilities, as the hero does, results in the development of overfunctioning characteristics in women, who

1. believe they know what is best not only for themselves but for others;
2. move quickly to advise, fix, rescue, and take over when others are in distress;
3. have difficulty restraining themselves and letting others struggle with their own problems;
4. avoid worrying about their own personal goals and problems by focusing on others;
5. have difficulty sharing their own vulnerable, underfunctioning side, especially with those whom they believe have significant problems of their own;
6. is frequently labeled by those who know them as "always reliable" or "always together."

Although the authors say these characteristics are typical only of women, I believe they would also apply to men who were childhood heroes.

Children who performed as scapegoats or rebels develop into adults who underachieve, and who often exhibit addictive behavior, whether those addictions are to alcohol or other drugs, food, smoking, or rigorous programs of exercise. As adults they may have difficulty maintaining stable employment as well as entering into and maintaining intimate relationships with others. There is generally a lack of permanence or stability in their lives; change is an ever-present characteristic.

Lost children develop into adults who are loners, who are socially isolated and socially awkward, and who also have difficulty entering into and maintaining intimate relationships.

Children who were mascots or clowns never seem to grow up. They continue the laughing and joking into their lives as adults and have trouble being serious, reliable, and dependable; they are usually taken care of by others in exchange for their humor and the diversion they provide from serious aspects of life.

There is a fuzziness in the literature about these roles in children and adults. The behavior exhibited by adults is really no different from the behavior they exhibited as children. It represents continuity, more of the same. Does playing the role of hero, for instance, contribute to the development of serious, reliable, dependable, compulsive adults or is this behavior, already exhibited by the child, part of what is really a fairly stable personality pattern over the life course?

There are many ways of thinking about the development of personality patterns. One can see personality as genetically determined, with behavior a function of physiology, a genetic legacy. From this perspective, genetics determines a range of behavior and where one falls within that range is affected by environmental and interpersonal factors. The physiological determinants of behavior are emphasized by adherents to what is sometimes called "sociobiology."

One can see the early playing of roles by children as gaining experience and expertise in assuming the role later as an adult. One learns and develops competence in playing a role that eventually constitutes a life script that can be changed, but only with difficulty if the behaviors have become intrinsic to the individual's pattern. This line of thinking concludes that the acquisition of roles is part of what is learned in the process of socialization. That is, we learn how to play roles in a sociocultural environment.

Families as Opportunity Structures

Families in which an alcoholic is present constitute an opportunity structure for the creation of parental and parentified children. Chase, Deming, and Wells (1998) used a Parentification Questionnaire to determine whether children of alcoholics reported higher scores on parentification than children of nonalcoholics and found that families in which at least one parent is alcoholic provide an opportunity structure for the creation of parental children (Goglia, Jurkovic, Burt, & Burge-Callaway, 1992). The alcoholic parent is incapacitated by their alcoholism and the other parent performs as an enabler, either as a drinking companion (also an alcoholic) or as a nonalcoholic enabler. The enabling parents are so busy taking care of the alcoholic—by being gainfully employed so that the family does not wind up homeless or by caring for the instrumental and expressive needs of the alcoholic—that they are exhausted, frustrated, and increasingly angry. The marital relationship can become so stressed by the alcoholism that attention is focused on the marital relationship at the expense of the children. The children get lost in the shuffle and must learn to care for themselves. This parenting gap is filled by older children, who function as parents to their brothers and sisters.

Impaired parenting is accentuated when there is only one parent and that parent is an alcoholic with no enabler around to help pick up the pieces. In this case, an older child functions as a spouse substitute and becomes an enabler by caring for both the alcoholic parent and the siblings. This caretaking is a form of enabling codependency, for the alcoholic is kept from realizing the negative consequences of his or her behavior by the competence of the enabling child.

Families in which at least one parent is alcoholic provide an opportunity structure for the creation of parentified children. The child has the opportunity to care for the physical needs of the alcoholic, such as putting him or her to bed, administering analgesic medications for hangovers, or cleaning up when the alcoholic vomits. The child has the opportunity to care for the emotional needs of the alcoholic by being a good listener when the alcoholic bemoans the stresses and strains, the pain, guilt, and remorse in his or her life. The child listens to the countless fantasies about doing better next time. This is all part of the child as therapist, friend, or confidante, part of being a parentified child.

The child is provided the opportunity to be a parentified child to the enabler spouse by also serving as a therapist, friend, and confidante when the enabler parent needs to dump or unload frustration, anger, disappointment, and fatigue as a mechanism for coping. Because the enabler is so exhausted from performing the work of two parents, the child has the opportunity to help out, to be "mom's little helper" in an attempt to ease the parent's burden. This helping out may include participating in cooking, grocery shopping, cleaning or child care, all part of the parentification of a child.

The next respondent echoes a theme that is voiced by many respondents, namely that alcoholism and domestic violence frequently coexist. Domestic violence creates a context for the development of parental and parentified children inasmuch as they seek to protect family members from the alcoholic's violence. Protection is a parental responsibility that children try to assume when adults cannot provide the protection that is needed. The following respondent had an alcoholic father who was more unpredictable when he was sober than when he was intoxicated because alcohol usually had a sedating effect on him.

CASE STUDY

I was eight years old when I first saw my father using alcohol as a way to escape his personal problems. At first drinking was very casual; it happened maybe once or twice a year, usually during celebrations, holidays, or special occasions. Later, he started drinking more often without any special occasion or apparent motive. Within three to five years, he started drinking heavily and constantly. Often he was too drunk to come home on his own own. There were times when I went to pick him up and brought him home. Most of the time, his friends and relatives brought my dad home when they found him passed out in the streets. My dad used to play baseball with a local team and sometimes he would take me with him during baseball games. After each game, he would start drinking to the point that his teammates would take him to the house heavily intoxicated. I asked him about the reasons for his drinking but he never told me. Nonetheless, I knew that something was hurting him for everytime he was drunk, he would cry.

As for my mother, I used to provide emotional support and companionship when she needed it. Sometimes my dad was absent months working in other states and at those times, I served as her companion. During arguments and domestic violence, I was there to comfort my mother as well.

I witnessed domestic violence when my dad was drunk maybe twice. My father never yelled nor hit me when he was drunk. I think he was more unpredictable when he was sober. One time my father asked me to bring some water to a friend of his who was working in the fields. I had some other plans for that day so I said 'no' and left. My father became outraged when I said 'no.' He said nothing else, instead, he charged after me. Once he caught up with me his belt went across my bottom five or six times. I learned to keep my distance when he was sober because of his unpredictability. Yet I became closer to him when he was drunk because I knew he was kind and generous. . . . My dad drank for many years, yet he never admitted having an alcohol problem. Twenty-five years later he still does not admit that he had an alcohol problem. . . . We always felt my father had the power to change his behavior but he refused to make changes. At the age of seventy, my dad finally stopped drinking. Occasionally he craves wine or beer but he has not consumed alcohol for three years now.

Questions

1. Give examples of situations in which this respondent demonstrates instrumental caregiving.
2. Give examples of situations in which this respondent demonstrates expressive caregiving.
3. When the father refused to admit that he had an alcohol problem, what is this called?
4. When people say "no" to others, what are they trying to establish?
5. What kind of boundaries usually exist between dependents and enablers?

Other Chemical Dependencies

The existence of alcohol abuse in a family establishes an opportunity structure for the creation of parental and parentified children. Alcohol is a drug. The abuse of other drugs such as heroin, cocaine (Inciardi et al., 1993; Waller, 1993), methamphetamines, marijuana, LSD, or PCP (angel dust) also creates opportunity structures for the development of parental and parentified children. Substance abuse impairs parenting competence, both for the abusing parent and for the spouse of the abusing person, whose energy and attention is diverted from the children to the abusing spouse. Often, when there is drug abuse in a family, the children are left to care for themselves as well as the parent.

> I can remember eating Cheerios for three weeks straight because there just wasn't money for food. Child support checks came and I cannot remember receiving the benefits from that added income. Still, I said nothing. And when my father would call I would lie and say everything was fine. I took care of everything. I would clean all day on Saturdays. I

cooked dinner and cleaned up after it. I made sure that we were keeping up with bills. I had a strict schedule that I was required to follow. If I deviated from this, there were huge sanctions to follow. At the age of ten I could successfully finish the laundry, clean the windows inside and out, garden, cook for three, take out the garbage, type out paperwork for jobs that weren't finished, decorate the house for Christmas . . . the list goes on.

Families that have a chemically dependent member usually have financial problems, because money is siphoned off to support the drug habit. Money has to be hidden or lied about to be available to support the household. The shortage of money sometimes forces children to hold jobs to financially support the family and keep its members from starving or being evicted.

Children in these families are witness to innumerable lies, from lies to the employer about why the employee was absent to lies about money and when bills would be paid to lies about drug use. Children in these families learn how to lie, committing both lies of omission and lies of commission, which adversely affects their ability to enter into and maintain intimate relationships in their adult lives (Stanton & Todd, 1982). Lies are barriers to establishing intimate and trusting relationships.

Children in these families are exposed to unpredictable lives; they can never anticipate episodes of stress or violence. Violence often exists when a substance abuser is coming down off a high (Cohen, 1995). The children are exposed to physical, emotional, and sometimes sexual abuse, either by family members or by friends of family members.

These children learn to be caretakers. They wake up the abusing parent when it is time to go to work. They are awakened in the middle of the night when a parent vomits in the bathroom from a bad dose of some drug and clean the bathroom floor. They learn to clean up the bloody nose of their parent from snorting cocaine. They learn to assess the physical appearance of the abusing parent and suggest changes to improve the parent's appearance, and help the parent bathe or shave or dress presentably. Parents who use uppers such as crank, cocaine, crack, or methamphetamines are up for days at a time, and have a disheveled appearance.

Drug treatment rehabilitation rarely occurs in a steady progression; relapses are part of the recovery process (Elster, 1999; Stanton & Todd, 1982). The occurrence of such relapses is part of the unpredictability of a child's life. Because little is predictable, the children caught in this environment feel a loss of power and control, although they desperately seek power and control to bring a sense of stability and order to the family's life. These children develop a need to control in order to feel safe and secure. "As children of chemically dependent or other dysfunctional families, we grew up in chaotic environments. To make sense of our world, to feel safe, we might have developed a deep desire to control everything and everyone in our lives" (Ray, 1989, p. 6). The need to control as an adult impairs their ability to create egalitarian relationships with other adults as well as their ability to establish and maintain intimate relationships in their adult lives.

In some jobs, work weeks of seventy to one hundred hours are not at all uncommon. How do people maintain the stamina to survive these grueling work weeks? Sometimes survival is aided by the use of uppers, particularly speed and cocaine and there are some companies where drugs are given by supervisors as a type of fringe benefit to maintain the productivity of the unit. Women, in particular, find it difficult to get off these drugs

(Mayers, Kail, & Watts, 1993, p. 92) because they receive little family support for entering recovery programs. These drugs also increase the metabolism, which keeps weight down. When women attempt to get off these drugs, they gain weight, violating cultural standards that expect them to be skinny.

The use of illegal drugs by parents represents only part of the picture of how chemical dependency impairs parenting. We live in a culture of drugs, as is illustrated by the increase of advertisements in all media for prescription drugs. Chemical dependency on prescription drugs represents one aspect of chemical dependency. People become addicted to pain-killing medications that impair their parenting or tranquilizers or anxiety-relieving medications that impair their parenting.

The willingness of the medical community to prescribe drugs, sometimes over the phone without an office visit, encourages parents to increasingly use prescription drugs to relieve both physical and psychological symptoms. The use of prescription drugs is widespread in U.S. culture.

Part of this is due to the cultural expectation that life should be fun, that life is a party, and people should not have to put up with things that spoil the party. Society should put science and technology to work to correct anything that interferes with life as fun. People should not have to endure droughts. Get those scientists to control weather patterns because droughts spoil the party. Scientists should be able to predict earthquakes to reduce the devastation they might create. Get those scientists busy on cures for cancer and AIDS and Parkinson's disease and Alzheimer's disease because these are inconsistent with expectations of what life in a postindustrial society should be like. Depression is inconsistent with the expectation that life should be fun, so anti-depressant medications are routinely prescribed to almost anyone who asks for them.

All medications have some side effects. The side effects of some drugs impair the effectiveness of parents who are taking them, such as when drugs induce drowsiness or reduce the alertness or vigilance of parents. Drug abuse by parents can result in losing custody of their children. The child then changes his or her residence to live with another relative or goes into a children's shelter or foster-care program.

The child often experiences guilt over this, asking what he or she did wrong to lose a parent. This is a symptom of parentification, because the process involves a blurring of boundaries. The problems of the parents become the problems of the child, and, when the child cannot control the substance abuse of the parent, the child often constructs a definition of him- or herself as a failure. The parentified child feels the need to care for, nurture, and solve problems. When the parent is incarcerated or when parental rights are revoked, the parentified children ask what they did wrong to bring this about.

Summary

The family of a person who is chemically dependent is an opportunity structure for the creation of parental and parentified children. Chemical dependency adversely affects the competence of parents. The dependent is impaired by the use of alcohol and/or drugs. The spouse is either also using alcohol or drugs or acts as an enabler who is preoccupied and fatigued from trying to fill the competency gaps created by the dependent's drug abuse. A parenting gap or vacuum is, thus, created within the family, a gap that is often filled by a child.

The child defines the family situation as problematic, infers that something must be done to address the problem, and perceives that he or she can help. The child acts as a parental child when he or she becomes a parental figure to brothers and sisters. The child acts as a parentified child when the child protects and nurtures either the incapacitated dependent parent or the exhausted, frustrated spouse of the dependent parent. In families that feature a chemically dependent member, children are caregivers of others and playing the roles of hero, scapegoat or rebel, lost child, or mascot or clown.

The caregiving patterns that children adopt in families with chemical dependency have legacies for these children that affect their lives as adults. Caregiving can become a life script that starts with childhood caregiving. These children may assume responsibility for controlling parental consumption of alcohol or drugs and may feel obligated to protect family members from physical and emotional violence, which burdens the child with responsibilities that are not age-appropriate. When the child fails to control the parent's drug abuse or violence, such failure can adversely affect the child's definition of self as competent, powerful, and worthy of parental affection, attention, nurturance, and support.

4

Parenting Vacuums

This chapter explores how parental and parentified children develop to fill a parenting vacuum created by some condition in a family that impairs the parents' competence. In dual-worker households, both parents may be so involved in their work that their gainful employment has them out of the home for most of their waking hours. When they are home, their energy may be so low that they have little time or energy left for their children. Their children get what is left over after their employer gets the best of what they have to offer. The children are left to care for themselves, creating parental children when older siblings care for younger siblings in the absence of a caregiving parent. Parents become so stressed and exhausted by their work that their children wind up being caretakers of their drained parents at home, creating parentified children.

When a family has a member who suffers from chronic physical or mental illness, one or both parents may have to spend so much time and energy caring for the ill member that there is little time or energy left for other family members. To fill this void, parental or parentified children develop. They may assist the parents in caring for the ill person. They may care for the caretaking parent, who becomes tired and frustrated and needs support to continue caretaking responsibilities. In the case of parental children, an older child may care for younger siblings so that the caretaker parent has fewer family members to worry about and care for; after all, they have their hands full already.

In families of recent immigrants to the United States, parents often have limited ability to speak or write English and this may create a dependency on children for communicating with the external English-speaking world. Children in these families are parentified when they serve as translators for their parents or when they conduct business for them. This is a form of caretaking. Both parents who are recent immigrants often work because they have low-paying jobs as a result of their limited English. The older children, in the absence of the parents, may become parental figures to their younger brothers and sisters, which may be culturally encouraged, as in extended families, in which everyone is expected to contribute to the group's welfare and survival. Many preindustrial societies of the world value collectivism over individualism. If parental income is low, the older children may become gainfully employed at a young age to support the family. This is a form of parentification inasmuch as the money the children contribute is a form of caretaking.

In large families where there are many children, managing parenting with employment is sometimes more than one or two parents can handle, so the parents enlist the services of older children to protect the health, welfare, and safety of younger siblings. Daughters may be called on to assume household chores, including child care, while adolescent sons may be called on to get jobs to help the family financially. Parenting in large families creates stress that can result in physical or psychological conditions, creating opportunities for the development of parentified children who nurture and care for their parents.

Life expectancy in this country is increasing. As a result, more and more adult children are being called on to care for elderly parents who may be physically frail or mentally impaired. The adult child may have to assume the role of "parent" to their own parents in terms of physical or emotional caretaking. The caretaking functions of adult children are not limited to kin, but also fall on the shoulders of family members related by marriage, particularly the wives of adult sons.

Blaming the Victim

In *Blaming the Victim,* William Ryan (1976) identifies the psychological process of blaming people for behavior that arises from their victimage in social systems. Ryan particularly focused on the poor and how the U.S. public generally blames the poor for their poverty, rather than seeing the poor as victims of institutionalized racism, gender discrimination, and shifts in the country's economy, over which average citizens have no control.

We must be careful in this chapter not to blame the impaired parents for their inability to give their children all the time, energy, nurturance, and attention that they might wish to give. These parents are often victims of forces external to them and beyond their control. The employed parents are working hard to maintain or enhance their standard of living, and their work in the present can be interpreted as entailing considerable sacrifice for their children's future.

In an economy that makes it difficult to maintain a comfortable standard of living, particularly as a function of escalating housing costs, working parents are doing what they believe they need to do to enhance their children's quality of life. And they may, indeed, be enhancing that quality of life. They just need some help from children to fill the vacuums that may be created within the family system, given that so much of the parents' time and attention is devoted to matters outside the home.

In families in which a family member suffers from chronic physical illness or mental illness, the people who care for that person are making a personal commitment and sacrifice. They should not then be blamed if a consequence of that caregiving is that others in the family are not getting what they might have received if there were no ill person in the family. The less-than-ideal parenting is a result of unfortunate circumstances, not negligence or intentional incompetence. The caretakers are doing the best they can under the circumstances, and require assistance from others. Nor should elderly parents who need to be cared for by others be blamed for their condition. Physical weakness, Alzheimer's disease, and senile dementia are common conditions of old age. The victims with these conditions do not want them and have no control over them. They should not be blamed for their inability to be totally independent and self-sufficient.

The frustration experienced by caretakers of the elderly is sometimes vented by blaming the elderly for their inability to be totally autonomous, which can lead to physical abuse, sometimes referred to as "granny battering." Physical abuse of the elderly is against the law, prosecutable as a misdemeanor—assault and battery—or, in some cases, as a felony if it is prosecuted as attempted murder or assault with a deadly weapon. States have increasingly seen the need to legislate protection against abuse of elderly people, once the public becomes aware of this formerly hidden form of domestic violence.

The Dual-Worker Family

In the first half of the twentieth century, most jobs were in manufacturing, the conversion of raw materials into manufactured goods, and people worked in factories where working conditions were harsh. Men were seen as being stronger and as having more stamina than women, so it was mainly men who were gainfully employed in manufacturing industries such as the steel and automobile plants. This helped to create patriarchal family structures, leaving women economically dependent on their husbands, which had the effect of keeping divorce rates moderate. Regardless of how unhappy a woman might be in her marriage, she could not afford to initiate a divorce. It would be very difficult for her to survive on her own in a male-dominated economy.

After World War II, the labor market changed and service-sector jobs expanded with new technologies. Robotics replaced some people in manufacturing industries. White-collar jobs in teaching, social work, law, advertising, public relations, leisure and travel industries, real estate, and the computer industry did not require physical strength. Success in these jobs depended on getting along with people and being liked, and here women were at no disadvantage.

The problem with these jobs for women was that entry into most service-sector jobs required some level of higher education, usually at least a bachelor's degree. Prior to World War II, however, many colleges and universities had quotas for women. After the war these quotas were dropped. At just the time that the job market was opening up for women, colleges and universities accepted them in larger and larger numbers so that they could obtain the training to get jobs in the expanding sectors of the economy. The result was that, from 1950 to 1991 in the United States, the number of married women with paying jobs more than tripled and, during the 1950s, 12 percent of children under age six had working mothers. In the early 1990s, that figure increased to over 57 percent (Bravo, 1995). The dual-worker couple is now the norm among families with children.

According to a U.S. Census Bureau report (2000), based on data from 1998, both spouses were employed at least part-time in 51 percent of the married couples with children, compared with 33 percent in 1976. One reason that mothers increasingly work is that it is virtually impossible to maintain middle-class status in the current economy without both partners working. Dual-worker households generally have greater financial resources than single-worker households. The census data indicates that 55 percent of the dual-employed couples had annual incomes of $50,000 or more, compared with 40 percent of the couples in which only the husband worked.

The data also showed that the majority of married or single mothers of very young children were likely to work at least part-time. Fifty-nine percent of the women with babies younger than a year old were employed in 1998, compared with 31 percent in 1976. The numbers were even higher for those with older children. Of the 31.3 million mothers aged 15 to 44 whose children were older than a year, 73 percent were in the labor force in 1998, and 52 percent worked full-time.

In past years, women with infants were substantially more likely to be employed if they had only one child than if they had two or more, but this gap is rapidly closing. In 1998, 61 percent of mothers with one infant held jobs, compared with 57 percent of those with two or more children, one of whom was younger than a year old.

Work Schedule Discontinuity

The United States has failed to adapt quickly to these changes, when mothers in families are increasingly employed outside the home. There is a discontinuity between the working schedules of children and the working schedules of their parents. Children go to school from approximately 8:00 A.M. to 3:00 P.M., depending on the age of the child. Parents, if they work full-time day shifts, work from 8:00 A.M. to 5:00 P.M., with the result that there is a two- to three-hour time span in the late afternoon, depending on commute time from work to home, when there is usually no parent at home to care for the children.

This results in the phenomenon of **latch-key children,** children who are given the key to the front door of their houses and told to go home after school and do homework or watch TV or play computer games until a parent comes home. This tends to be socially isolating for these children because they do not interact with other children during this period, and it can be anxiety-producing for those who are expected to keep themselves and the residence safe in the absence of an adult. It may be more than some children can comfortably navigate, given the level of their competence and sense of security. This sets up an opportunity for the development of a parental child when the oldest sibling becomes a parent figure taking care of younger siblings.

> I clearly recall instances of cooking dinner for my two sisters and myself; us three would commonly finish our dinners by the time my parents got home from work, at which point they would be so tired that I would serve them dinner at the table, catering to such needs as getting drinks and utensils for them. I remember helping my parents into bed, taking off their shoes for them as they were too tired to do it for themselves, or comforting them when an upsetting day at work had made them emotional . . . I remember feeling like it was up to me to keep the family in harmony; I was the glue that held my family together.

When this respondent took care of her sisters, she was performing as a parental child. When she took care of her parents in their exhaustion, she was playing the role of a parentified child.

If parents are to avoid creating latch-key children, they must find a good and inexpensive after-school child-care program. The shift of U.S. families to two-worker households has created a demand for schools to either expand the length of the school day or provide after-school activities. If the school provides after-school activities, it must often charge significant fees for this service. Additional staff must be hired to replace regular teachers who have ended their work day. Additional insurance premiums must be paid to cover children in after-school activities and these fees are often high because children are more apt to be injured playing than working in the classroom. Additional janitorial services are needed to cover the extra time the school is used. Additional supplies are needed as the children's time must be filled with activities of various kinds. In the absence of sufficient and affordable after-school day care for children, parents must explore other alternatives for child care while they work. Librarians of city libraries tell me that increasingly parents are instructing their children to walk from school to the library and do their homework there until a parent picks them up after work. What is assumed is that the library is a relatively safe place and librarians will supervise children and protect them if necessary. Relatives are another alternative to after-school child care. To what extent are fathers and grandparents being used as child-care providers by working parents?

Fathers and Grandparents

Census data indicate that fathers and grandparents are increasingly participating in the parenting of children in the United States. The Survey of Income and Program Participation (SIPP), taken in 1993, reveals that one in five fathers in married-couple families with children aged 0 to 14, whose mothers were gainfully employed, provided care for at least one child under age 15 while the mother was working (Casper, 1997).

When mothers are gainfully employed, fathers are more likely to care for preschool-age children than grade-school children. Almost one in five fathers were primary care providers for preschool children while one in nine fathers were primary care providers for grade-school children during the time that mothers worked (Casper, 1997). Casper attributes this to the fact that preschoolers are generally seen as needing more attention and supervision by virtue of their age, so parents may be more willing to juggle their work schedules to care for them than are parents of older children (creating **split-shift households** when parents stagger their work schedules). Furthermore, grade-school children have the supervision of school personnel during school hours. Older children are likely to have older parents who have higher earning power by virtue of their longevity on a job, and these parents have greater resources to hire caretakers.

The nature of the economy affects fathers' participation in child care. In times of economic recession, unemployed fathers increase their child-care participation because they are available as resources to working mothers. Fathers who do not work or who work part-time or at night are more likely to participate in the care of preschoolers while mothers work. Casper (1997) suggests that the role of fathers in families continues to be defined in the society as primarily performing the **instrumental function,** providing the family with food, clothing, and shelter, financially supporting the family through gainful employment. Recently, however, these fathers seem to be increasing their caretaking functions, at least for preschoolers.

Fathers in poor families are three times more likely to be caretakers of their children than are fathers in non-poor families. Generally, fathers in families with lower incomes are more likely to care for their preschool children than are fathers in families with higher incomes. It would appear that fathers who are less able to perform a viable instrumental role for their families are compensating through caretaking, even if they are working full-time. Note that many poor are working poor, people who do have full-time, but low-paying jobs.

Fathers in service occupations, where salaries are low—occupations such as maintenance, police, firefighting, and security positions—are about twice as likely as fathers in other occupations to be taking care of preschoolers while mothers are working. These occupations tend to be twenty-four-hour-a-day operations where people rotate in shifts, allowing workers to work non-day shifts so that they can create a split-shift household, alternating caretaking of children with their spouse in a synchronized dance.

Fathers residing in central cities and in rural areas were more likely to caretake preschoolers compared to fathers who resided in the suburbs (27% to 22%). Suburban fathers are more likely to have higher incomes than fathers who live in central cities or rural areas and, thus, can better fund child care while mothers are working.

Fathers with two or more preschoolers are more likely to be caretakers of preschoolers compared to fathers of one preschooler. In 1993, one in three fathers cared for their preschoolers if they had two or more, whereas only one in five fathers cared for their preschoolers if they only had one. They were more likely to be primary caretakers of their children as well as more likely to provide some child care. With more than one preschooler, the expenses of outsourcing child care were likely to be too high, creating an economic motivation for more fathers to engage in child care themselves.

Despite the fact that fathers seem to be increasing their participation in childcare, the percentage of fathers who provide some child care for their children is not very impressive, less than one in five fathers (Smith, 2000). In 1995, grandparents cared for preschoolers almost as much as fathers did while the mother was working (15.9% vs. 16.6%).

One may well ask why extended kin are not used more to care for children after school. Hertz (1986) answers this in three ways. First, grandparents and other kin are likely to live geographically far from where the children live. Second, middle-class families are expected to be self-sufficient and independent, which mitigates against asking kin for assistance. Thirdly, parents in two-worker households are apt to wait to have children until rather late in their lives, giving them time to develop their careers, which means that, by the time the children are of school age, grandparents may be too old to want to or be able to perform much child-care. One might add that high geographic mobility might have kin living too far away to provide after-school day care on a regular basis.

Older Children

In the absence of relatives to provide free child care, and in the absence of affordable and good after-school child-care programs, parents turn to another source of free labor for child care, their oldest child. The alternative of having older children care for younger siblings after school provides cheap supervision as these children are usually unpaid for their services.

> I would occasionally hear my parents arguing about money—specifically the lack of it—which would encourage me to redouble my efforts at keeping peace within the family and caring for my two younger sisters. I felt sure that if we, as a family, could just get enough money in the bank, my parents would never argue about it again. Although my parents

tried not to get us kids involved in their financial matters, kids know and feel things—more than they are given credit for—and I knew that money was a major stressor to my parents.

Older children also provide supervision that is performed in a style likely to please the parents because they were trained by their parents, and know what their parents like and do not like in parenting styles. Older children provide parents with trustworthy and predictable child-care service.

Not only is it older children who are called upon to care for younger siblings, but it is female children who are called upon more than male children. The following female respondent was the oldest child in her family and was called upon to care for her two younger brothers when both her parents were at work. This respondent developed more parental hierarchy as a caretaking sister than the parents were able to create with the boys.

> I was always mature and because of this I was seen as a huge role model for my two younger brothers. I am the oldest and am the only girl. I was cooking and cleaning since I was quite young and cooked my first pot of beans when I was in the fourth grade. I have been like a "mom" for most of my life or at least from the time that I was about ten years old. I come from a two-worker household . . . I have been there for my brothers and family in good times and in bad. I have had to learn how to balance out my gender and social roles from a young age. I have learned how to be a daughter, a sister, a student, a cook, a housekeeper, a counselor, a tutor, a role model, an employee and most of all a huge caring icon for the family. I became a parentified child because of the fact that both of my parents have worked ever since I can remember. They have worked since they were kids themselves and had a lot of responsibilities placed on them from their families. Due to the fact that both my parents worked, I feel like there was a time when I kind of took over a lot for my parents. I helped them out a lot. I remember having to wake my brothers up and get them fed and ready for school. I would drive them to school (even when I didn't have a license), go to school myself, and pick them up after school once I got out. I would take them home, fix them a snack, and make sure that they started their homework. I would get one ready for karate practice and drive him and drop him off. I would go home, pick him up at the scheduled time, and then we would go back home. I would start dinner and get them showered and make sure that their homework was completed. Mom or dad would come home and I would then go to my room and do my homework. This was my routine for many years, so I kind of feel like my brothers are my boys too. I feel this in my heart. Even to this day sometimes the boys listen to me more than they do to my own parents. Sometimes my parents need to have me 'talk to the boys' to talk some sense into them because my parents know that they do listen to me and value what I have to say.

The next respondent, also female, describes her experience as both a parental and parentified child in a dual-worker household. Note that this respondent interprets her considerable caregiving responsibilites as being ultimately beneficial to her, making her "a more mature person" who developed "the ability and understanding to handle many things at a time." Note also the observation of this respondent, and cited by many others, that she was a sister at some times and a parent at other times to her brothers, so she assumed multiple roles relative to her siblings. This respondent grew up in a relatively affluent family, though the wealth did not spare her from caretaking responsibilities.

Growing up for part of my life in a dual-earning family came with it great advantages as well as its somber disadvantages. My family was probably a little different than others who had two working parents because my dad was not only a full-time working parent, but he was also one who worked out of town from Monday to Friday. He came home on Friday afternoons and left again on Sunday afternoons. This set-up left me being the oldest child in the house, with more responsibility. In fact, I did take my Dad's place in the family, and I continued to help my mom out with the normal things that I already helped her with. I believe that these experiences made me a more mature person and also gave me the ability and understanding to handle many things at one time.

I became a parental child when I took my dad's place in the family. I was no longer just an older sister to my younger brother, but I was also a parental figure whom he could always count on. When I was fourteen, I took my driver's education classes, and then when I turned fifteen, I applied for a hardship license. Texas has a policy that if your child plays an instrumental role in your family, then he or she can apply to get a license before they turn sixteen. As a result of my father's everyday absence, I was granted a license soon after my fifteenth birthday. After I got my license, I got my own car. As a result of getting my own car, I was in charge of taking my brother to school and picking him up. I took him to his extra-curricular activities and music classes. I took myself wherever I needed to go. I did all the grocery shopping, dropping off and picking up of the dry cleaning, and attended to landscaping around the outside of the house. I regularly did the cooking, made lunches in the morning for my mom, my brother, and myself. When I came home in the afternoon, I made sure that there was a snack for my brother to eat. Everyone knows that growing boys eat a refrigerator's worth a day. I would plan a menu sometime during the beginning of the week and make sure we had all the ingredients ready. I'd have dinner ready most of the days by the time my mom was back from work, and the table would be set as well. On the weekends or days when I got home from school early, I would do some of the vacuuming and dusting and cleaning of the house. We had a maid who came to our house regularly, but if we knew we were going to have company before she came, I had to make sure everything was clean and neat. My brother would let me know if there was something specific he needed to wear for school or a game, and I would have to do the laundry in time. If there was a festival or an occasion coming up, I went out and bought new clothes for the whole family. I would send in the RSVP's and make appointments for doctors, dentists, and cleaning services. I would check the mail each day, sort out all the bills and important mail. My mom would keep a checkbook with her signatures already signed so that I would just have to fill in the blanks with the names and amount and out went the bills . . . paid. On garbage days, I went around the house and collected it . . . then put everything outside the night before.

I have come to realize that somewhere along the way, while I was functioning as a parental child for my younger brother, I turned into a parentified childd and began taking care of my mom. I talked to her about all kinds of things, whether it meant something funny, serious, or extremely personal. One summer while my mom was working and I was taking a class in summer school, we ended up having a funny kind of relationship. I ended up playing the mommy role and she played the daughter role, what I mean is that I continued to make sure that she had a lunch, that dinner was ready, and that she had all the things she needed to take with her to work. In our house, if anyone lost something or needed to find anything, they knew whom to call on. Ask Deborah, she'll know where it is or she'll find it for you in a jiffy. Soon I became an indispensable person to my family. I believe that is why it took me longer to launch from home.

This respondent perceived a role reversal with her mother, where the child became a caretaking parent and the parent became like a needy, dependent child. Who a child is and who a parent is in a family has nothing to do with age. "Child" vis à vis "parent" are roles and involve behavior (how people act), so this respondent observes that she acted as if she were the parent and her mother acted as though she were a child. The parentification of children involves role reversals where children are caregivers to their parents.

The next respondent, also a female in a dual-worker household, was not the eldest child in her family. She had an older brother and a younger sister, but as the oldest girl in her family, she was assigned caretaking responsibilites even to her older brother. Notice the resentment that is displayed in this account over the responsibilities she was asked to assume.

> Being the middle child and oldest female, I have incurred many responsibilities. My parents often worked thirteen-hour days, therefore I was to wake and dress myself and my sister, fix breakfast, and walk my sister to school. After school I was in charge of watching over my sister and had a list of chores that were to be completed before my parents came home. My brother, on the other hand, had half the responsibilities that I had despite our four-year age difference. While I was expected to stay home with my sister, my brother played with his friends. Being the oldest female child in my family meant that I was to fulfill the role of our mother.

Grollman and Sweder (1986) studied parental children in dual-worker households and found that many were angry at being taken for granted by their parents because they rarely received compliments or expressions of appreciation. They often resented having to baby-sit siblings day after day, having no time for themselves, and complained of having no time to spend with their friends. These children complained of social isolation and loneliness. "For these children, being home alone for two hours or more exacerbates their feelings of inadequacy. They are forced to deal with a situation that is overwhelming for them—caring for themselves [and siblings] for long periods of time each day without proper supervision or emotional support" (Grollman and Sweder, 1986, p. 26).

These children generally do more household chores than do children in intact nuclear families where one parent is not gainfully employed or works part-time. They often try to help out their parents at home by cleaning the house, doing laundry, washing dishes, or cooking meals and so assume adult responsibilities as children. As a result, they grow up fast.

There are two ways of looking at this situation. A more positive analysis is that these children have to learn to be independent, self-sufficient adults sooner or later, so they are learning valuable skills that will serve them well as adults. The following account from a respondent reflects this optimistic perspective. This respondent's caretaking responsiblities as a child carried over into her adult life. Her childhood caregiving did not stifle her desire to work with and care for young children.

> Looking back at those years of my life, I can't see any long-term negative effects of having to take care of my sisters. At the time it sucked, but now I have a different perspective. Although I did do a lot of chores and missed out on some social events, I still managed to

have friends and fun. I was able to keep good grades in school and never got into drugs or alcohol. From this experience, I think I became a more responsible and independent person. I can take care of myself and don't fall apart during the rough times in life. I think this also brought about my love for teaching and helping children. Currently, I am studying to be a teacher, teach pre-school, and am also a nanny for two young girls.

A more pessimistic analysis is that the responsibilities these children assume rob them of their childhood. They are often overburdened by responsibilities that are not appropriate for their age. They are not free to go out and play with friends nor do they really have downtime to be alone. They are so busy attending to the needs of others that their own needs cannot be met. In fact, these children have no time for introspection to determine what their own needs are. This perspective is reflected in the following account which conveys the anger and resentment this respondent experienced being burdened with adult responsibilites as a child.

Imagine you are entering the sixth grade and you find out your mother has to start working (Dad already works). You're not only adjusting to the new teachers, friends, and workload of middle school but also to the responsibility of taking care of your three- and seven-year-old sisters. Afternoons of watching TV and attempting your homework turn into days of making snacks, cleaning, preparing dinner, and attempting to control your sisters. This scenario was my life as an eleven-year-old. . . . Cleaning, watching my sisters, and cooking were not my idea of fun. I hated that I had to do so much for the family and I hated my parents for it too. I felt I wasn't allowed to have a social life because my parents worked. Even on some weekends, I would have to take on a second shift. My parents were worn out from work (and still very young) and wanted to go out. This left me with more responsibilities: cleaning up after dinner, getting everyone bathed and into bed, then I could start or finish up my homework. I remember being very bitter and cold toward my parents. I felt the whole situation was unfair. But they kept telling me, 'Life's not fair!'

Parental children become so trained to attend to the needs of others that it affects their personalities as adults. They are apt to develop what is known as the "caretaker syndrome," capable only of relating to people they can take care of, either physically or emotionally. They have to be "one up" to another who is "one down," a phenomenon I will discuss in the last chapter of this book.

Outsourcing Child Care

For dual-worker parents, an alternative to using older siblings to supervise younger children at home or a way to reduce their burden as child-care provider can be to employ a variety of after-school activities for the children. Parents sign up their children for soccer leagues, baseball and softball leagues, piano lessons, dance lessons, foreign language instruction, church bible study, an array of activities whereby some other adult is responsible for supervising children after school. Soccer, baseball, swimming, and gymnastic coaches provide a valuable service for working parents by providing supervision for the many children of working adults. Census statistics from 1995 (Smith, 2000) indicate that 39 percent of grade-school children, nationwide, participate in extracurricular activities such as sports, lessons, and clubs. Such activities afford the children social interaction with age-appropriate peers that the latch-key child does not have as well as the supervision of adults who will insure their safety.

These after-school providers of activities for children become surrogate extended family, like members of the family, adult figures who serve the same function as grandparents or aunts and uncles might. In postindustrial societies, we deconstruct the concept of "extended kin" so that it includes people who are not related to the family by blood or marriage but who function "as if" they were family members, supporting children, teaching them skills, affecting their self-esteem, supervising them, and, often, providing them the afternoon snack that might be provided if the child went to grandma's house.

African American families often contain "fictive kin," people who are assigned kin titles such as auntie, cousin, niece, or nephew even though they are not really related to a family by blood or marriage. The title allows the person who is taken into the family to have a sense of belonging. It is a gesture of welcoming the person into the fold as well as a way of avoiding stigmatization of the new family member.

In some ways, professionals and volunteers who care for children in our society become "fictive kin," not in the titles they are assigned but in the duties they perform for children and in the relationships they develop with children and their families. They are a vital support system for the family of each child. For the duration of the season, and sometimes beyond, they are treated like members of the family. This meta-familial relationship often is reciprocal as the coach or piano or music teacher comes to treat the child as if he or she were their own, or at least as if the child were a member of his or her own family.

It is particularly when we look at dual-worker households that we come to see how the world external to the family system is brought into the family to, for some period of time, become a member of the family, and to serve as an important resource of social support and nuturance.

The Split Shift Household

One way in which parents sometimes avoid using older children for after-school child care is for the parents to stagger their work schedules. One parent would work a day shift and the other a swing shift. This means that there is usually one parent at home to supervise children during their waking hours. This creative solution requires excellent communication between the parents so that there is continuity for the children. The parent who starts a caretaking shift needs to be reminded of medicine that must be taken or a birthday party that the child is going to attend or the time of a soccer game scheduled to be played.

The downside of the split-shift household is the precious few hours that the spouses spend together in the course of a working week. This arrangement gives them little time to communicate with each other, to nurture their relationship as spouses. They see each other very little and when they do see each other, one or both of them is usually exhausted, which undermines the quality of their interaction. These adults are spending so much time attending to the other's needs, and they have very little time or energy left to attend to the needs of each other as spouses and they have very little time and energy to spend on themselves—to exercise, meditate, read a good book, watch TV, or take a nap. They rarely have time or energy to "recharge their batteries," just take time out and relax or attend to their own personal needs.

Part-Time Work

A second alternative tried by some couples who can afford it is for one spouse to work part-time so that somebody is home for the children when they return from school. One problem with this is that companies often exploit part-time workers by refusing to give them health care or other employee benefits. A company may offer a person a half-time job knowing full well that company policy prescribes that an employee must work at least 51 percent to be eligible for health-care benefits. Half-time employees only work 50 percent and so are ineligible for such benefits.

Another alternative for parents who work in high technology industries is to ask for flexible working hours such that they work at home on their computers in the late afternoons when their children are home from school. Some companies permit this, others will not.

In *The War against Parents* (1999), Hewlett and West explain that families in the United States are so fragile and have so many divorces because there is little institutional support for them in U.S. society—little support from the government and little support from corporations. Although a growing number of corporations are providing on-site child-care services for preschool children of employees, most companies do not. Although Congress passed a family leave bill, family leave is unpaid time off the job. Most postindustrial countries have some form of paid leave, particularly for both parents after the birth of a baby, but not the United States. In this country, families are left to their own devices to provide supervision and care for children, and the effect of this absence of external support is that families often call on older children to perform these services, thereby creating parental children.

Unemployment

Capitalism as an economic system is noted for creating peaks of prosperity and valleys of recession and depression over time. During times of economic recession, employees are laid off. Katherine S. Newman's book, *Falling from Grace* (1989), describes what happens in middle-class families when one or both parents lose their jobs. According to Newman,

> children in downwardly mobile families find themselves drawing closer to their families because they feel they cannot "desert a sinking ship" and because their parents lean on them for emotional support. When they do pull away from the family—even temporarily, they feel guilty. Willing but unwilling, they become psychologically and emotionally bound inside a familial cocoon (p. 104).

The unemployment of a parent causes great internal family stress. The family wants to keep the unemployment a secret from the outside world because the unemployment is stigmatizing. This secrecy is much like the secrecy of families with a chemically dependent member or a family, in which its members are physically or sexually abused.

Parents may spend many hours looking for work, which takes them out of the household for long periods of time. The children want to help out in this time of crisis, so older children find themselves cooking, cleaning house, doing laundry, and caring for their younger siblings. This creates social isolation for these children: the more they do at home, the less they interact with the outside world. They do not maintain friendships because they spend less time interacting with friends.

These children become parentified as they seek to be a source of emotional support for parents. They become the confidante of either parent, as both parents may seek the comfort of an older child to assuage their fears, concerns, and anxiety. As one or both parents get depressed by the unemployment and the financial hardship it entails, an older child may seek to play the role of therapist or comic to help reduce a parent's depression or anxiety.

> For downwardly mobile families, it is the parents who need their kids' emotional support. The parents have become dependent on their offspring in weathering the crisis. Their children want to be more independent, but a sense of responsibility and obligation pulls them back [within the family] (Newman, 1989, p. 105).

What Newman describes is the parentification of children in downwardly mobile families. There is a role reversal when older children become caretakers of their stressed parents. They may seek to ease the anxiety of their parents by spending less money themselves in order to ease the economic burden. They may put off buying clothes or music. They make their lunches rather than buying them at school. They might seek part-time employment after school and contribute their income to the family's financial resources.

A parent's unemployment adds to a child's workload as the child tries to help the parents cope. Some of these children become overburdened by the responsibilities they assume but are developmentally unable to execute. Newman describes one child who had to be hospitalized in a psychiatric facility as a function of being overwhelmed by the family responsibilities created by a parent's unemployment. If the unemployment lasts over a long period of time, the parentification of a child can adversely affect his or her ability to leave the family of origin as an autonomous adult.

Immigrant Families

Technically, the only nonimmigrant families in the United States are families of Native Americans. All other families contain ancestors who, at some point, came to the United States from someplace else. The United States is a nation of immigrants. In the eighteenth and nineteenth centuries, most of those immigrants came from European countries. Particularly in the later part of the twentieth century, as globalization became increasingly evident both economically and politically, immigrants came to this country from all over the world. By the year 2000, there were 28.4 million foreign-born people residing in the United States (Lollock, 2000), who represented 10.4 percent of the total U.S. population.

Among these foreign-born people, 51 percent were born in Latin America (including Mexico), 25.5 percent were born in Asia, 15.3 percent were born in Europe, and the remaining 8.1 percent were born in other regions of the world.

The recent migration of families to the United States often results in intergenerational conflict for people within the families. For the parents, it becomes increasingly difficult to socialize their children in a new land with a different language and culture. The process of socialization is a multigenerational process of parents passing on to their children the values, language, and customs of their culture. It involves teaching children norms for behavior. It requires a parental hierarchy in which parents are the experts who teach while children learn. But often in immigrant families, children do not want to learn what their parents have to teach. What the parents have to teach is the language and customs, the traditions and history of their homeland, which their children do not see as valuable in America.

The parents who come to the United States from some other country are known as first-generation immigrants. They cook and eat the foods of their home country. They often speak the language of that homeland and are knowledgeable about its history, customs, and holidays. They still have relatives there, communicate with people in that country, and sometimes visit it if they have the financial means to do so and if they can visit without legal or political reprisals. They often are proud of being from that country, which is a source of identity for them.

The children of first-generation immigrants are second-generation immigrants. Their focus is on integrating into a cohort of peers (Jensen & Chitose, 1994). To integrate into their schools, for instance, they feel they must be seen as no different from their peers. They must sound no different from these peers, so they work hard on losing any accent they may have. They must dress like their peers, which may be more risque or flamboyant than their parents would like. The clothes these children want to buy may often be more expensive than their parents can afford. The primary objective of these children is to "fit in," to assimilate into the mainstream of U.S. society, which often involves discarding any signs of their ethnicity. These children have no interest in learning the language of their parents. They have no interest in learning to cook the foods their parents cook. They have no interest in returning to the homeland of their parents. They have no interest in celebrating holidays that are linked to their parents' homeland. They want to be 100 percent American.

The third-generation immigrants, the children of the second generation, find that to be 100 percent American gives one no sense of cultural identity. The United States is a very young country with few national traditions or values that are truly a unique source of ethnic identity. The third generation has an interest in returning to its ethnic roots, of learning the language of its grandparents, of learning to cook the foods its grandparents know how to cook, of visiting the country from which its grandparents came. There is a joke that is well known among family therapists. It starts: "Why do grandparents and grandchildren get along so well?" Answer: "They have a common enemy, the generation in between."

What the above descriptions indicate is that ethnic families in the United States experience intergenerational conflict. It appears to family members that this conflict is personal, between father and child, between mother and daughter, but, in fact, it is often cultural conflict manifesting itself as intergenerational conflict. Each generation is an advocate for a culture and defends the values and customs of that culture.

First-generation immigrants defend and identify with the culture of the land from which they came. The second generation defends and identifies with the culture of the land into which it wants to integrate. Inasmuch as these two cultures conflict in their values, the people, each of whom is a representative of his or her respective culture, will be in conflict. It is really a conflict of cultural values (Rumbaut, 1994), and it gets played out as intergenerational conflict in immigrant families.

First-generation immigrant parents may want their children to come home after school and study, in the belief that to get good grades in school is the beginning of a prosperous future. When their children comply with their wishes, this is congruent with their cultural values in that children respect the wishes of their parents. Generational hierarchy may be valued, respect for elders may be valued, scholarship and academic success may be valued, but the children may refuse to come home after school because they value autonomy and independence, values of the United States. The children want the freedom to "do their own thing." The child may also resist parental hierarchy in favor of egalitarian values. The conflict between parents and children reflects a conflict of cultural values, but is experienced by the participants as personal conflict.

Portes and Rumbaut (1996) maintain that intergenerational conflict in immigrant families is not inevitable. Rather than seeing intergenerational conflict in such families as normative, Portes and Rumbaut describe a continuum that ranges from intergenerational congruence to intergenerational dissonance. Where a family will fall on this continuum is a function of congruent or differential levels of acculturation between members of the first and second generation as well as the impact of the immigrant community that surrounds the family. These authors maintain that generational consonance occurs when (1) both first-generation parents and their second-generation children remain unacculturated to Western culture, or (2) when members of both generations acculturate at roughly the same rate, or (3) when the immigrant community encourages selective second-generation acculturation.

Conversely, intergenerational dissonance is maximized when second-generation acculturation is neither guided nor accompanied by changes in the first generation (when their rates of acculturation become discrepant). It is exactly this scenario that leads to role reversals between parents and children, when the parents lack sufficient education or integration into an ethnic community to cope with the outside environment and, thus, become dependent on their children. The ability or inability of the parents to integrate into an ethnic community is an important intervening variable affecting the dependence of parents on their children. Integration of parents within such a community is apt to reduce parental dependence on their children.

Intragenerational Conflict

Cultural conflict does not just exist between immigrants of different generations. It can also exist between people of the same generation. If a husband and wife come to this country, and the wife assimilates to Western culture faster than does her husband, they may experience marital conflict. This is really cultural conflict manifesting as marital conflict when the wife becomes a spokesperson for Western values of independence, autonomy, individualism, and freedom. She may want to be gainfully employed and have an independent income. Her husband may feel threatened by this, and he may want her to be a homemaker, to stay home and care for their children. He may voice the values of a culture that encourages collectivism, interdependence, and familism. So they argue about whether she becomes gainfully employed or not.

Labor and the Status of Children

The power of women in a household is enhanced by gainful employment. Generally, the more money a woman makes, the more power she has in determining how money is to be spent. How people are perceived by others in postindustrial societies is based on what they do and how they behave. Women gain prestige in the eyes of family members by achieving success in their work. But many immigrants come from societies that are preindustrial or in the early stages of industrialization, when prestige is based on attributes such as age and gender. In many of these societies, males tend to have greater status than do females and elderly people have more status than younger people.

Parents in families that recently immigrated to the United States usually expect deference from their children based on factors such as age and gender. They believe they deserve respect from their children by virtue of their age and the wisdom they have accumulated by virtue of that age. But the wisdom they have mainly came from experiences they had in their homeland, so that wisdom may not be seen by their children as very useful in the United States. From this perspective, the children may not see the basis for treating their parents with deference, particularly when they define parental wisdom as obsolete or irrelevant in the new country.

When families have recently immigrated to the United States, the status of parents and the elderly tends to remain high because status will be based on age when the values of the homeland still predominate. The longer the immigrants are in this country, however, the more the prestige of parents and the elderly may deteriorate as members of the family become more acculturated to a Western society in which status is based on one feature, one's successes and accomplishments. As the children learn to do more and more things that their parents do not do, from knowing English to driving an automobile, the more the status of parents and grandparents may deteriorate and the perceived value of the parents may diminish in the eyes of the children. Increasingly, the parents and grandparents become dependent on their children as a function of their differential competence in their new world. If the behavior of children toward parents is constructed in the minds of children, then the interpretation of parents by children as having obsolete or irrelevant knowledge or skill leads to behavior that lacks deference and respect.

The process of acculturation involves learning and internalizing the language, values, norms, and customs of a culture. The greater the level of acculturation within an immigrant family, the more the status of children will be enhanced through their labor as parental or parentified children, because status is more apt to be based on one's behavior or the labor one provides to the family.

The lower the level of acculturation in an immigrant family, the more likely it is that the labor of parental and parentified children will not produce greater status for them because status in families who have recently immigrated will likely be based on age and gender. Despite the fact that these children are providing valuable resources to the family, they are still children, often female children, which will keep their status low.

Valuing Individualism or Collectivism

The ground rules that govern social interaction differ in preindustrial societies and highly industrialized societies (Parsons & Bales, 1955). Life in preindustrial, agriculturally-based societies is apt to be difficult and involve a struggle for survival. Sometimes it is hard to survive as an individual. The chances of survival increase if one is a member of a group in which members are interdependent on one another. If you have fish today, you share it with others. If others have fish the next day, they share it.

Interdependence is expected among family members. As elders cared for infants when they were fragile and dependent on others for survival, so it is expected that, when those infants develop into adults, they will repay the elders for earlier nurturing by caring for them in their old age.

The following account illustrates the concept of interdependence that operated in a family originally from Mexico. This account is interesting because it includes two contexts that will be explored later in this book, both of which create opportunity structures for the development of parental and parentified children. One context is when a parent is incarcerated and children adapt to this by assuming many of the responsibilities that were held by the incarcerated parent, including caretaking the remaining family members. The other context is when a parent becomes ill and a child adapts to the illness by assuming many of the responsibilities formerly assumed by the ill parent.

Most migrant children learn adult responsibilities from an early age, and they use their knowledge to survive in life. These responsibilities may be working in the fields or performing household chores. However, some parents push their kids to carry out these responsibilities beyond the young children's physical and emotional capabilities. I remember the case of my cousin, who at age eight, used to care for her siblings and her mother as well. This young girl would get up at five-thirty in the morning to make lunch for her brother who worked in the fields and two siblings who stayed at home. Every morning my cousin began her day making tortillas and preparing food for the entire family. During the day, she would care for her mom who was very ill. My aunt had been very sick and could not care for herself, therefore my cousin provided personal care along with companionship. My cousin had learned to become the parental and parentified figure in the household. My aunt lived three years or so with her illness before she passed away. Yet even after her mom had died, my cousin continued caring for the rest of the family. As for her education, she could not attend school because of the many responsibilities she had to tend to. My cousin's father had been out of the picture since he had been incarcerated for two years before my aunt became sick. At an early age, a male cousin worked in the fields from six in the morning until three or four in the afternoon. While he contributed financially, his other siblings contributed emotionally and financially as well. The younger siblings worked for other families in domestic jobs. Sometimes they were cleaning houses, delivering food and providing companionship to the elderly. With the money earned, they used it to buy groceries, pay bills and buy medicine for their mother. Somehow, the entire family worked hard to contribute financially for the survival of the household.

In many Asian societies, the concept of **filial piety** is an important cultural value. Filial piety is the expectation that younger people will respect and care for elderly parents and grandparents. Filial piety becomes very important in societies where there is no governmental social security system to provide care and financial support for the elderly. In most Asian societies, one's children provide one's social security. This is one reason why it is so important to have children and that these children are successful in their adult lives, because the success of one's children affects the quality of the parents' lives in their old age.

In postindustrial societies, individualism is a cultural value. One looks out for oneself. This focus on self in Western cultures contributes to high rates of divorce. If a person is not happy, if his or her needs are not being met, the person may leave a family. If that is difficult or inconvenient for spouse or children, that is their problem. This is the thinking of someone focused on self.

In a society based on individualism, the goal of the socialization process is for families to raise independent, self-sufficient, autonomous adults who will succeed by their own intelligence, skill, and hard work. Most postindustrial societies have a social security system whereby the elderly are provided for by the government in the absence of families that care and provide for needy relatives.

Immigrant children, as they acculturate to Western ways, tend to abandon caring for older relatives. They may well think that, if they were back in Vietnam, where there is no government care for the elderly, family members would take care of elderly people. But here in America, where the government does care for the elderly, each person is expected to care for him- or herself. If he or she cannot care for him- or herself, the government will assist in providing the funds to acquire care, so children often feel no obligation to care for elderly parents and grandparents in the United States.

Elderly immigrants often feel abandoned and rejected by their children and grandchildren in the United States. Acculturation often entails the abandonment of cultural rules from one's homeland. Norms of filial piety are often ignored as children acculturate to the West.

What I am suggesting is that the process of acculturating to Western cultures works against the development of parental and parentified children in families. When the acculturation process is incomplete, when there is still adherence to the values and norms of one's homeland, one may well see parental and parentified children in immigrant families. This is a function of intergenerational loyalty that still exists in these families as well as adherence to values of familism, interdependence, cooperation, and collectivism. As acculturation becomes more complete for children of immigrant families, these values of the home culture are abandoned and the young are less likely to support the elderly.

In the next account of a Latin American adult female, note the ambivalence and anger generated by the process of parentification for this respondent. Although she still attends to her mother, one could easily anticipate a time where this respondent abandons her parentified role.

> as I have grown older, I have noticed that my responsibilities toward my mother have become more and more of me being the parent and she becoming my child. A reason for this is the fact that the more I grow up, the older she gets. The fact that I have been raised in the

United States and that I know the language and how to get around makes her more dependent on me. There have been times when I find myself making sure she has eaten, taken her high blood pressure pill, has a way to get to work and from it. I've also heard my voice raised at her, treating her as a child, where I need to tell her what is the best thing for her to do. I've also noticed that I am sure she has an umbrella when it rains or I've given up my rain jacket to her so that she doesn't get wet when it rains. The fact that she really never learned how to speak the language and that she is not getting any younger as the years go by make her depend more on me. I have to make her doctor appointments for her as well as taking her to them. This right here has made me become knowledgeable of certain things that I shouldn't have to know about her and my step-dad. I have to go to the appointment and serve as an interpreter when I cannot get one for her. A function of this is that I know how to deal with people and I know what I have to do to get the treatment I need from certain people. A recent thing that I had to deal with was the purchasing of a home and how stressful it can be, but now I know what I will need when I buy a home of my own. The stress that I went under recently was uncalled for. The only stress that I should have right now is school. Given the fact that I live at home, I'm not married and I do not have any children or any bills to worry about. The fact that I have found myself treating my mother as my child scares me sometimes. I'm not ready to be a mother, which is why I have not had any children of my own, especially if I'm to become my mom's mother. I'm the child, a grown child, who is to be the child of my mother, not the other way around.

If the process of acculturation works against the development of parental and parentified children in immigrant families, the question then arises, for children who are less acculturated and who do assume the roles of parental and parentified children in immigrant families, what do they do in performing these roles?

Language

First-generation immigrant parents speak and write the language of their home country. The fact that the parents often have limited facility with English sets up an opportunity for parentification: children take care of their parents by providing a communication link between the family and the outside world. As Portes and Rumbaut (1996) write:

> One of the poignant features of immigrant adaptation to a foreign society is that the roles of parents and children are often reversed. In these situations, children become, in a very real sense, their parents' parents. This happens when their learning of the new language and culture has moved so far ahead as to create a vast gap with the first generation, forcing elders to rely on their youngsters for guidance (p. 240).

The children often assist their parents in conducting business, whether that be going to a bank or setting up phone service or electricity for the household. They may accompany their parents to grocery stores because signs in English must be read, labels may need to be read, and groceries must be paid for, which means communicating with a cashier. Children accompany parents for all government-related business that requires communication in English, from registering a car or getting a driver's license to conducting business with immigration officials or the social security administration. The role of translator, of communicator for the family, is one of the most important ways in which my immigrant respondents saw themselves as being parentified.

> One of my roles as a parentified child is being my parents' translator. I have always been their translator, and they have learned to depend on me. Although I feel that my parents have acquired sufficient English, they feel intimidated by the American language. Every time my mother has a doctor's appointment, she wants one of my sisters or me to accompany her. We do not mind. We are used to this. When she schedules her appointment, she makes sure it does not conflict with our own personal schedules. Sometimes we are beside her in the doctor's office without saying a word. She rambles on and tells the doctor everything she wants. I hardly ever say a word. However, she needs me there to symbolically hold her by her hand. It is for reassurance.
>
> My father knows less English than my mother. His language skills are weak in Spanish and in English. Therefore, he depends on me a lot more. As a child, he did not have the opportunity to attend school. I am always filling out forms, writing letters, making telephone calls and more for him.

The following respondent points out that children, when they arrive in this country, are quickly put in school. This accelerates their facility with English so they acculturate faster than their parents, who are often socially isolated from the English-speaking world by virtue of their limited English.

> As far as I can remember my mother has always relied on me to do all the talking for her in places that do not speak Spanish. I came when I was five and was put in school as soon as possible. I was still young and I learned the language in a matter of months. It was not easy but when you have to go to the bathroom and you need to say it in English, you learn it fast. . . . The fact that I knew the language and I spoke it clearly made her depend on me in getting the message out to the other person. I remember that I would write my absence excuses for her to copy in her handwriting.

All of the respondents above are female. Ekstrand (1980) found that girls are generally better than boys in acquiring a second language, particularly if they start learning that second language before the age of seven (Fieldman, 1997). Ekstrand also found that girls are more likely than boys to be called on in immigrant families to serve as translators. One of my respondents concurs when he writes:

> Based on personal experience, I have also found that girls in many immigrant households are called on to become translators. My parents would quickly call on my sister to translate for them. In other immigrant households that I know of, ranging from Nicaraguan to Chinese, the same was true for the females in those families. They were asked to fill out papers, read medication labels, and act as an interpreter for their parents' conversations with employers. In the absence of a competent female in the sibling subsystem, a competent male sibling would be called upon as translator.

Valenzuela (1999) identifies three roles frequently played by children in immigrant families. The first is the role of tutor, when the child is called on to serve as a translator or teacher of the parents or other siblings.

My parents knew a minimal amount of English whereas my sister had quickly acquired the language. She would constantly be called upon to act as a translator for my parents. As soon as I was old enough to start speaking, my parents began teaching me Spanish. That meant that it was up to my sister to teach me to speak English and make sure I was prepared for American society.

The second role Valenzuela finds immigrant children performing is that of advocate. In this role, children were called on to intervene or mediate on behalf of the family in difficult, troublesome situations. This can range from being an advocate with governmental agencies to negotiating with a school over the behavior or academic performance of a child.

When problems would arise for my friends and me at school, they would always call on our older siblings for assistance before they would call upon our parents. Our siblings would speak to school officials or teachers and they would decide upon the next course of action. In a sense, they were playing parents, making decisions regarding our lives.

The third role Valenzuela identifies children playing in immigrant families is the role of surrogate parent. Here a sibling is a caretaker of brothers and sisters, meeting their physical as well as emotional needs. This role is particularly apt to exist in families when both parents are gainfully employed. Because the parents may lack facility with English, the only jobs they may be able to find are low-paying jobs, so they may have to work multiple jobs to make ends meet. Their long hours of employment may make them absent from the home for long periods of time, leaving a parenting gap that gets filled by an older child. When they return home, they may be too exhausted from work to perform parenting functions in an efficient manner.

Within the context of my family, I would wait for my sister after school and we would go home. She would then partake in the family chores, while watching over me. She would prepare dinner for my parents and myself. After taking care of my parents' needs, she would focus her attention on me, making sure I had taken my shower, finished my schoolwork, and so on.

In my immediate family, I am the oldest child. My parents have always worked. I consider my household a heaven when compared to other immigrant children's households. My parents have been great and their parenting has been filled with love. For the same reason that they wanted to see their three daughters have a better life than them, they worked constantly. My mother and father would alternate shifts so they could save money on baby-sitters. Even with their time management, I still ended up taking care of my two younger sisters. For the longest time, I was the one that would wake my sisters up in the morning for school. I made sure they had breakfast and that our room was clean. I also washed the dishes and cleaned up the kitchen. After my sisters had brushed their teeth, I combed their hair. When we were finished getting ready, we would walk to my aunt's house next door. She would take my cousins and us to school. Reality is that as many responsibilities as I had, I did not mind. I have always thought of it as part of my family role.

Valenzuela (1999) found that girls, more than boys, were likely to perform the above three roles in immigrant families. The oldest child was also more likely to perform these roles than were younger siblings, regardless of gender. Children of immigrant families, by taking on parental and parentified roles, enable the family to cope with the stress of relocating by allowing the parents to focus primarily on taking care of the family's basic needs. As the following account suggests, one consequence of caretaking by children is that such children are socially isolated from nonfamily members because they do not have much opportunity as adolescents to interact with peers from school. They leave school to come home and assume familial duties.

> The older sisters became parental figures to the younger siblings since both parents had to work long hours. When the parents arrived home, the older daughters had prepared and served the food. The routine was always similar, the parents would come from work, go to sleep and wake up for the next waking day. Rarely did the parents have the opportunity to play, read a book or spend time with the children. Although the kids were doing better in school, they could not participate in sports or after school activities. Many times they wanted to enroll in extra-curricular activities but they were unable to because the younger siblings were at home waiting. The girls did not mind these types of responsibilities for they had learned to assume these responsibilities when they lived in Mexico. Mexican families teach young girls to care for their younger brothers and sisters. Also, these young girls learned to do household chores as part of the personal responsibilities, therefore, when they arrived in the United States, carrying out these responsibilities became less difficult. In migrant families, it is common to see children, nine years old and up working in the fields with their parents.

If the parents cannot provide for the family's physical needs through gainful employment, it often falls on older male children to work and supplement the family income.

> Most of my cousins from lower class families had part time jobs as soon as the law permitted them to work. Usually their paychecks would go to the parents. If the households featured only a female single parent, it was usually up to the oldest son to provide the family with income. In households featuring only a male single parent, it was up the oldest daughter to take care of the father and siblings. Her tasks would usually include cooking, cleaning, and taking care of the father's needs.

Most immigrant families are nuclear family units rather than extended families (DeGenova, 1997; Landale, 1996; McGoldrick, Pearce, & Giordano, 1982; Mindel, Habenstein, & Wright, 1998). Sometimes it is an adult male who first comes to the United States, initially leaving his wife, children, and kin at home and sending money home. Eventually, he brings the members of his nuclear family to join him when he achieves some level of financial stability. The elderly often decline immigration, feeling that it would be too hard at their age to acculturate. Because most immigrant families are nuclear family units, these families have limited resources to help with child care. The nuclear family system facilitates the development of parental children because older children constitute the only resource available to perform parental duties when parents are away working.

One of my cousins was and still is a parental child. She took on the responsibility of her baby sister right after her mother had to go back to work in order to make a living to put food on the table. My cousin made sure that her little sister was bathed, dressed, fed, changed, and was well taken care of while mom was at work. My cousin gave up playing mommy to a doll and became a mother to her baby sister. She did her role so well that sometimes she says that her sister should call her mom.

This is another illustration of how the concept of "social role" incorporates the idea "as if." The caretaker is a child but is performing tasks "as if" she were an adult. The caretaker is a sister or is a cousin but is functioning "as if" she were a mother. In any discussion of parental and parentified children, there is an implicit "as if." Parental children act "as if" they were parents to their siblings, and parentified children act "as if" they were the parents of their own parents.

Social Isolation

As a country, I think we do a better job of acculturating immigrant families than assimilating them into the mainstream of society. One can learn the language, values, norms, and customs of a new country and still not be assimilated into that society. **Assimilation** involves being socially accepted and integrated into the society. The waves of immigrants that have entered the United States over the past several decades are not unique to the United States. Waves of immigrants have also turned to Canada, Australia, and most countries in Western Europe.

These immigrants are often ghettoized into ethnic communities where they largely interact with each other rather than truly integrating into the broader society. One finds Chinatowns or Japantowns in many large cities. One finds whole shopping centers featuring stores run by and servicing Asians. When one goes to a school yard, one can see ethnic diversity but there are separate groups of students and each group is ethnically homogeneous.

Particularly for recent immigrants, difficulty with English and the lack of an automobile or a driver's license socially isolates them from the outside world. The following account from a Vietnamese student makes this point poignantly.

'I stay home for all day long,' my mom said to me, 'I don't know what happens out there. Like a deaf and dumb [mute] person, I don't know anything. Please tell me anything you know about the world.' Her words are acids that drip on my soul. 'Mom,' I said to myself, 'I have to work to support the whole family, otherwise I would stay home with you and tell you all the things I know.'

The reader may be impressed by the difficulty faced by immigrant parents with limited English skills, limited job opportunities, and low levels of pay for extraordinarily hard work. According to Matuk (1996), the levels of stress among immigrants sometimes cause them to turn to alcohol. Matuck found that immigrant men drank more than women and alcohol use was most prevalent among immigrants with a higher level of income and secondary levels of education. If immigrant parents come to abuse alcohol as a way of dealing with their stress, it creates a further avenue for the development of parental and parentified children.

Immigrant parents were often highly skilled and highly respected in their country of origin. They may have been verbal and eloquent in their native language. They may have been government officials or prosperous entrepreneurs. They may have been revered for their knowledge of history or philosophy or religion, but the skills they have are often of limited value to them in the United States. The newly acquired skills of their children are more valuable, often undermining the sense of power or competence of the parents. Parents become dependent on the skills or labor of their children, setting up a situation that is ripe for the creation of parental or parentified children. Whether or not the skills of the children enhance their power in the family system is largely a function of how acculturated the family is to Western culture. The more acculturated the family, the more status will be based on the behavior of people, on their contributions to the family, based on what they do rather than who they are [as when status is based on age or gender]. The more Westernized a family is, the more the labor of the children will enhance their status in the family.

CASE STUDY

This account comes from a Vietnamese female. When she was eleven years old, in the fifth grade, her family separated to live in different states. She lived with her father in an apartment and this is her story.

> Due to some problems in my family, my mother had to leave California to move to Colorado with my brothers and sisters . . . thus my father and I moved out of my older brother's house to live in an apartment. Since my mother was not around to take care of my father and me, I took over her role to take care of my father.
>
> When we first arrived at the new place with a new neighborhood and a different environment, I was nervous and not used to living with just my dad. I went to school during weekdays in the morning and came home in the afternoon. My father was the one who cooked for us when I got home from school. I would help him with the cooking and cleaning up after dinner such as putting the dishes away and washing them. Then, I would do my homework and watch television if it was still early before bedtime. On the weekends, my father and I went grocery shopping for food, drinks, and other supplies that we needed at home. My chores at home were to clean the whole house. On Saturday, I would start cleaning the bathrooms, vacuuming the carpets, mopping the kitchen floor, and sweeping the back yard. Also, my dad and I went to laundry location to do our laundry. We did not have washing and drying machines at home. Even though we went together—because obviously my dad was the legal driver and was the only one who could take me there—I did everything once we got to the place. I placed the dirty clothes in the washing machine, took them out when they were ready, and placed them in the dryer for drying. My dad did not have to do anything. Sometimes he helped me fold the clothes together and place them in a basket. Thus, I felt like I was a housewife, but at the same time I

gained skills at taking care of daily tasks at home and feeling good that I was helping my father out when my mother was not there for him.

Since my father was not good at English and could understand just a little bit of it, I was the one who translated English into Vietnamese whenever there was someone who spoke English to him. Especially when my father had to make an appointment with a doctor who was not Vietnamese, I would have to call for my dad and go along with him to the doctor in order to translate English into Vietnamese and vice versa. My father has high blood pressure, so he often needed to visit the doctor. I did these things for my dad on a regular basis. The time I stayed with my father and lived alone with him lasted close to two years. My mother moved back to California and lived with us after that. Although at times I felt kind of tired from doing all the housework when my mom was not available, I was proud of myself for being a good daughter. I believe that the time I was being a parentified child was short in duration and that it did not have negative effects on me. If my mother had stayed in Colorado for another year or so, I would have definitely become exhausted and faced many problems such as experiencing social isolation from my peers.

Questions

1. Using Jurkovic's four dimensions of parentification (infantilization, healthy non-parentification, adaptive parentification, or destructive parentification), which dimension does this account illustrate and how do you justify your choice?
2. Using Valenzuela's description of three roles that children play in immigrant families, which roles are illustrated in this account? Describe what this respondent does in each of the roles you selected.
3. In symbolic interaction terms, what are the "indications" this respondent makes to herself regarding her experience as a parentified child? Does she see herself as a victim or a survivor? Does she perceive the experience to be harmful or helpful to her?
4. What does this respondent identify as a primary factor that prevented her experience from becoming "destructive parentification"?

Large Families

Family size decreased throughout the twentieth century in the United States. Large families with four or more children became increasingly rare because children in a highly industrialized and urbanized society create a significant economic burden inasmuch as children generally are not economically productive. Large families tend to have many children either because the parents wanted a large family and achieved their goal or because the parents wanted a small or medium-sized family and produced more children than they intended to have. In the latter case, it is the youngest children who are more likely to be unexpected "surprises" rather than older or middle children (Lloyd, 1994). Unplanned pregnancies and the presence of many children that add to economic stress can adversely affect marital adjustment, which tends to be poorer with increased family size

(Rossi, 1972). The stresses on a marriage created by many children contribute to high rates of divorce and single-parent households, both of which are also conducive to the creation of parental and parentified children. Large family size, divorce, and single-parent households are all inversely related to social class in that, the lower the socioeconomic status, the more likely are all three phenomena.

Family size tends to be inversely related to social class. The lower the social class, the more likely one is to find large families. According to Wagner, Schubert, and Schubert (1985, p. 66): "the family of six is living at a lower SES level, farther down the poverty line with severely limited resources (unless, indeed, the husband's income is quite substantial) than are smaller families." Poor families are more likely to have larger families by virtue of their limited access to education and the medical technology that can manage fertility.

Research indicates that family size affects the style with which children are socialized by parents. In larger families, there are more rules and regulations and deviance tends to be more punitively sanctioned (Bartow, 1961). There is more corporal punishment of children (Nye, Carlson, & Garrett, 1970), partly because, in a large family, there are more people who will be adversely affected by deviant behavior so there is more need to control such behavior. Girls are less harshly treated and more protected than are boys (Wagner, Schubert, & Schubert, 1985).

Children from large families generally do less well in their lives than do children from small families. Large families more frequently produce children who exhibit delinquent behavior (from truancy to more serious crimes) and who do poorly in school, both behaviorally and academically (Jones et al., 1980), and are more at risk for smoking and alcoholism (Conley, 1978; Wagner et al., 1979). These children manifest poorer self-images and are more resentful and angry compared to children raised in small families (Wagner, et al., 1979). What is unclear is the extent to which these phenomena are a function of family size, socioeconomic status, parental competence and style, types of discipline, or other variables.

Large families are opportunity structures for the creation of parental or parentified children. Older siblings in large families are likely to function as parental surrogates or "little helpers." Older girls are often given many of the household chores while older boys may be withdrawn from school or be expected to help support the family financially after school (Assmen, 1981). The parents may be burdened by exhausting, minimum-wage work so they have limited resources for child care outside the family. As a result, older siblings are enlisted to insure the supervision and protection of younger siblings. Advantages for the family of enlisting older children for child care include the supervision and protection of children at no cost, the support of parents by the older child, relieving them of some of the stresses and fatigue of combining work and parenting, and the addition to the children of another parental figure who can provide nurturance, help with schoolwork, and who can provide food and security during anxiety-producing times of parental absence.

One potential negative consequence of inducting a child into that role is that parental children tend to be favored by the parents because of the valuable services they provide. The status of parental children is elevated, so younger children may feel they are less favored, loved, or valued than the parental children, which can lead to scapegoating of the parental child by younger siblings or feelings of anger or resentment directed toward the parental child. When a parental child is established, the status and parental treatment of siblings is not equal, which can prove detrimental to the self-esteem of the younger children.

Poor parental health can create a parenting vacuum in large families. Women who have had many children are more likely to develop hypertension with accompanying high blood pressure (Feldstein, Harburg, & Hauenstein, 1980), stress symptoms, gall bladder disease, diabetes, and postpartum depression. These women are also at greater risk for developing cancer of the cervix, digestive organs, and peritoneum, but are less likely to develop breast cancer than are women who had fewer births (Wagner, Schubert, & Schubert, 1985). Fathers of large families are more at risk for hypertension and peptic ulcers (Wagner, et al., 1979). These medical issues remind us that physical and mental illness in parents can create opportunities for the development of parental and parentified children. Such children try to compensate for loss of the ill parent or to help that person's partner, who is so busy caring for a spouse that he or she cannot devote sufficient time, attention, and energy to other family members. Parental children pick up the slack in caring for siblings, while parentified children provide physical and emotional caretaking of ill parents or of the parent who supports and cares for the ill spouse.

Lastly, with many children in the household, it is more than one or two parents can manage to care for those children. They need help from others and it is an older child who is readily available at no financial cost to them.

Chronic Physical or Mental Illness

Chronic physical illness and mental illness often coexist with one another. For instance, it is not unusual for a person who experiences chronic physical pain or chronic physical illness to also experience episodic depression. It is also not unusual for people who experience chronic pain or illness to also be chemically dependent on alcohol or prescription or other drugs.

> I grew up with a mother that was physically disabled; she had many medical problems/conditions. Foremost among those problems was a heart condition that left her feeling weak and useless and depressed a lot of the time. The first heart attack that she had that I can clearly remember was when I was in the fifth grade, and her problems just continued to get worse. And progressively, other medical problems were added. She was, and continues to be, a very unhealthy, very unhappy, depressed, and pessimistic person. In addition to this, my father was a military officer and an alcoholic. Being in the military meant that my father was often gone for six months at a time, leaving my brother and I with my mother. Being an alcoholic meant that when he was home, he was drinking—and my mother joined him in the drinking, even though it was not a wise decision on her part.

Many of the issues we discuss in this book coexist with other phenomena. The stresses and strains of adapting to a new country can influence mental illness among members of immigrant families. The mental illness can then lead to divorce, creating single-parent households. Furthermore, the existence of alcoholism in a family can lead to divorce, and drug abuse can lead to premature death and widowhood.

E. M. Brown (1989) sees dysfunctional families as creating environments conducive to the creation of parental and parentified children. She states that, "Life in a dysfunctional family . . . often encourages a child to enter into a role reversal with his or her disturbed parent. The child will frequently become a little parent, worrying about the needs and limitations of the adults. Since their own wishes for care and guidance cannot be met, such children tend to bury their needs in order to take on this caretaker role. The result is a 'parentified child'" (p. 1).

For children of parents who are emotionally disturbed, parental and parentified children develop as an adaptation to the absence of a parental safety net for the child.

> If you grow up with a disturbed parent, you may have found—to use the simplest example—that you lacked a parent who would prevent you from falling down the steps. Perhaps your parent wouldn't stop you, in a constructive way, from hurting people around you when you were having a tantrum. You may have had a parent who, when you hit him or her, hauled off and hit you back. Or perhaps your parent took a two-year-old's frustrated fit as a personal affront and burst into tears, asking you, 'Why do you hate me so much?' Or you may have had a parent who didn't respond to you at all, who didn't seem to notice what you were going through, or who didn't reflect it back to you in a way that showed you that he or she understood your needs (E. M. Brown, 1989, p. 10).

In the absence of parental protection and competence, children learn that they have to depend on themselves, not their parents, for protection. They realize that they themselves are all they can count on for survival. This can prove frightening to them.

> Most of you attempt to provide the safety for yourselves. Since you can see that your parents don't have the necessary control, you have to get into the driver's seat. There is no other solution if you're to continue to grow, develop, and move on with your life. But providing the support for yourself at such a young age and in the face of so much fear can only be accomplished at a cost. What you sacrifice is the right to feel and express the whole range of human emotion: fear, anger, even love. You learn to control your feelings. In a dysfunctional family, you quickly discover that your feelings are a source of danger. You provide safety for yourself by clamping down on your emotions. . . . You squelch your anger and your sadness and your fear. Since the response is anything but comforting when you turn to one of your parents in tears looking for comfort, you begin to avoid the rebuffs by not turning to them (E. M. Brown, 1989, p. 7).

In the following account by one of my respondents, the struggle of sharing a child's burden with others is nicely revealed. Jennifer was in the fifth grade and had an older brother who was in the sixth grade. Jennifer's parents were incapable of dealing with her brother's ADHD (Attention Deficit Hyperactivity Disorder) and thus the burden of caretaking fell on Jennifer's shoulders. Jennifer was saved by a supportive grandmother and supportive teachers, whom she was able to lean on for support. Often the difference between a parental or parentified child surviving the burdens of this role and being overwhelmed and paralyzed by those responsibilities is the existence of a guardian angel, a grandparent, some other relative like an aunt or uncle, a teacher or neighbor, who comes to the aid of the child and supports them in their struggle.

It was difficult to believe that Brian was a sixth grader, not only because of his small size but also because of his behavior. He had been diagnosed with ADHD and tended to act immaturely. In fact, he usually played with the second and third grade boys because boys his own age didn't want him around. Both parents worked long hours, and Jennifer and Brian were enrolled in a group care situation when they weren't in school. The parents seemed to have a hard time keeping up with their kids. The one who had it all under control was Jennifer. She was the one who woke up the rest of the family in the morning so that no one would be late. If she didn't make lunches for Brian and herself, they wouldn't have any lunch at all. Many times, she had to call her grandmother and let her know there was no food in the house; her parents had forgotten to go shopping. Grandma also got called when their parentts forgot to pick them up from after school care. Brian had a hard time controlling his behavior, and was on Ritalin. It was Jennifer who made sure he had his pill on time, and when his behavior was getting out of bounds, she would stick next to him to keep him in check. Even though she was the younger sibling, she was the one who held it all together. It took a long time for Jennifer to learn that she could trust the teachers in after-school care and ask for help. Once she felt comfortable, she would begin to pour out her worries that there would not be food to eat, that her grandmother would die and leave her without someone to call for help, that her brother would get into more trouble than she would know how to fix, that her parents would be late for work, lose their jobs, and blame it on her for not getting them up. She felt she was literally holding her family together with the help of her grandmother.

For the child of parents who are chronically physically or mentally ill, an issue that must be dealt with is control. One must control one's own emotions and one tries to control the feelings and pain of the parent. Here we see a blurring of personal boundaries—the problems of the parent are taken on as problems of the child. The child tries to ease the burdens of the ill parent, and, if the child cannot do this, it is the child's failure to control the situation and the child experiences guilt and powerlessness.

> As you gain control over your own feelings, you attempt to take control of your parent's chaos as well. In other words, you try to take care of your disturbed parent . . . motivated by the desire to help and heal your caretaker so that he or she will be able to take care of you. . . . 'If I can only make Mommy feel better, then she'll be here for me; she'll be able to take better care of me.' You hope that if only you can give enough support, maybe you will finally get some (E. M. Brown, 1989, pp. 8–9).

Whitfield (1987) gives an example of a child who becomes fused with her mother when the personal boundaries between parent and child were blurred.

> I survived as a child by being obedient, doing well in school and focusing on my mother . . . I took on a caretaker role. As a teenager I went to the library and read everything I could find on psychology in an attempt to cure my mother and father. In my recovery in psychotherapy and in my self-reflection, I learned that I was fused with my mother, that our boundaries were so merged that I literally woke up every morning and didn't know how I felt until I looked at how my mother was feeling.

The effect of not being able to bring about improvement in the parent's or family's situation can have profound repercussions on the adult personality of the child who grows up in a family with chronic illness, according to E. M. Brown (1989).

The sad truth is that most of you are fated to fail in your task. And as you do, your self-esteem becomes more and more eroded. You have a deep feeling of aloneness and deprivation because your parent isn't providing reliable and loving contact. And you feel terrible about yourself because you consider it your fault that you aren't being adequately taken care of. In the midst of this massive struggle there is little room to be a playful, light-hearted child. The result is a typical profile of the parentified child—serious, responsible, intense, unusually sensitive, and often readily hurt (p. 11).

We will be analyzing the consequences of parentification on the development of adult personality patterns in the last chapter of this book. As we will see, assuming the roles of parental or parentified child leaves legacies that these children tend to exhibit as adults.

Part of the legacy of growing up in a family in which one or both parents has some chronic illness is a lowered sense of self-esteem (Wells, Glickauf-Hugh, & Jones, 1999). This comes from the experience of having no control over one's environment as a child. No matter how nice, helpful, or competent the child is, the child cannot avoid unexpected emotional outbursts from the ill parent. These outbursts are often abusive and the child is the object of vitriolic cursing of everyone and everything in the parent's life. The child is called incompetent and worthless because he or she cannot ease the parent's pain or distress. The child internalizes this because he or she wants to ease the pain and suffering of the parent but cannot, and so feels guilty over this and is thus vulnerable to attacks accusing him or her of being incompetent and useless.

Self-esteem is also under attack from the absence of love, attention, and affection from the ill parent. The child often asks why he or she does not get the love, attention, and affection that other children seem to get. Such children may conclude that they are not really worthy of this love, attention, or affection. That is, that they do not get these things because they do not deserve them. Such thoughts are emotionally self-mutilating as the children try to understand why their childhood was as it was.

However, as a symbolic interaction theorist would tell us, the impact of parental illness on a child is partly a function of the "indications" the children make to themselves about the illness. The impact is affected by the children's interpretation of events. The impact of parental illness is affected by how the children define and make sense of that illness. The following student's mother was stricken by a debilitating illness, which he adapted to by becoming a parental child to his sister and a parentified child to his mother.

When I was an adolescent, a situational problem forced me to care for my mom (diagnosed with Huntington's Chorea). My mom would fidget with her fingers, stumble and lose her balance easily, forget where she put things, and had a hard time going to the bathroom without falling to the floor. Upon the diagnosis of her illness, I began doing the household chores my mom once did. I had to care for my sister making sure she went to school and came home afterwards. Also, I had to prepare breakfast, lunch and supper for my mom, because she wasn't able to function due to her illness. Thus, I had to go to school, maintain the household and care for my sibling, because my mom wasn't able to care for us like she used to. My other parent wasn't around to assist the family with emotional support. My grandmother was around to care for us by purchasing groceries for my mom so all we had to do was prepare it for her. However, my grandmother had only limited funds, so she wasn't able to buy enough groceries for everyone in the household. As a result, my siblings and I had to buy our own clothing and food.

This respondent's family provided a good deal of support to the children and currently provides emotional support to the mother.

> My mom is currently getting treatment in a nursing home where she is still visited by her mother and extended family members on holidays. She is receiving counseling/therapy, behavioral cognitive stimulation, and she has a facility to nurse her 24 hours a day.

Note that this respondent interprets his caretaking responsibilities as a form of reciprocal exchange. He is grateful for the care and support that others have given him in the past and, thus, sees his own caregiving as a reciprocal payback. He also engages in anticipatory reciprocity, hoping that someday, when he may be disabled himself, that others will treat him with the same devotion as he is treating others now.

> I am still faced with the parent role responsibilities of taking care of my younger sister because she doesn't have a high school diploma, which is limiting her access to resources. I believe it is my duty to take on the tasks my mother once had, such as taking care of my sister. My grandmother has encouraged me to take care of my mother (visiting her as much as possible, checking in on family members on a monthly basis) . . . because someday I too will be in my mom's shoes (physically disabled) and it would be nice to have someone around to care and spend quality time when I become disabled. Both of my parents and extended family members contributed to my survival and understanding about life and I feel it is my duty to return the favor by caring for them and being there for them until they depart from this planet.

This respondent's sense of duty helps him avoid feeling overwhelmed or overburdened by the responsibilities of caring for his sister, his mother, and his grandmother. His interpretation of his situation helps him continue to provide support to others at considerable sacrifice to himself.

Children of parents who are blind or deaf or visually or hearing impaired, when the child does not experience such impairment, often become parentified children, providing the parent with their eyes and ears. The impaired parents become dependent on the children, making it difficult for them to leave the family of origin to become an autonomous adult. The parents become dependent on the child, who experiences guilt at the thought of leaving the household.

Protection becomes an important theme in families when a member is physically or mentally ill. One way in which protection is given is by keeping the illness a secret from the outside world. Secrecy is maintained sometimes by telling lies regarding the illness, much as family members keep secrets and tell lies to hide alcoholism or drug addiction. A child may not reveal to nonfamily members the existence of a parent's multiple sclerosis, for instance, or a child may hide from other family members the difficulty that parent had in a grocery store while trying to shop for food as a result of that illness. A habitual pattern of keeping secrets and lying in childhood can adversely affect the development and maintenance of intimacy in that child's later adult life. Intimacy involves sharing thoughts and feelings with others, being open and honest with others, and keeping secrets or lying creates barriers to the development of intimacy.

Children in families in which a parent is ill may stay home from school to care for their parent. This happens when the other parent is away at work and there is nobody else to care for a needy parent. The child worries about the health and safety of the parent and sacrifices his or her education to care for that parent. This not only adversely affects the child's school performance academically but also impairs interpersonal relationships the child has with schoolmates as a result of discontinuous attendance and interaction with peers.

Advantages for children growing up in a family in which a member is chronically physically or mentally ill is that they are less apt to be critical of others, less apt to expect perfection from others, and are more tolerant of the limitations people exhibit. They are less likely to see everybody as being the same, and they develop a tolerance and understanding for people who are different. They are more likely to accept people for who they are. Their experience as caregivers has them growing up quickly as they assume adult responsibilities as caretakers of others. As one respondent wrote, one who was a caregiver child to a disabled father:

> the socialization process I have gone through has taught me many things that will help me to be a responsible adult in society. Of course, there are some bad things, such as getting yelled at for no apparent reason (apparent to me at least) and having to help my siblings with their homework because I was the oldest. But all in all, I feel like I have grown stronger because of the events I have experienced.

Sudden Illness

When a parent becomes ill suddenly, it can result in an adaptive response within the family whereby children become either parental or parentified for some period of time. In an era when divorce rates are high and families are having fewer children, a single parent often has to depend on his or her children when he or she suddenly becomes ill, forcing the children, at least temporarily, to become parentified.

> In January, 2000, my mom had a heart attack and was rushed to the hospital. The doctor told me she had a 15% chance of living but fortunately, she made it through the surgery. I was terrified when she was lying on the hospital bed, because I did not want to lose her after everything she has done for me. After one week, she recovered and went back home with me. I prepared her meals, cleaned the house, made sure she took her medication, and was there when she needed to talk. I had lots of responsibilities because I am the only one who she can depend on.

When children are required to assume responsibilities for a limited time, as a short-term adaptation to parental infirmity, it can prove a rewarding and gratifying experience for them. They experience their value as caretakers of others and have an opportunity to pay back their parents for all their parents did for them when they were younger. They have an opportunity to get in touch with their own resilience and strength in overcoming adversity in times of crisis. They have an opportunity to hone their skills as physical and emotional caretakers of others as well, which can prove valuable to them later in their lives. The following respondent, although overburdened for about six months, interprets the experience of caretaking in crisis as difficult but helpful in her own personal growth and development, making her ultimately "stronger and more responsible."

My mother had to go to the hospital to have an operation. She went through the operation just fine, but had complications when it came to healing. Because of this, I was called upon to take care of her. I had to help her with anything that she needed. This included giving her a bath, going to the bathroom and just daily activities. My father had to continue to work his normal shifts and was not readily available. My sister was part of a dance team and had to be taken and picked up from practice. I would take her and drop her off. Then I would come back home and fix dinner. My dad would come home and then my mom, dad, and I would eat dinner. After dinner I would go and pick up my sister from practice. She would be very hungry when we would get home so I would fix her a plate. Sometimes my dad would have the dishes cleaned and put in the dishwasher. When he didn't, I would usually do the dishes and leave a few for my sister. I didn't have much time left in the evenings. I would do some homework and then help my mom to bed, and then myself. This cycle went on for about six months. Looking back, I see I did a lot for my family. When it was all occurring, it was what we *had* [respondent's italics] to do in order to function. I don't believe that the experience negatively affected me, because it was for such a short time. Actually, I believe it made me stronger and more responsible.

This illustrates Jurkovic's (1997) contention that, if parentification is of short duration and if the efforts of children are acknowledged and verbally appreciated by family members, that parentification is not necessarily detrimental for them. When the physical or mental illness of parents results in parental or parentified children for a long period in a child's life, however, and when his or her efforts are not recognized and appreciated by family members, the roles of the parental and parentified child can prove traumatizing and have long-term detrimental effects.

Families with Alcoholism and Mental Illness

Children who grow up in a family in which one or both parents are chronically mentally ill have many of the same experiences as do children who grow up with one or both parents who are alcoholic. There is unpredictable emotional volatility, which often ranges from depression to rage. Because of this, they can never relax, can never take anything for granted, can never count on any routine or predictability.

Mental illness, like alcoholism, is potentially stigmatizing for the family, so family members often hide the illness from the outside world and boundaries around the family tend to be closed. Children in families where a parent is mentally ill usually do not feel free to invite friends to the house and they do not usually reveal to others in the outside anything that happens within the family. Secrecy is maintained, which has the same consequence for these children as secrecy has for children in families of alcoholism. Keeping secrets maintains resistance to change and diminished external resources that could support family members.

There are often norms of silence in families where a member is mentally ill and family members are forbidden to talk about what they see and hear. They are expected to keep their thoughts and feelings to themselves and not share them with other relatives.

As a child, I tried desperately never to have a problem because our family had so many. So I became perfectionistic and hid my fears, concerns and needs from everyone. On the outside, I always appeared strong and self-assured, able to handle anything. But I developed a lot of shame (Marsh & Dickens, 1997).

The norms of silence, coupled with norms of secrecy, have the same impact on adult children of the mentally ill (ACMIs) as they do for adult children of alcoholics (ACOAs). These adults have difficulty establishing intimacy with others. They have difficulty sharing their thoughts and feelings with others because they were taught in their families of origin not to engage in such sharing. As adults, they have to learn new ways of relating to others in an intimate way because the norms in their families discouraged intimacy.

These adults have difficulty maintaining intimate relationships because they learned not to trust others, only themselves. They were taught to be self-sufficient, independent, and competent because they were the only ones that they could count on. They also have difficulty believing that people will do what they say they will do, that people sometimes do tell the truth, and that people can be altruistic, competent, and thoughtful of others.

> Another stressor, which affected my brother and I more than it did my parents, was the fear of becoming close to others. It affected us as teenagers when we had few good friends, and invited very few people to our home. And it has affected us as adults in our relationship failures. Tied in with this is learning to discount feelings and needs. In my case, I completely shut down any feelings, was always very even-tempered and did not acknowledge having needs or desires at all. Because my brother and I had no other experience of "family" except our own, we had irrational belief systems. We did not have realistic ideas about relationships, love, or marriage. As a result, both of us made mistakes in our personal lives that I often wish could have been avoided.

Children in families with a mentally ill parent have difficulty as adults pairing with people who are not dependent. These ACMIs are so used to caring for others that they are attracted by the familiar, and so are attracted to people who need to be taken care of. ACMIs may be attracted to alcoholics or other chemically dependent people, the mentally or physically ill, or people who thrive on being dependent on others, who seek to be taken care of by others.

ACMIs are often the caretakers in their own families of origin. If a parent is incapacitated by illness, the other parent may devote him- or herself to caring for the ill partner, leaving little time or energy to care for the children, who are left to care for themselves. This can make a parental child of an older sibling, one who becomes a parental figure to younger brothers or sisters.

When One Parent Escapes

If a parent is incapacitated by illness and the partner cannot cope with the stresses of caring for that partner and the children, that individual may escape to work or desert the family as the only coping mechanism for dealing with the stress. Furthermore, it is not uncommon for the family with a chronically ill person to become a single-parent household when the caretaking parent disappears into work, abandons the ill spouse, or divorces the person who is sick.

so where was the father one might ask? In the beginning he, like the rest of the family, was very optimistic about his wife's recovery. Then weeks turned to months and months to years; slowly he found himself at work more, and the hospital or home much less. With mom and dad flaking out on their parental duties, Susie found herself taking on both their roles. She shopped, cooked, cleaned, helped her little brother with homework, and even signed report cards. This is not the life of a typical American teenage girl. It is a life Susie did not pick but was chosen for her. She admits at times that maybe if her mom had been successful in her suicide attempts, life would have been easier.

When a parent escapes from such a situation, it leaves a parenting vacuum in the family that is usually filled by an older child who parents siblings and the ill parent. In parenting the siblings, the caretaker child becomes a parental child and, by caring for the ill parent, also becomes a parentified child.

I took care of my mother and made sure that the house and the subsequent chores got done. I became the mother of my own mother. I took care of her, I made sure she took care of her personal hygiene, I made sure she took her medicine and kept her doctors' appointments, and I took care of the household chores when she felt unable to do so. I tried to cheer her up when she was depressed, which was much of the time. My earliest memories are of doing those things because I was embarrassed that our house was not always clean, that our clothes were not always ironed and neat, of having company come over and finding my mother still in her bedclothes and not showered. And also because it was just expected of me, and to a lesser extent, of my brother. I am eleven months older than my brother is, so there was minimal care required there; we were both pretty independent and self-sufficient. We pretty much accepted things in our home as normal; we did not realize that other families were not like ours.

Many children who become parental or parentified report that they just fell into these roles because there was nobody else in the family to assume the responsibilities of holding life together. Nobody else stepped forward to assume a leadership position so they took on these roles by default. This is illustrated by the following respondent.

I moved into it [the role of caretaker for her mother] because all of my older siblings [she is the youngest of six], they weren't around, so I ended up with the job that they had been doing. My dad was always away working, so I was alone with my mom. [This] all started when I was about nine. Almost every day, my father would make out lists of things that had to be done and also my mother would just ring a bell for me anytime she needed anything. She would just lie in bed and ring a bell and every time the bell would ring, I would have to come and see what she wanted. I would buy her a new bell every Christmas because I was so sick of hearing the same bell. To this day, I can't stand the sound of bells.

Because of closed boundaries, children in families of disabled parents tend to be socially isolated. They do not socialize much with peers because they come home after school and perform the caretaking duties. They do not visit other peoples' homes so they have no sense of what normalcy in family life is like. They tend to assume that what happens in their house is happening in other peoples' houses, also. It is only through extensive interaction with other people that they come to realize that what happened in their homes was not what was happening elsewhere.

As in the child of the alcoholic, there is a fusion between the parent and the child, a blurring of personal boundaries so that the problem of the parent becomes the problem of the child. The child's problem is to make the parent happy or well. When the parent is not happy or well, it is the child's failure. The child is full of good intentions but, simultaneously, is filled with feelings of powerlessness, worthlessness, sadness, grief, and guilt over their inability to make things better (Jurkovic, Jessee, & Goglia, 1991). At the same time, they never give up the battle and keep trying.

Marsh (1998) cites several effects of growing up in a family where one or both parents have a serious mental illness. Such children may shut down their own feelings to protect themselves from feeling sad, powerless, or worthless in helping their parents. This blockage of feelings can adversely affect their ability as adults to enter into or maintain intimate relationships.

They can also develop an unrealistic sense of power over others if they believe that their own actions had an effect on their parents' relapses or symptoms, particularly if they feel their own actions had a positive effect on their parents' ability to function. They then see themselves as working well with others who need help and develop an exaggerated sense of their ability to control the behavior of others. These people often are very controlling of others and may seek professions that are congruent with their need to control the behavior or emotional states of others, such as social work or psychology.

The need to control sometimes stems from their experience as children that they were the only person in their family who could be counted on to be competent, reliable, and dependable. They have learned that to trust others to perform well is to face disappointment. So, as adults, children who grew up in families with parental illness cannot trust others to come through or follow through competently. They feel that they are the only ones who can do the jobs that need to be done. This assumption can also adversely affect their intimate relationships with other adults. They cannot trust others or accept offers of help because they doubt that others will follow through, just as their parents or siblings were never able to follow through. What is happening here is the process of generalization. Such individuals can only believe that what happened within their family of origin will happen elsewhere in the world.

What children of ill parents must learn as adults is that the coping styles that helped them survive within their families of origin may not be functional for them in surviving in the external world. Their coping style may undermine their ability to experience satisfying, mutually rewarding interpersonal relationships.

Siblings

I have, thus far, focused on families in which a parent is physically or mentally ill, but what of situations in which a sibling is physically or mentally ill? What is the impact of this on other siblings?

Siblings may take a very protective stance toward the ill brother or sister. In being protective, they assume a parental responsibility.

I had an older brother that had heart problems. When I got old enough I took over the role of the hero for the family. Although he was able to live close to a normal life, I was to be the one to use my physical abilities to do the dirty work. I was taught to defend my brother in any situation. I was to do all the physical labor around the house. I can remember when our family bought the house we live in, I was cutting the lawn at the age of six. I loved the responsibility. I fit into that role very easily. I wanted to be like my father. There was no room for failure. I had to cut the lawn until my father was satisfied. I was soon to become a perfectionist in everything I did.

Siblings who are not ill feel obligated to protect their brothers or sisters from barbs and arrows, flung by insensitive others who may taunt and tease the ill relative. Physically impaired or emotionally disturbed children are often teased by classmates in their schools. The theme of protection is highlighted in the following of a sister, whose younger brother suffers from allergies. This sister became a parental figure to her younger brother.

One seven-year-old girl became fiercely protective of her four-year-old brother when her mother decided to go back to work. She helped him with potty-training (he trained late). She kept track of his long list of allergies better than either of her parents. She hovered over him, teaching him manners and giving him "time outs" when he misbehaved. She took it personally when he was teased or threatened by another child. Her behavior changed somewhat when one of her parents was around, but she did not know how to just be a sister to him.

The sibling tends to take adaptive roles relative to the ill sibling. One of those roles involves compensating the family for the sibling's disabilities by becoming an extraordinary hero, taking on all the tasks that the sibling might have done in the family. This hero role might involve doing things like mowing the lawn, as is illustrated in the above account, or by being an academic hero who brings the family a sense of pride and accomplishment and who serves to distract others from the stress and anxiety of caring for a "special needs child." The hero may adapt by becoming an athletic hero, a musical hero, or a "star" in some other capacity.

Some children, however, find the role of hero to be guilt-provoking. They feel guilty garnering the attention and adulation that their ill sibling cannot generate. They wonder how they can achieve success with relative ease when their brother or sister struggles mightily just to stay alive.

Should the sibling in fact not stay alive—should a sibling die from an illness—then other siblings have the issue of survivor's guilt to deal with. They feel guilty being allowed to resume their lives and enjoy the pleasure and fun of those lives when their sibling can no longer experience the pleasures, successes, and joys of life. Survivor's guilt tends to surface at the very times that are most joyous, most satisfying for the siblings who remain.

A sibling response to illness may also be jealousy and anger at all the attention the ill child is getting. The parents are often so busy caring for a sick child that the other children in the family get lost in the shuffle. This can create feelings of rejection and abandonment for the healthy children, who may resent the sick child and the parents for what they feel they need but are not getting.

Worry is part of the life of a parental or parentified child. The parental children spend much time and energy worrying about their sick sibling or parent, which can distract them from schoolwork. Caretaking siblings may worry that their ill siblings will not be able to manage if they leave home to go away to college or marry or live on their own. They worry that their parents, who relied on their labor for caring for the ill child, will not be able to manage when they are gone.

The worry of parental and parentified children intensifies as the parents become elderly. If the physically or mentally ill family member is a child, caretaker children worry that their parents are becoming too elderly to adequately care for the sibling. They worry that the stresses and strains of caretaking, which the parents may have done for decades, will become too burdensome to them. Sometimes, out of this concern, a caretaker child who is living independently returns to the family domicile to assume the role of caretaker parent to a needy sibling. Or, if the physically or mentally ill family member is a parent, the parentified child worries that the partner to that parent is getting too elderly to care for the partner and the parentified child returns to live with the parents to care for both of them.

The worry of parental and parentified children can adversely affect their attempts to leave home. The element of personal sacrifice is often a component in the roles caretaking children play and parental children often sacrifice their futures and their independence to stay at home and care for others.

The existence of a physically or mentally ill family member constitutes an opportunity structure for the development of parental and/or parentified children. The special needs of ill family members require special time, energy, and attention. If it is a parent that has these needs, a child may become parentified in providing the support needed to care for the parent. If it is the marital partner that is meeting the needs of a parent, a child may become parentified and provide support for the caretaking partner of the ill parent. If the child is the ill member, a sibling may become a parental child who protects, supervises, and cares for the brother or sister. If parents assume the major caretaking function for the ill child, a sibling may become parentified and provide psychological support for the burdened and stressed parent. Children can become parental or parentified well into their adult lives. The dynamics of creating parental and parentified children continue throughout the life span of families because parental and parentified children can be created as the parents age and become less able to assume caretaking responsibilities they have successfully executed for decades. It is this phenomenon that we examine next.

Caring for Elderly Parents

U.S. Census (ST-98-40) figures for 1998 indicate that there were over 34 million people over the age of 65 in the United States, 12.7 percent of the total population. Partly as a function of improved medical technology and preventive medicine, which keep people alive longer, the elderly, that is people aged 65 and over, grew from just over three million people at the turn of the century to more than ten times that number today (Briggs, 1998). In 1998, there were over four million people, or 1.5 percent of the total U.S. population who were 85 years old or older.

There was a significant drop in births during the Depression years, so the population of people currently aged approximately seventy to seventy-six was artificially reduced by virtue of lower birthrates. The biggest age cohort group in the United States is the baby-boom generation, people who were born between 1946 and 1964. This is the group that is currently serving as caregivers for the old; they are the children of the old.

Life expectancy in this country is increasing. People are living longer and longer. Most of the people over sixty-five are women because they tend to live longer than men. For people over sixty-five, there are three women for every two men. At eighty-five and over, there are five women for every two men. Given that women have a longer life expectancy than men, 5.3 years longer, and that husbands are usually about two years older than their wives at the time of their marriage, it is likely that women over sixty-five will live alone unless they are taken in by their children or cohabit with other elderly people. In 1995, 9.8 million people aged sixty-five or older lived alone. Eight in ten were women.

The number of people living alone increases with age. Among noninstitutionalized people age sixty-five to seventy-four in 1995, 64 percent were married and living with their spouse and 24 percent were living alone. Among those aged eighty-five and over, only 21 percent lived with a spouse and 54 percent lived alone (U.S. Census, 2000).

It generally costs society less when the elderly maintain their residence than when they receive institutional care. With institutional care, housing must be provided and workers must be provided who will attend to the physical and emotional needs of residents. These workers may do everything from janitorial work to medical functions. Workers are also needed to provide food—dietitians, cooks, servers of the food.

Social or educational or recreational programs are needed for residents as well. Creating and maintaining these programs presents problems over time, because, as the residents of a facility age and develop infirmities, there are fewer people in the facility who can participate in these programs. As fewer people participate in the programs, those programs deteriorate in their quality and become more expensive on a per capita basis.

If the government generally supports older people who continue to reside in their homes, the question becomes, Who will care for these people, most of whom will live alone? Because of the prohibitive expense of bringing professional caretakers to the home to care for the elderly, the government counts on family members to provide the physical and emotional support the elderly need. This means that children will provide a great deal of the support their aging parents need, and this provides a structural opportunity for the creation of parentified children. Male children of elderly parents are more likely to help their parents financially as well.

Female children of elderly parents are more likely to help their parents emotionally, such as calling the parent frequently to touch base and giving the parent social contact with the outside world. One problem of elderly parents living alone is their social isolation. Particularly when the elderly are no longer able to drive, their access to the outside world is restricted. I am told that, in Norway, postal workers are expected to deliver mail to people over 65 personally, ringing the doorbell of all elderly residents on their route. This is often the only human contact this person receives in the course of a day, and the elderly eagerly look forward to the delivery of mail and the arrival of the postal worker on a daily basis. It is the highlight of their day. This daily contact is a societal effort to protect the health and safety of the population of elderly citizens, because the postal worker makes sure that the resident is alive and well and asks if there is anything he or she needs and gets assurance from the contact that the resident is functioning adequately.

In addition to making verbal contact with a parent, female children often do most of the "hands on" caretaking for these parents, from helping with grocery shopping to helping them clean house to chauffeuring them for doctors' appointments or to banks or other business meetings. This caretaking is not only done by biological children; it is often done by children through marriage. Daughters-in-law are often asked to assume the same responsibilities as might be expected of biological children of elderly parents and they sometimes resent the expectations placed on them. They never expected when they married that this would be part of the deal.

I often tell my students to take a good look at their prospective mother-in-law because they will probably be called on to take care of her someday. It is more likely that children will have to care for mothers-in-law rather than fathers-in-law because women live longer than men.

As the next writer testifies, the caretaking of elderly parents is not only difficult for the adult caretakers but also affects people who have to work with these adult caretakers, because the caretakers sometimes have to take time out from their work to care for elderly parents. This absenteeism affects employers, supervisors, and coworkers who also have to adapt to the crises, sometimes by assuming more responsibilities, as well as expending time and energy "covering" for the employee who must leave, sometimes with little or no notice, to deal with an emergency. This respondent works with two coworkers, both of whom are the primary caretakers for elderly parents.

> I work for two wonderful people who are parentified children themselves and since there is only three of us in the office, I not only get to see what it's like, but if one of them or both of them are gone, it affects the company greatly. They are a married couple. Pam owns her own food brokering business and her husband, Bob, is the vice-president of the company. I am their secretary. Pam lost her father due to a massive heart attack at a young age and frequently cares for her now eighty-year-old mother. Bob lost his mother to cancer and cares for his eighty-nine-year-old father. Bob's father can still drive his car, but recently he got sick and had to be put in the hospital, so Bob had to take time off of work to go and take care of him. Bob has an older sibling but he lives too far away and works too much to care for his father. It is frustrating for Bob because there are many times that if his father has a scare, they will wake him up at the crack of dawn to ask for help. He often loses sleep and gets restless after he's been out all day running around to get his father's things done.
>
> Since Bob is the beneficiary of his father's accounts, he manages his father's checkbook and all his father's legal affairs. Of course, now his brother is outraged by this because he feels left out from the money but not once does he come around to help care for his father!
>
> Pam also leads a similar life. Her mother lives alone and at times hyperventilates. Pam takes time out of her work schedule to care for her mother and ninety percent of the time her mother goes to stay with them, especially during the holidays. If Pam and Bob are gone at the same time, I get stuck taking care of the office, not that I mind because I understand that they are helping their parents live long, healthy lives, but sometimes people call with questions that I honestly can't answer and it's hard. I figured that they would switch caring for parents if they could, but I think that they feel more comfortable caring for their

own parents because both parents have their own specific needs. So that is their crazy life in a nutshell.

Note that caregiving for elderly parents not only adds stress to the life of their co-worker but also adds stress to their marriage, as each partner is in competition with a parent for time, attention, affection, and energy from a spouse. Each partner may, over time, come to question where he or she stands in the partner's priorities. This is a marriage that is challenged to create a balance so that everyone's needs are met.

There is a growing literature on the survival of caretakers (Berg-Weger, 1996; Hansson, 1994; Ryff, 1996). The caretaker role can be exhausting and depressing, particularly when there is blurring of personal boundaries between the caretaker and the person being taken care of. The caretaker role can be so absorbing of time and energy that caretakers can lose themselves in the process and often forget to take time out to take care of themselves. Numerous self-help books, with titles such as *How to Care for Your Aging Parents and Still Have a Life of Your Own* (Dolan, 1992), *My Turn: Caring for Aging Parents and Other Elderly Loved Ones* (Haymon, 1996), and *Caring for Yourself While Caring for Your Aging Parents: How to Help, How to Survive* (Berman, 1997), promise to help them. Caretakers often believe they cannot afford to take time out from their caretaking responsibilities to recharge their batteries and replenish their energy. They forget to give themselves time to walk on the beach or take a walk in a forest. They can't allow themselves the opportunity to take time out to have lunch with a friend. Like most parentified children, they sacrifice themselves for the care of another, which limits their ability to perform their caretaking duties with a cheerful spirit, without resentment and hostility, and limits their ability to be a caretaker over the long haul because they do not pace themselves as long-distance runners learn to do.

One of the most important messages that sociologists can provide to the public is the importance of integration into social networks. One of Emile Durkheim's findings in his study of *Suicide* (1893) is that people get depressed and suicidal when they are not incorporated into social networks, which results in what Durkheim called "egoistic suicide," which occurs as a function of social isolation because caretakers of the elderly often cut themselves off from their peers.

The concept of synergy implies that the more time and energy we spend interacting with others, when that interaction is rewarding, the more time and energy we seem to have in our lives for other things. Synergy is sometimes referred to as the principle of $2 + 2 = 5$, because energy is added through the positive interaction of people who enjoy being with one another. Less can sometimes involve more, because the production of energy is not a zero-sum game. We can generate more energy and enthusiasm by expending energy in productive ways. What constitutes a productive way of expending energy can be deceiving because the walk on the beach may seem like a "waste of time" but, in fact, it generates more energy for being productive after the walk. Having lunch with a friend can seem like a "waste of time," but it generates energy and enthusiasm when one returns to the task at hand.

We are witnessing an expansion of support groups for the caretakers of others that provide for social interaction and the regeneration of energy. These support groups remind members to maintain personal boundaries and to look after themselves because, if they get exhausted or sick, they won't be available to the person who might need them. The trick is learning to take time out from caretaking without feeling guilty.

We know we are creating personal boundaries, protecting ourselves from unreasonable outside demands, when we are able to say "no." When we say "no" to a boss who wants us to work overtime, we are establishing boundaries. When an organization wants more volunteer time from us and we say "no," we are saying "I need time for my family and time for me and I will not allow you to gobble it up." Saying "no" is incredibly difficult for many people. It helps to take pride in our ability to establish boundaries. Caretakers of the elderly must also learn to sometimes say "no," and give themselves time out, giving themselves permission to take care of themselves or others who might need them (spouses, children, friends, etc.).

Taking Charge

What happens when elderly parents can no longer live independently in their own residence? This can occur as a result of physical disability or dementia or Alzheimer's. In such cases, the elderly parents must move but may not be willing to move or they may not be aware of the need to move because they are oblivious to the risks to their health and safety by continuing to live alone.

Parents often make decisions for children who may be too immature to make good decisions for themselves (you are not going to that event or you are not going to play soccer this year, you are already overloaded). With elderly parents, the role is often reversed and the children have to make decisions for the parents because they cannot make good decisions for themselves. This is one dimension of the parentification of children: they become the parent figure, telling their impaired parent what he or she must do. This role reversal can be gut-wrenching for the adult child. Perhaps the parent wants to continue living independently in his or her residence, but the adult child sees this as a threat to the health and safety of the parent. The child then has the unenviable responsibility of protecting the parent and, at the same time, moving the parent against the parent's will. This is extremely difficult because, for decades, the parent had power and control over the child. Now the child is taking power and control over the parent because of the parent's impairment. This role reversal comes with guilt, anguish, and regret for the adult child. For the elderly parent it can cause anger.

If the elderly parent is to be moved, where is that parent to go? One option is to move in with one of the children. Another is to have the parent move to a facility where there is supervision and assistance. There are, however, many options, and each one has financial complications. Some facilities have assisted living and intensive care options with gradations of care, others do not. Some facilities require buy-in programs with enormous down payments (some refundable, others not) while others do not. Who decides where the parent is to live?

Most families have one child who is primarily responsible for the care of an elderly parent. Does that child make the decision unilaterally? To what extent is the parent part of that decision, particularly if the parent doesn't want to move anywhere. Are siblings consulted and included in the decision-making process? What happens if the siblings have different interests and cannot agree among themselves concerning the available options? These decisions have the potential of creating significant rifts in the adult sibling subsystem.

If the parent moves into the home of the caretaker adult child, power issues often ensue. The parent has always told the children what to do, and will not give up being the boss easily. There is a loss of privacy and a loss of autonomy for all parties as well. The parent is moving into the child's house but may resent having to live by the child's rules. The parent may be critical of what he or she sees, either in the relationship between spouses or the relationship between parents and grandchildren. This creates stress for elderly parents who have to live with things they do not like but have little opportunity to say anything about what they see or to change family dynamics. When an elderly parent lives with an adult child, the adult child is increasingly pushed into the role of parentified child, in charge of seeing that medications are taken, in charge of the parent's health and safety, in charge of seeing that the parent eats properly, gets to doctors' appointments and other social activities, and in charge of the parent's overall well-being.

If the decision is to have the parent live in a facility, questions arise as to how often the child is to visit and how much involvement the child is to have in the life of the parent. What are the responsibilities of the adult child and what are the responsibilities of the facility? These boundaries get fuzzy. Often the adult child assumes the role of advocate for the parent with the facility, negotiating to get the parent's needs met. This requires the parental child to be a mediator between the parent and facility. The stress of this role intensifies if the behavior of the parent becomes problematic for the facility. In this case, the facility might request the child's help in controlling the behavior of the parent. This is what parents normally do with children; children are not usually called on to control the behavior of parents. In this kind of role reversal, the facility places the child in the role of parentified child.

Even if the parent lives in a facility for elderly persons, the child may become parentified as a chauffeur, a chief source of entertainment and social interaction, a supplier of food that is more enjoyable than what the facility provides, or as a major source of emotional support when the child performs the roles of therapist, best friend, chef, comedian, and provider of books, magazines, movies, or cosmetic supplies.

The Future

Over time, baby boomers will become the very old, straining societal resources to care for the large numbers of elderly people. The U.S. Census anticipates that, between 1990 and 2020, the population aged sixty-five to seventy-four will grow 74 percent while the population under age sixty-five will increase only 24 percent. By 2020, the baby boomers will be between fifty-five and seventy-four.

The population of children that will exist to support the elderly will be low because of falling fertility rates in the United States. These falling fertility rates are, in part, a function of the costs of raising children to the age of eighteen. It costs a family that earns approximately $60,000 a year approximately $317,000 to raise a child to the age of eighteen.

Rates of immigration among the young will not compensate for the loss of young people through low birthrates.

Another reason for the low fertility rates is the fast-paced style of life for adults in a post-industrial society. Married adults are not having children because they realize that both of them have to work full-time to attain the standard of living they desire; this leaves insufficient time to attend to the needs of children. Rates of voluntary childlessness among married couples is increasing in the United States (Eshleman, 1991).

Soaring divorce rates in the 1960s and 1970s also contributed to low fertility rates. The adults who are not considering having children are, in large numbers, children of divorce who are skeptical about the stability of marriage (Wallerstein, Lewis, & Blakeslee, 2000). They do not want to have children who experience what they had to experience as children. They realize that marriages are still fragile in our society, in part because parents have little waking, alert, fun time to spend together as couples to nurture their marital relationship. They realize that society gives very little institutional support to family life, so that married couples get little help from corporations or governments to sustain stable marriages.

Another factor that influences voluntary childlessness is the perception that having children interferes with one's own happiness and personal freedom. The fact that people are marrying later in their lives also affects childlessness. Older women may not be able to become pregnant; also there is the fear of birth defects among women in their forties, or complicated pregnancies or deliveries that they do not want to risk. They may feel that they are too old to start a family if they will still be parents to adolescents at age sixty.

The future holds the prospect of many elderly parents existing to be cared for and relatively few children to care for them. This "graying of America" will create a question of who is responsible for caring for the elderly: the family and children or the government? If the family is to care for the elderly, there will be fewer children available to share the caretaking burdens. If the government is responsible, the cost to the government of housing, feeding, and providing medical and emotional care will be extraordinary given the number of elderly to be served.

Mainland China today is struggling with this issue. Their one-child per family policy—initiated to curb the population—creates huge burdens on these only children who must care for two parents and four grandparents. One of the key principles of Chinese culture is filial piety, the expectation that children are to respect, honor, and care for their elders in their old age. The children are voicing outrage at the government, claiming that this is too much of a burden for them and so are pressuring the government for greater assistance and support in caring for the elderly. There is a possibility that the one-child policy may be relaxed in the future to give children siblings who can share the responsibility of caring for aging parents, because the government seems unwilling to assume this responsibility.

As parents age, their ability to live independently and autonomously becomes impaired by physical or psychological infirmity. Their adult children are presented with the opportunity to become parentified, becoming physical or nurturant caretakers of their elderly parents, responsible for protecting their health, safety, and welfare. The caretaking of elderly parents is one more context in which the parentification of children occurs.

Summary

This chapter describes five contexts in which opportunity structures exist for the development of parental and parentified children. In all five contexts, situations exist that can impair parenting effectiveness and competence, leaving a parenting vacuum. That vacuum can be filled by a child, who assumes parenting functions either toward their siblings or toward one or both parents. In dual-worker households, the parents spend most of their waking hours attending to needs of employers and coworkers and come home exhausted, having given the best of their energy and skill to work. One huge problem for families in which both parents work is the lack of congruence between the school schedule of children and the work schedule of adults, leaving children to fend for themselves until a parent gets home. When an older sibling cares for younger siblings in the absence of a parental presence at home, that child becomes a parental child. When the child cares for an exhausted, drained parent by cooking dinner or serving the parent as companion, friend, therapist, or cheerleader, the child is functioning as a parentified child.

In families in which a parent is chronically ill, with either a physical or psychological impairment, the child who becomes a caretaker for that parent is a parentified child. Parentified children also care for the adult caretakers for the ill parent when the caretakers get frustrated, exhausted, angry, or stressed. When it is a sibling who is chronically ill, a child can become parental by becoming a parent's "helper" in caring for the ill sibling or when they serve to protect their sibling from danger or demeaning behavior from others.

In families that have recently immigrated to the United States, children become parental children when they acculturate their siblings to Western culture. They become parentified when they serve as mediators between their parents and the outside world, when they speak for their parents, represent their parents, or chauffeur their parents to appointments. They also become parentified when they work to help financially support their parents.

In large families, the burdens of parenting can be more than one or two parents can manage on their own, so they enlist the help of older children to become parent surrogates for younger siblings. Parents in large families are more prone to health problems than are parents with fewer children. With limited financial resources, they may have difficulty getting those health problems medically treated and controlled. This creates opportunities for the development of parentified children who care for the ill or stressed parent.

Children also become parentified when they are the caretakers of their elderly parents. As age impairs the ability of parents to be truly autonomous and independent, an adult child may assist the parent so that he or she can maintain his or her own residence. When the parent can no longer maintain the residence, adult children become important sources of external support when they visit, take the parent into the external world for outings or for family functions, and spend time comforting, listening, and emotionally supporting the parent. Over time, adult children may have to make critical decisions for the parents, who become unable to make reasoned, responsible decisions themselves. In such cases, the parentified child makes decisions for the parent, just as the parent made decisions that affected the lives of children (such as what school they will attend).

In the next chapter, we examine how parental and parentified children are created as a function of divorce, and will revisit several themes touched on in this chapter, such as how employment of a single parent or how the pain and sadness of divorce can impair parenting. Divorce presents yet another context in which parental and parentified children provide adaptations to change.

5

Children of Divorce

Divorce involves the legal termination of a valid marriage contract. It is usually a painful experience for both parents and children, painful because all family members usually experience some sense of loss. With the loss of the marriage comes the loss of dreams, fantasies, and expectations that the marriage would last a lifetime. There is a loss of hope that somehow the couple would find a way to work through its difficulties. The divorce symbolizes a loss of love or a loss of faith and confidence that both partners might have had for one another at an earlier time.

All members experience the loss of a sense of family structure. That family structure provided security and support, and all members experience that loss of structural support, but in different ways. A marital partner may experience divorce as a loss of financial support, for the partners will usually no longer financially support one another, which results in a significant decline in the standard of living, particularly for women and children. Financially, divorce usually means the loss of the standard of living that the family had in marriage (Maccoby & Mnookin, 1992; Teachman & Paasch, 1994; Weitzman, 1985), and this loss is something that most women, prior to the divorce, never anticipate; they don't expect it.

While most women and children experience financial loss, most men experience a loss of companionship, emotional support, love, sex, and support services from others (nobody cooks his food, cleans his house, does his laundry, or washes his dirty dishes, all of which for him are symbols of love and emotional support). Many men lose contact with their children, which is another loss in their lives.

Children experience the loss of family structure as a loss of support and caretaking. Children worry, "Who is going to take care of me?" Their concerns differ depending on the child's age (Wallerstein & Kelly, 1980). Three-year-olds worry about "Who is going to feed me?" They worry about who will be physically present to provide them with a sense of protection, safety, and emotional nurturance. School-age children worry about who will help them with their homework and who will get them to and from school. Teens worry about who will support them when they are old enough to go to college.

Judith Wallerstein is a California social worker who has done longitudinal research following the parents and children of sixty Marin County families in their post-divorce experience over a twenty-five-year period (Wallerstein, Lewis, & Blakeslee, 2000). She finds that these children are absolutely correct in worrying about the things that concern them because divorce for children results in a long-term falling away of social and emotional support from parents, from extended kin, from neighbors, congregants, and friends.

Research literature on the effects of divorce on children reflects different focuses over the past five decades. The literature of the 1950s and 1960s generally downplayed the negative effects of divorce on children. Louise Despert's book, *Children of Divorce,* for instance, cites the fact that children of divorce sometimes feel a sense of relief that the fighting, stress, and anxiety will be over. She states that children of divorce are better off than children who are trapped in families characterized by conflict-habituated but stable marriages, because they can never escape from the conflict and anger. They are imprisoned in a battlefield where the fighting is constant; it is just the intensity of the conflict that varies over time.

Of course, the context of divorce was very different in the 1950s than it was in the 1970s and 1980s. In the 1950s and early 1960s, nearly 90 percent of all children lived with both of their biological parents until they reached adulthood (McLanahan, 1999). In the 1970s and 1980s, nearly half of all American children spent some of their childhood in single-parent households, most created through divorce (Glick & Lin, 1986). It is predicted that more than half of the children born in the twenty-first century will experience life in a single-parent household before they become adults (McLanahan, 1999).

The majority of children whose parents divorce will eventually live in stepfamily households as their parents remarry (Furstenberg, 1990). Second marriages are generally more fragile than first marriages, because they have the remnants from the first marriage to deal with. There are children from previous marriages who may not support the stepparent or the second marriage because it is a barrier to the biological parents getting back together again and reconciling. If reconciliation were to occur, the family of origin would be reconstituted, which is the only family in the minds of the children. Children of divorce cling steadfastly to the myth of reconciliation. Parental remarriage violates the myth of reconciliation. The new stepfamily has ex-spouses to deal with, who may prove intrusive or unreliable and undependable. There is child support arising from the previous marriage that may or may not be paid on time and may arrive as only partial payment. To the parent paying child support or spousal support, this may create stress and strain on the new marital relationship because family resources are going elsewhere. Spousal support payments that are expected monthly may or may not be paid or may be paid in whole or in part. Visitation schedules must be contended with, and a visiting parent may or may not show up for visitations, may show up on time or late. All this adds stresses and strains for a subsequent marriage that may not be able to survive. If these subsequent marriages do not survive, children of divorce are subjected to divorce again; 62 percent of remarriages in the United States end in divorce (Sorrentino, 1990).

The research of the 1970s, 1980s, and 1990s was generally more dire in stressing that we formerly underestimated the negative, traumatic effects of divorce on children (Hetherington & Clingempeel, 1992). Some researchers state that divorce creates single-parent households and that children from such households are more likely to be poor, are more likely to drop out of school, experience teen pregnancies, and exhibit juvenile delinquency (Blankenhorn, 1995; Popenoe, 1988, 1996; Whitehead, 1993).

Other researchers link the negative effects of divorce on children, not to the divorce, but to poverty created by a divorce (Skolnick, 1991; Stacey, 1993). Duncan and Hoffman (1985) found that half of women have their total family income cut in half one year following the marital separation. Women whose predivorce income was below the national median are particularly hard hit, with about 40 percent of children in these families living below the poverty line one year after the divorce. Often the economic situation of divorced mothers only improves when they remarry (Furstenberg, 1990).

Others state that children of divorce do less well in their lives, not as a function of the divorce itself, but as a result of the conflict, stress, and anxiety created by the poor marital relationship that preceded the divorce, a stress-filled environment in which the child was immersed, often for years prior to the divorce, and over which the child had relatively little control (Ahrons, 1993; Johnston, Gonzalez, & Campbell, 1993; Johnson & O'Leary, 1987). From this perspective, the source of problems for children lay in the quality of the parents' marriage before the divorce—the conflict and, at times, violence—not the divorce itself.

Mega-analyses of many research studies on the effects of divorce on children tend to show that, although children of divorce do less well in their lives than do children from intact nuclear family systems, the level of difference between these children is relatively small (Amato & Keith, 1991; Grych & Fincham, 1990). Many studies show that the greatest level of difference becomes manifest in the first two years after a divorce, with the differences decreasing thereafter. The major difference was that children of divorce tend to externalize problems through aggressive or delinquent behavior (Amato & Keith, 1991). Significant, but smaller, differences showed up in areas of academic achievement, social adjustment, self-image, and the tendency to internalize problems, which results in increased depression and anxiety for these children. There is so much variability in the response of children to divorce that researchers have increasingly focused on asking which factors enable one to account for good adjustments and which enable one to account for poor adjustments to the divorce process.

Factors Affecting the Adjustment of Children

Grych and Fincham (1990) find that children who adapt poorly to divorce are those whose parents continue to fight, whose relationship with their parents are conflictual or distant, who experience a number of negative life changes, such as moves, and who experience severe economic hardship. Children adapt better to divorce when the parents cooperate and agree about parenting issues or resolve conflicts that arise between them, when the children maintain close relationships with both parents, when they can use active coping strategies, and when their lives are relatively stable after the divorce. In general, adjustment to divorce is better when children are socially supported by parents, siblings, and a network of extended kin, neighbors, and friends.

McLanahan (1999) links the differential outcomes of children raised in intact nuclear family units and in single-parent households to three primary factors. About half of the differential, she believes, is attributable to the fact that a single-parent household, one disrupted by divorce, usually has fewer financial resources to devote to a child's upbringing and education. In addition, single parents, who often have to function as both mother and father, as breadwinner and nurturant caregiver of children, usually have less time and energy to nurture and supervise children than do parents in intact nuclear family units. According to McLanahan:

> Forced to play two roles, that of father and mother, single mothers experience stress and often depression, which can adversely affect their parenting. With their time, energy, and spirits stretched, some single mothers become too lenient, others become too rigid or strict (p. 135).

What the single-parent household often lacks is a system of checks and balances between two parents, so that neither becomes either too permissive and neglectful or too rigid and harsh in discipline. Without critical input from another parent, single parents are more prone to parenting at either extreme of the parental spectrum or may be more prone to exhibit uneven or inconsistent parenting behavior compared to parents in intact nuclear family units.

Thirdly, McLanahan says that single parents, because they have to give so much attention to the needs of both employers and children, often have neither the time nor energy to reach out to community resources that might supplement and support them. The fact that they are apt to be socially isolated reduces their effectiveness as a parent, because they are trying to do everything themselves without external support.

Deater-Deckard and Dunn (1999) cite risk factors that may predict poor adjustment to divorce in children including poverty, neighborhood crime—which is usually associated with poverty—violence, the child's gender and temperament, and illness in the family. Male children in mother-custody households tend to have more difficult adjustment compared to female children in mother-custody households (Warshak, 1986). Problems in parenting and problems in the home environment are also predictors of poor adjustment of children to divorce including maternal negativity, depression, parenting stress, and the use of harsh physical punishment (Deater-Deckard and Dunn, 1999).

Ahrons (1994) cites two factors that differentiate between children who are and are not damaged by divorce. First, children benefit from maintaining the familial relationships in their life that were important and meaningful to them prior to the divorce, and they do better in their post-divorce adjustment if they are not abandoned or rejected by a parent. The importance of maintaining familial relationships extends not only to parents but also to extended family such as grandparents. Secondly, children benefit when the relationship between their parents—whether married or divorced—is generally supportive and cooperative. This dovetails nicely with the work of Janet Johnston and colleagues (1987), who researched how children of divorce suffer when the post-divorce relationship between the parents is conflict-habituated.

Hart (1997) is among the more positive, optimistic authors regarding the effects of divorce on children. He finds that the increased caregiving required of children of divorce, both of the custodial parent and siblings, promotes the development of responsible behavior in these children. Caregiving can lead to greater resilience and competence in children who are contributing, productive members in a family of divorce, a position supported in the work of Teyber (2001).

The research of Paul Amato (1993, 1995) reflects slight differences in the development of children raised in an intact nuclear family system and in a single-parent household. Children of divorce raised in single-parent households tended to do worse in their lives if they experienced the loss of a parent in their lives because they also lost the knowledge, skills, resources, and support from that parent. Children of divorce did less well if there was poor parental adjustment to the divorce (Amato, 1993, 1995). The mental health of parents affects the mental health of children, and this is particularly true for the parent who has primary custody of the child.

Children of divorce also did less well if there was deteriorating parenting competence in parents who helped them develop (Amato, 1993; Amato et al., 1995). This parenting competence includes physical and emotional caretaking, being present for emotional support and stability, being able to set limits for the child, and enforce established rules. Limit setting provides a source of security for children, the security of having a parental figure who is in charge and in control of the family environment.

Amato (1993) finds that the greater the economic loss for children as a consequence of divorce, the less well they are apt to do in their lives. Children in single-parent households are not as likely to have economic resources available as children in intact nuclear families are.

Children of divorce did less well if they were exposed to parental conflict prior to, during, and after the legal divorce. The extent to which children were exposed to parental divorce affected their well-being and development.

Divorce creates life stresses for children, which is often linked to their having to change residence after the divorce. At a time of great anxiety and stress, the move means that these children lose important sources of support. They are torn away from neighbors who may have known them all their lives. They leave their school, leaving supportive teachers, counselors, janitors, secretaries, and classmates they have grown up with. Often the parents of their classmates were instrumental sources of support and contacts with these parents are severed in a move. These children also lose contact with congregants who were supportive throughout their lives. Wallerstein described divorce, for children, as a period of acute stress coupled with a falling away of social support, and this intensifies if the divorce involves a residential move.

Wallerstein's twenty-five-year longitudinal research illustrates the tenor of the more recent research on the effects of divorce on children. Wallerstein would add that, not only is divorce traumatic for children, but that trauma has long-lasting effects on their lives. These children are generally less likely to do well in their adult lives compared to children who grow up in intact nuclear family units (Hetherington, 1999; McLanahan, 1999; Whitehead, 1993).

They are apt to have difficulty entering into and maintaining intimate relationships in their own adult lives as a consequence of fear related to issues of abandonment and rejection. Children of divorce are reluctant to jump into intimate relationships with both feet. They are cautious and guarded (Wallerstein, 2000). The development of intimacy requires courage by both partners to share their thoughts, feelings, and themselves with another and the trust that, by doing so, they will be accepted and valued by the other. Boys who experience parental divorce are apt to ask, "If she knows me will she love me or will she leave me?" Out of that fear, they are reluctant to self-disclose to their partner, which creates a block to intimacy. Girls whose parents divorced are apt to ask, "Will he leave me as my father left my mother; will I be rejected and abandoned?" They are apt to be defensive in their relationships and unlikely to jump into relationships. This guardedness also is a barrier to the creation of intimacy in adult relationships. Wallerstein uses problems with developing and maintaining intimacy by adult children of divorce to illustrate that the legacies of divorce are long-lasting, pervading the adult lives of children of divorce decades after it occurs.

Financial Loss

For families in the bottom third of families socioeconomically, there is not a huge loss of family income from divorce. When a spouse leaves, there is approximately a 10 percent reduction in the standard of living, which tends to be matched by a 10 percent loss of income for wife and children. Because the husband's earning power was not high when the family lived together, his geographic mobility is limited, which maximizes the ability of courts to implement court orders relative to child and spousal support.

Inasmuch as working-class families are not apt to be geographically mobile, there may well be extended kin, such as grandparents or aunts and uncles or cousins, living nearby who can assist with child care, which reduces the child-care expenses of a mother who may need to work two jobs to make ends meet.

The post-divorce loss of standard of living is most severely experienced for women and children coming out of families that lived in the top third of the socioeconomic ladder in the United States. For these families, when a spouse leaves, there is about a 10 percent drop in the costs of living for a family maintaining its family residence. Although utility bills and phone bills may drop slightly when a family member departs, most family expenses are fixed, such as mortgage payments. Some drop in utility bills may be more than offset by the increased costs of child care.

While the cost of maintaining a household drops by about 10 percent, the income of a newly divorced mother and her children drops by about 40 percent, creating a mismatch in the ratio of cost to income (Weiss, 1979). In the United States, women make approximately seventy-five cents to every dollar a man makes performing the same job. This imbalance generates a political agenda for feminists who demand equal pay for equal work.

The likelihood is that wife and children will not receive from a court order any more than 50 percent of a husband's net income in combined child and spousal support. Women in many states will not receive anything in spousal support unless the marriage has lasted at least seven years.

Even if a court order mandates that the husband pays the wife child and/or spousal support, there is no guarantee that she will receive what the court has ordered. Billions of dollars are spent by taxpayers in this country each year supporting women and children via welfare programs who are on welfare because court-ordered child support has not been paid. There is a high incidence of noncompliance with court orders relative to child and spousal support, particularly by men who can afford to be geographically mobile, thereby escaping law enforcement authorities. Whole divisions of district attorneys' offices exist to prosecute violators of support orders. Despite this, recovery of the moneys owed is minimal.

To recover some of the lost income, most newly divorced mothers must be gainfully employed to a much greater extent than they were when they were married and where two spouses shared the financial burden. If they were homemakers, they become gainfully employed. If they worked part-time, they work full-time. If they worked one full-time job, they may work more than that. Census data from 1998 show that the gainful employment of mothers with infants is affected by their marital status. Fifty percent of the separated, divorced, and widowed women with infants were working full-time in 1998, compared to 39 percent of those who were married, and 24 percent of those who had never married (U.S. Census Bureau, 2000).

Newly divorced mothers often provide a source of profit for greedy employers. They may have had their employment history interrupted by childbirth and childcare, which employers may use as an excuse for offering them low wages that do not reflect the competence and maturity that they bring to employers. If they can only work part-time, they are employees who do not have to be paid fringe benefits, such as health-care insurance.

These mothers can be hired cheaply because they often cannot afford to travel and leave their children for long periods of time. They often are not available for overtime or unexpected, unscheduled work to deal with corporate crises. They may not be willing to work nights and weekends attending corporate social functions for clients or corporate parties designed to enhance work team morale, so they may be perceived by supervisors as not being "team players." Often these newly divorced women hit the glass ceiling in their work because in the competing interests of work and family they opt to be present for their children. They may be deprived of administrative positions, which serves employers by keeping the employee's salary low. Often these divorced women turn down promotions voluntarily because they are not willing to travel or work nights and weekends or to assume additional management responsibilities that they feel are more than they can handle given the family management responsibilities they already have.

Discontinuity in Parent/Child Work Schedules

The employment of the newly divorced woman creates a parenting gap in the single-parent family. Given her hours of work, who will care for the children? In the United States, parents face a child-care crisis, in part because the schedules of school children are not congruent with the work schedules of their parents. Children go to school from roughly 8 A.M. to 3 P.M., but their parents work from 8 A.M. until 5 or 6 P.M., leaving afternoon hours when the children are not in school and the parents are not available to care for them.

This situation puts pressure on school districts to provide children with after-school supervision, allowing children to stay safely at school until their parents can leave work to pick them up. For school districts, after-school child care is expensive because of increased insurance premiums that must be paid to insure children for additional hours, often in activities such as sports, in which there is an increased risk of injury. Teachers are paid for a teaching day that does not extend until 5 or 6 o'clock, so additional staff must be hired to provide the supervision and activities if children are to stay in school until the early evening.

In 1997, I had the opportunity to visit major cities in mainland China, where preschool hours are from 7 A.M. to 7 P.M., which gives parents societal support in parenting.

Children receive three meals a day: breakfast, lunch, and dinner. The preschool teacher becomes like a member of the extended family, functioning as a grandmother or aunt (the teachers are primarily women).

Some families in the United States rely on extended kin as caretakers for their children. This provides an alternative to paying professional caretakers a sizable percentage of one's income. Working-class families, in particular, who have limited geographic mobility, are most likely to have extended kin available because the nuclear family unit has not moved far away from them. As African American, Mexican American, and Vietnamese families are heavily represented among working-class families, and as these cultures support use of extended kin to support nuclear families, we often find extended kin used for child care in these ethnic groups (Kamo, 2000).

Kamo suggests that there are significant differences regarding who might be available as child-care resources in these ethnic groups. Asian cultures stress filial piety as an important cultural value. Filial piety is the expectation that children will respect and care for family members in their old age. They are likely to take in parents and grandparents and include them in the household, which potentially makes elders available as resources for supervision and care of grandchildren.

With first marriages tending to be delayed until later in peoples' lives, grandparents may feel that they are too old to assume extensive care of their young grandchildren. Also, with people not being able to financially retire early, grandparents may well be working and unavailable to assume child-care responsibilities.

African Americans place importance on caring for the young. If parents are not able or available to care for children, families will take in children as "fictive kin," incorporating them into the fabric of their family life (Ebaugh & Curry, 2000; Stack, 1974). With many children around and with limited financial resources, some African American families may constitute opportunity structures for the creation of parental and parentified children, using older children to care for younger children while parents work.

Mexican American families are likely to exhibit what Kamo calls "horizontal" extended family households, in which parents' siblings—aunts and uncles of the children—or godparents may be available for child care. In horizontal extended households, the extended kin used as resources tend to be members of the parents' generation. As the following Filipino respondent relates, however, as younger siblings begin to marry and create families of their own, they may become less available to nieces and nephews over time. The availability of extended kin may not be constant as the lives of family members are continually changing, which requires frequent adapatation of the family to find new alternatives for family support.

> When I was born, my parents were already divorced. . . . My mom had lots of resources to turn to because she lived with her kin and they helped her take care of me while she had to work. Her younger siblings started to marry and started to attend college as they grew older and that was when she did not have lots of resources to turn to.

An alternative to the use of extended kin, when none is readily available, is to pay for professional child care. This often is expensive if the child-care facility is of high quality. If the divorced mother is making limited wages, then a sizable percentage of her earnings may be turned over for child care, leaving her with little money to show for her extensive labor. If she has limited funds, she may have to make gut-wrenching decisions. One option may be to send her child to a facility she cannot really afford. She does this when she is not willing to compromise on the quality of the care her children receive. Or, she may send her children to facilities she can afford, but that are less than desirable in terms of the quality of care the facility affords. The price the mother pays for this option is guilt and concern for her children while she is at work.

As with health care, this society does not provide its citizenry with sufficient quality child-care facilities at affordable costs to parents. The supply of quality facilities falls far short of the demand for such services. Child-care workers, in even the best facilities, earn very low wages, resulting in high rates of employee turnover that can prove traumatizing for children, who often experience heightened anxiety and fear and a loss of security due to frequent changes in their lives. Children whose parents have recently divorced already have heightened sensitivity to issues of abandonment and rejection. Rapid turnover of child-care providers can prove unusually traumatizing for this population of children.

Latch-Key Children

If child care is either too expensive or of inadequate quality, the parent may opt to leave the children at home to care for themselves. This creates the phenomenon called "latch-key" children, who have possession of or access to the key to the front door of their house and who are told to come home after school, lock the front door, and stay at home until the parent returns home from work.

Latch-key children are left, for some part of each weekday, to care for themselves, presenting an opportunity for the creation of parental children, older children who provide younger children with supervision and discipline, help with homework, and snacks or dinner in the absence of a parent.

> When I was around seven years of age, I learned how to wash dishes, make my own lunch for school, vacuum, dust, wash windows, and do various other household tasks. I began to do my own laundry around age nine or ten, in addition to making my own dinner on frequent evenings when my mother came home from a long day of work much too tired to even think about cooking. I would also make sure certain of my brother's clothes were washed if I was washing general loads of laundry—such as socks and underwear—that could be thrown in together rather easily. My mother would wash his regular clothes so she could make sure to get out every spot of dirt (we had little money for new clothes). I took plenty of care to keep my own clothes neat and clean. As for making dinner for my brother, I would heat things up for him in our microwave if I was already making something in there for myself so my mother would not have to do it . . . when my mother came home exhausted from work.

When older children attempt to discipline younger children, it can create considerable sibling conflict and resentment. The following respondent describes what it was like for her to have a divorced mother who was frequently away at work and an older sister who attempted to assume some of the supervisory and protective responsibilities of the absent mother. This respondent did not appreciate having two people assuming mothering roles and fought the protective efforts of her sister.

> My parents divorced while I was still an adolescent. As is the case with many divorces, my dad moved out while my sister and I stayed with my mom. We sold the house and moved into a condo in a nearby planned development. My mom was fortunate enough to have a job she enjoyed and which paid her very well, but it required her to work long hours. Some days she would leave for work before I got up for school and not come home until after I was already in bed. She was always bringing work home with her at night and on weekends. My sister is two-and-a-half years older than I am, and she took it upon herself to watch over me. I don't know if she really knew what she was doing however. She would make dinner if mom wasn't going to be home in time, but everything else that she did really bothered me. She always wanted to know where I was going and when I would be home. Mom's working a lot caused me to grow up quickly as well. I thought I was old enough to go and do what I wanted without anyone needing to know about it. So when my sister asked where I was going, I usually had a smart remark like, 'None of your business!' or 'Don't worry about it!' She was always telling me to do my chores and clean up after myself. Now, as I look back on it all, I know she was just looking out for me and trying to help my mom. But at that age you view it as mothering, and I was always telling her to 'stop mothering me!' My mom would tell her the same thing, but she [mother] was probably glad she [sister] did as it made her [mother's] job easier. Needless to say, my sister and I were always fighting.

Here we have another illustration of a child who is really a sister but is playing the role of the mother. When sisters mother their siblings, they play the role of "parental child." If a stranger were to ask the respondent, "who is this?" and point to the sister, there might be a moment of confusion in the response. One wants to call her a sister but she acts like a mother, so maybe one would respond, "This is my sister who acts like my mother." This is one illustration of family systems as complex phenomena. This confusion of status and role is further illustrated by the next respondent, who realizes that she acted like a mother to her younger sister.

> After my parents divorced my mother remarried and had two children. My mother decided after the second child was born that she needed to go back to work for about six months. I was twelve years old and had been babysitting for a few years prior. I was very physically and mentally mature for my age. So my mother decided to leave me home with a six-month-old baby and a four-year-old child for three hours a day, three times a week, which made me a parental child. I had no difficulties with this, but because I was left with them, I became more of a mother figure to them than a sibling. I was allowed to discipline them. To this day, I am more of a mother figure to my youngest sister; we do not have a sibling relationship.

Children of divorce often pride themselves on being part of a team effort at survival. While the mother is at work, performing the instrumental function of providing for the family's physical needs, the child takes pride in performing the expressive function of caring for the siblings' emotional and psychological needs as well as, at times, providing for their physical needs such as food. She saw her mother as working very hard and the next respondent seemed proud to be able to help her mother out. Notice that this mother voiced her appreciation of her daughter's contributions, something that reduces the degree to which this child felt overburdened.

> As I was growing up, I made our breakfast, lunch and dinner because I did not want to bother my mom. I knew my mom had a hard day at both her jobs she was holding and I did not want to give her anymore stress over cooking. The meals I prepared were not fancy but my mom appreciated that I tried to help her and she would always give me a hug and a kiss in the end. At an early age, I realized that my mom sacrificed a lot just to raise me because she worked two jobs and she hardly had any free time for herself. She told me she worked so I would have food, shelter and clothing like my other peers.

The single-parent household created by a divorce experiences a shortage of money that colors the quality of life in that household. There is a shared struggle for economic survival. This has the effect of bonding the single parent with the children in their economic plight. As the following respondent shares, the absence of money affected her childhood and made her feel "different" from children in intact nuclear families.

> Being a child of divorce with little money, I unfortunately had to be exposed to certain problems in our household that many parents with higher incomes tend to shelter from their children, and those problems involved money and our lack of it. I constantly heard the word "no" while in the supermarket when my brother or I wanted some sort of junk food in particular followed by the words, "we don't have the money." I went without many toys, games, clothes, and school supplies while other children at my school seemed to have everything and then some. I learned as a child (from my mother) that my father was to blame for much of our money problems due to his resistance to pay child support.

As this respondent continues her account, she shows how many children of divorce feel the need to help their family financially by becoming gainfully employed themselves as soon as they can find a job. They go to work at very young ages, often out of a desire to ease the financial burdens of their parent.

> Despite the child support debate that went on between my parents, I simply received the primary food, shelter and medical necessities from my mother while receiving very little financial assistance from my father. His meager child support checks helped to provide my brother and I with these necessities while various extra expenses—such as school supplies, clothing, cosmetics, yearbooks, etc.—came right out of my own pocket as soon as I reached the age of sixteen and secured my first of three jobs. At first it was exciting to earn my own money; however, I soon learned that money did not go very far unless spent extremely wisely. After a while, a resentment toward my father began to build up in response to his fruitless efforts to provide for his own children—leaving me with the stress of having to work hard for just about everything I needed regarding school expenses. It seemed so unfair when I saw that other classmates had a plethora of free time to spend on homework and extracurricular activities while I seemed to possess only a fraction of that time. Now, after working in retail for roughly four years so I could fund my own college education, I still harbor some resentment for my father's financial shortcomings. At the same time, however, I am proud of all that I have struggled for and achieved because it planted

in me a sense of strength and survival that I am unsure exists in those same classmates I once observed—who had their parents to provide for nearly everything they wanted and needed. I have always been able to get good use out of my ability to cook and clean and would actually prefer to learn it all over again if given the chance—even if my mother were able to stay home and I never had to learn these tasks.

This respondent illustrates what Wallerstein describes as the long-lasting effects of divorce for children of divorce. Wallerstein wrote that, "Divorce is deceptive. Legally it is a single event, but psychologically it is a chain—sometimes never-ending chain—of events, relocations, radically shifting relationships strung over time, a process that forever changes the lives of the people involved" (1989, p. xii). In the next section, we will see how divorce sometimes sends parents into a depression that adversely affects their ability to parent. We will explore a post-divorce phenomenon that Wallerstein describes as a "diminished capacity to parent" and how that creates an opportunity structure for the development of both parental and parentified children.

The Diminished Capacity to Parent

Marital separation can be emotionally traumatizing for all family members. Wallerstein estimates that approximately one in three persons goes through a period of severe depression following the marital separation. The parents are hurt; they feel rejected and abandoned. They are pained. They are wounded. Sometimes they are angry; sometimes they are sad.

The emotional pain that parents experience from the marital separation leaves them in a state of paralysis. The emotional pain creates what Wallerstein calls "a diminished capacity to parent." The parent is unable to go grocery shopping, unable to cook meals, unable to do laundry, unable to set limits for the children, and unable to discipline children when they violate rules. It is as if the parents are so depressed that they just want to crawl in bed, turn up the electric blanket, and hibernate to lick their wounds for a year or so.

As the next respondent writes, the depression of a parent is of great concern for the children. They worry about how long the depression will last. They worry about where the depression will lead. In her depression, this respondent's mother threatened suicide, which was a huge source of fear and concern for this daughter.

After the divorce process started, my mom became a basket case. She went into depression, accompanied by fits of rage and then sobbing. I quickly learned how to do the laundry, and since dinners suddenly came to a standstill, I learned how to cook and fend for myself. I took out the trash, vacuumed, brought in the mail and so on. A typical day consisted of my mom coming home from work and immediately going to her room. She would lock herself in and then enclose herself in the closet with the phone. My sister and I would have to wait to use it until she had finished calling her parents, friends, and anyone else who would listen to her gripe and moan about life. It was very difficult. We had become second in line to the divorce. . . . When in rages, she would tell us how close she had been to going to our backhouse, taking down my brother's shotgun and shooting herself. I worried and worried and worried. First and foremost on my mind was the question, 'What can I do to prevent her from actually following through with it someday?'

This child became a parentified child because she saw it as her responsibility to take care of her mother. She saw it as her job to prevent her mother from killing herself. She worried about her mother as a parent worries about the safety of a child.

When parents withdraw as a function of their depression, the children often feel a sense of loneliness. They feel that their parental safety net has been pulled away, which heightens their sense of anxiety. They feel a removal of parental support, which is one of Wallerstein's most consistent findings in her research. Children experience divorce as a time of stress, anxiety, and trauma, with a pulling away of support.

There is a removal of parental support and a removal of support from relatives, friends, and congregants. People shy away. They are afraid of saying the wrong thing, They don't want to look like they are taking sides in the divorce. They don't want to get involved in other peoples' business, because families are seen as private arenas where outsiders should not intervene without invitation.

Parents often are reluctant to ask for help or support from others. Particularly people in helping professions want to see themselves as strong, as the helpers of others, rather than people in need of help or support themselves. So they hide to lick their wounds and try to heal. They want to convey their strength and resilience to others; it is part of the denial process, a denial of their own vulnerability, their own pain, their own need for support. The result of this withdrawal from the outside world is social isolation, not only for the parent but for the children as well. The family unwittingly closes itself off from the outside world, denying themselves the opportunity to be supported, nurtured, and helped by others. This social withdrawal often lengthens the grieving process for all family members.

Depression

Respondents consistently reported on the depression of one or both of their divorcing parents. This depression leaves a parenting vacuum that is filled by a child. Children of divorce experience decreased affection, communication, control, and monitoring as part of their diminished capacity to parent (Hetherington, Cox, & Cox, 1982; Hetherington, Stanley-Hagan, & Anderson, 1989; Wallerstein, 1985). Sometimes the child compensates for the paralysis of a parent by becoming a parental child.

> His parents divorced when he was about twelve years old. Dan took care of his two younger brothers, age ten and four. After their father was gone, their mother was the initiator of the divorce, which emotionally demolished their father. As a result, he could not handle responsibility of his children let alone take care of himself. Their mother returned to the dating scene at nearby bars. She was at work from early in the morning until early evening and then home for a short time only to eat and then get ready for a night out. Dan was responsible for waking his brothers in the morning, feeding them and getting them ready for school. After school he took part in and managed the daily household chores. Their mother's only assistance with the housework was to provide the boys with a checklist of what needed to be done around the house, including laundry, vacuuming and other miscellaneous cleaning responsibilities several times a week. Once these tasks were completed, he was responsible for completing his own homework, as well as assisting in the

completion of his siblings' homework. All these things had to be completed by six o'clock in the evening in addition to Dan preparing a meal for his mother and siblings. The only quality time that the children received from their mother was at dinnertime and weekend afternoons. After dinner, she could not be bothered while in the bathroom applying makeup and getting ready for a night out. This was a daily ritual for them unless she was ill. Dan recalls that because of their daily routines and the lack of their mother's presence, they became self-sufficient and became used to not having her around. All three boys were sacrificing typical after school play and interaction with others. In Dan's situation, he was forced to quit playing football because he had to come home right after school to take care of his brothers. Dan never really had a normal childhood; he was too busy playing the parent role around the house.

In this case, Dan moved from becoming a parental child to his sibling to a parentified child, taking care of his father. This case demonstrates how children sometimes become quite mobile after divorce, moving from place to place and have no sense of stability or really belonging anywhere.

After a year of this, Dan became tired of the responsibility. Their mother had become engaged to marry a man that Dan could not accept. He took the opportunity to live with his father, leaving his brothers to fend for themselves with their mother and soon-to-be stepfather. When he went to live with his father, he found his father's emotional wounds had not healed. Dan was no longer responsible for his brothers but soon learned that his father needed help with day-to-day life. Though Dan no longer had a list of chores, he soon took over many of the same responsibilities he had before, living with his mother. His father did not expect Dan to complete hours of chores or prepare meals, but his father did not complete these necessary tasks either. Unfortunately, these things did not get done unless Dan did them. After work, his dad usually went out and drank excessively to numb the pain of his emotional problems. The only dinner Dan would get would be fast food unless he prepared dinner for both himself and his father. At times, Dan's dad would come home drunk at night, stumbling in the door and Dan would have to put him to sleep. This went on for a year or so until Dan moved on.

Dan's father met a woman whom he decided to move in with and Dan did not feel like he belonged. His mother's violent and failing marriage was coming to an end. Since he did not have anywhere else to live, he decided to move back in with his mother and assumed his previous responsibilities. He continued to live with his mother until he was sixteen. He had enough of taking care of everyone and himself so he ended up living on the streets or with friends. He began to get into trouble with the law. He started to burglarize and became involved in gangs. He never really thought about the results that could come from his actions because he did not really care. There was no one to look out for and enforce values of what was right or wrong.

This sad story illustrates how children can develop a sense of worthlessness when they are not nurtured and cared for by adults. They internalize the neglect, feeling that they were not worth a parent loving them, spending time with them, caring for them.

Dan's turning to a gang was an attempt to find a family. Gangs often appear to be an appealing alternative to their own family when the gang can offer attention, affection, excitement, and money that one's family of origin cannot provide.

Parentified Caretakers

Dan's taking care of a needy, alcoholic father is just one of many stories my students tell of their parentification as part of a post-divorce experience. After a divorce, approximately 90 percent of children live primarily with their mothers. Mothers are usually the primary custodial parent. Some students wrote about the post-divorce depression of their mothers and how they became unable to care for either their children or themselves. The children were left to care for themselves. They often were caretakers of their mother. One student writes about her half-sister, Judy, and Judy's mother, Eileen [fictiitious names].

> After the divorce, Judy's mother Eileen became physically and mental incapacitated. Eileen was very dependent on drugs. This caused Eileen to forget about caring for the needs of her daughter. After the divorce, Eileen became greatly depressed and was diagnosed as 'suicidal.' This was very difficult for Judy. Since Eileen was physically and mentally incapacitated, Judy had to take care of her mother. There were times that Judy stood in the living room and could hear her mother crying in the bathroom because she could not handle life. It was the responsibility of Judy to talk through the door and calm her mother down. She would tell her mother that everything was going to be all right and that she would help with the household chores to ease the burden. Eileen was very dependent on many things, such as drugs and alcohol. But most of all, she depended on her daughter, Judy. It was Judy who would act as the parent. She supported her mother, instead of her mother supporting her. Judy encouraged her mother to start to get dressed everyday and get a job so she could keep busy and so she could meet new people who would have a positive influence on her.

This account illustrates Wallerstein's (1985) description of a parentified child as "burdened by responsibility for a troubled, needy or depressed parent and who have been cast by that parent or by both parents into the psychological role that the parent requires" (p. 119).

The next account is written by a student about a friend of hers. Steve was so absorbed in caring for his mother's psychological needs that he was unable to leave his family. He sacrificed his own future to stay home and care for his needy mother.

> Steve has been a parentified child since the age of 14. His father left and left his mother without anything. Steve's parents married when they were young and all the friends that his mother has are friends of her husband's. She did not have friends of her own, because she was caught up with the marriage. The only person that Steve's mother had was Steve, who she leaned on for support. She began to drink heavily, got fired from her job and gained 35 pounds. Steve decided that he did not like to see her like this, and he helped her get through this hard time. He joined a gym with her and she soon quit the smoking and drinking. They spent a lot of time together, going to dinner, movies and hanging out together. When Steve wanted to go out with his friends, his mother wanted to tag along. She put a guilt trip on him and it made him feel sorry for her. He decided to stay home. When he did go out, he would feel bad because she would be home alone. Steve is now 24 and he decided to stay here to go to college to be closer to his mom. He worries about her often and is still living at home with her.

I have also filled a parentified role with my mother over these years. In the times when she could not handle the stress of single parenting, I was the one who provided the shoulder to cry on and the ear to listen. To this day, my mother confides in me differently than with my siblings.

The experiences of Dan, Judy, and Steve with their mothers is reinforced in much of the literature on the effects of divorce for women and children. Some of that literature winds up bashing mothers, as is illustrated in the tone of the following excerpt:

> The mother who has not remarried is often too dependent on and too involved with her children, without meaning to do harm, the mother often turns her children into her counselors, best friends, or confidantes—unintentionally encouraging them to pity her, to shoulder too much responsibility for solving her problems, and to provide the emotional intimacy no adult is providing her. Sadly, these children and their mother end up too involved in one another's lives (Nielsen, 1999).

Several points can be made regarding the hostile press that divorced mothers have received. First, my students tell me that fathers, not just mothers, are the objects of a child's parentified energy. Fathers often become needy, incompetent, and dependent following a divorce and, though they may not overtly reach out to their children for help, they still are on the receiving end of their children's nurturant caretaking.

> My dad had a very difficult time adjusting to the idea of my mom wanting a divorce. My sister told me that there were numerous times in which he would cry like a baby and she would hold him and console him. I never experienced this because my role was that of the counselor. Imagine your parent coming to you and asking advice about the divorce, more specifically, how to handle your mom because she's turned into a ball of rage and resentment. What is a kid supposed to say?

The fact that some mothers experience depression as part of their post-divorce experience can in part be attributable to the failure of fathers and husbands to financially support their former wives and their children after the marital separation. U.S. Census figures for 1997 show that, throughout the country, mothers who were primary custodial parents received only 60 percent of the court-ordered child support they were due (U.S. Census Bureau, Current Population Survey, April 1998). Stress in the lives of women and children could be reduced if fathers did a better job of paying child support and if law enforcement agencies did a better job of prosecuting nonsupport.

The fact that some fathers do not pay child support in full or at all places great pressure on divorced mothers to economically survive. They generally put in a very long day. They wake up at approximately 6 A.M., get themselves ready for work, wake their children, get their children ready for school, which often involves feeding them breakfast, making their lunch, and getting the children dressed if they are young. They get their children off to school and leave themselves for an eight-hour workday. They get home from work, prepare dinner, eat dinner with the children, clean up from dinner, interact with the children, perhaps help them with homework, get the children bathed and ready for bed, perhaps doing some reading with the children and then putting them to bed.

Then comes a magical hour, the one hour in the course of the day that single parents have when they are not attending to the needs of somebody else. They are not attending to the needs of an employer nor to the needs of a child. This is their time, time to be alone, time to recharge the batteries, time to relax. Should a child not go to sleep when he or she is supposed to, or should a teen not go to bed when he or she is supposed to, the parent is deprived of the only real "downtime" in the course of his or her waking day.

Single parents maintain this schedule five or six days a week. On a day off from work, they are doing special tasks such as grocery shopping, laundry, cleaning the house, or tending to yard work. It is not that they cannot maintain this schedule day after day, week after week. They can and do maintain this arduous schedule. It is just that they are working to the maximum of their capabilities, so they are exhausted and living on the edge of their ability to cope. When a crisis arises, such as a child getting sick or a car breaking down, the demands of their life may seem overwhelming and they experience "role overload." Role overload involves an emotional "flooding out," crying, feeling depressed, and overwhelmed, and it results in temporary paralysis during which the single parent feels that he or she cannot carry on.

One contributing factor to this sense of being overwhelmed is the social isolation of single parents. They are working full-time and the rest of the time is devoted to their children, so there is little time to attend to maintaining or developing friendships. Single parents often have few sources of support in the outside world.

As a result, they tend to rely on their children for support. As the going gets harder and harder for the parent, one or more of the children is apt to step up and attempt to help out. This might result in a parental child if an older sibling tries to help the single parent by becoming a parent figure to younger siblings. The following student learned of his parents' decision to divorce when he was eleven years old.

> Upon learning of my parents' decision [to divorce], the first words I spoke to my mother were, 'I guess I'm the man of the house now.' Though my mother assured me that I was not expected to fill that role, I naturally shifted to it of my own accord. Since then, I have actively tried to present a good male role model for my brother, who is six years my junior. I have attempted to give him the male mentoring and companionship I believe he lost when my parents divorced and my father moved out. I constantly seek out activities that we both love to do. I also try to share my experience and wisdom of age with him to help him with where he is in life. My younger brother is also one of the main reasons why I chose to stay at home for college, so I could continue to support him.

When fathers leave a household, it is common for male children to step up in the structural hierarchy of the family to assume the role of "man of the house." We see this happening when a father is deployed in the military and an elder son steps up to fill the position of "adult" male. We also see this when a father is removed from a household through incarceration and an adolescent son attempts to take his place in the family system.

As in the case above, the child became a fatherlike figure to his younger brother, becoming a parental child. Sometimes these children become a spouse substitute, being a partner to the mother, a confidante, a companion, a supportive cheerleader. This phenomenon is called spousification (Sroufe & Ward, 1980), when a male child climbs the hierarchical ladder to assume a coequal status with the remaining parent. The relationship between parent and child has many of the same qualities as do marital relationships without a sexual component.

The next respondent describes her observation of a classmate who, through the divorce of her parents, became a parental child to her siblings.

> Tammy was a parental child as a function of divorce at the age of 12. Her father and mother divorced as Tammy's mother had to begin working. I met Tammy in the seventh grade in one of my classes and she always seemed to be really concerned about her siblings, but she never mentioned her mother or father. She would periodically miss classes. She was missing classes because she had to take care of her younger siblings. I went over to her house one day after school, and I noticed that she was in charge of her younger brothers and sister. She got home, went to the bus stop, picked up her younger siblings and took them home. When they got home, they got a snack and began with everyone's homework, including Tammy's. Tammy had to be available to help all three of them with homework questions, entertainment and preparing a healthy dinner for them. Karen's mother came home about 7:30 and ate dinner, put the younger kids to bed and tried to relax. Tammy finished up her homework and went to bed around 9:00. In the morning her mom usually wakes up Tammy about 6:30 or 7:00 so that she has time to get ready and get the others prepared for school. Tammy's mother worked in the city, so she had to leave by 6:30. Tammy got herself ready, prepared breakfast, usually cereal for herself and her siblings and got them to the bus stop or ready for the carpool. Tammy, now 22, is still helping out with her family. She attends [a local community college] where she can be close to her family. Her father lives in Utah; she has not seen him in five years. Her mother has not realized that if it weren't for Tammy, the family would not have been able to stay together. Tammy is glad that she was able to help out her family and help her mother out because she knows that her mother would do the same. This has proven to make the relationship between her mother and Tammy stronger. At the beginning, it was tough and created a lot of frustration between them. Now, Tammy and her mother have both grown and Tammy has been able to see the importance of being a parental child as a function of divorce. In the end, she helped her mother and helped raise her younger siblings.

According to Weiss (1979), because the labor of children is so critical to the survival of single-parent households, children hold much more power in these households than they do in intact nuclear family units. The children are likely to be asked what they want for dinner, when they want dinner. To an outsider this looks like a very permissive household with egalitarian relationships between the single parent and the children. There is a diffuse boundary in such households, with all people having their responsibilities that must be done if the family is to survive. In conflict theory terms, the labor of children in single-parent households is an important resource to the single parent. Providing this resource—labor—generates power for children in single-parent households.

Weiss states that approximately one fourth to one third of single parents start out as single parents, making what he calls "the single parent's inaugural address." This address goes something like this: "Kids, before I was the parent and you were the children. Now we are all just going to have to be people each doing their jobs. I can't be after you to get your jobs done. They just have to get done if we are to make it. We're all going to have to pull our own weight. There are lots of jobs that have to be done, and we all have to pitch in to get them done." Inasmuch as there is no newsletter that goes out to single parents telling them to make this speech, it is fascinating that so many single parents give this speech independently.

Integration Problems

The close bonding between single parents and their children, coupled with the egalitarian status of children in single-parent households, creates problems when the single parent starts to date. The children often have their mother all to themselves during the time she is not working. They have mother's time, attention, affection, energy, and money. A suitor symbolizes loss for the children, because, when she starts to date again, they have to share mother's time, attention, affection, energy, and money with an outsider. They often see the suitor as a threat, as the enemy, and their goal is to vanquish the enemy, to throw the enemy off their turf.

Children often invest a great deal of energy sabotaging relationships the single parent initiates with others so that they can have mom to themselves. This sabotaging persists until at least one of the children reaches the age of sixteen-and-a-half or seventeen years old. This late-adolescent then does a magical about-face and begins to exhibit great interest in having the mother remarry. This reversal of goals is a function of self-interest. If the mother remarries, the child can leave the family of origin without guilt. If the mother remarries, there will be somebody to care for her and the child is relieved of his or her parentified role. He or she can go away to college or leave town to establish an autonomous life without worrying about how mother is going to survive.

The single-parent household, in which single parent and children are highly integrated by virtue of their history of shared struggles, makes integrating a stranger, a new spouse, very difficult when the single parent remarries and creates a stepfamily. The remarriage symbolizes the children's failure to conquer the enemy. This is not apt to endear the new spouse to the children.

The new spouse who looks at the structure of the single-parent household sees that the children have too much power. He is apt to believe that the mother disciplines neither well nor enough. To the mother, everything the stepfather says sounds critical of her parenting. This may well create a fragmented parental system in which the new parents sabotage each other. The stepparent often comes off as the "heavy," seeking to provide discipline, rules, boundaries. The stepparent tries to return the children to their role as children, creating hierarchy between the parental subsystem and the sibling subsystem.

As the stepparent disciplines, the children run to their biological parent for nurturance and support. They are apt to tell their biological parent that marrying this jerk was the worst thing she ever did. They look to the biological parent for help. To the biological parent, the stepparent is too harsh in his discipline. To the stepparent, the biological parent is too soft. The parents begin to work against each other, weakening the other's power. The result of this conflict is sometimes out-of-control children, with more power than either of the parents. The out-of-control children in stepfamilies exhibit high rates of school truancy, get poor grades in school, may get into trouble with the law, may be involved with gangs, may be consuming large amounts of alcohol and drugs, and may be sexually promiscuous; their parents may be unable to effect changes in these behaviors (Whitehead, 1993).

Divorce as Gendered

Much of the literature on divorce tends to have gendered bias, either being prowomen and antimen or the reverse. The prowomen literature tends to focus on the absence of financial support women get from former husbands, the way in which former husbands abandon their former wives in terms of lending them parenting support, and how former husbands abandon their children in terms of spending time with them and nurturing them.

Children of divorce suffer greatly from their fathers' remarrying faster than their mothers and seeing these fathers financially and emotionally supporting their stepchildren far more than they financially support them. This is a blow to the self-esteem of these children, and symbolizes their abandonment and rejection by their fathers, which generates considerable anger and pain for these children.

The gendered literature on divorce depicts the struggle of women in their post-divorce experience, as they suffer from too little money, too much work, in both providing for the family financially and nurturing the children, a shortage of energy and stamina, as well as a shortage of social support.

Literature that focuses on how men suffer in divorce tends to focus on how they are seen by their former wives and by the courts as a wallet, a financial provider. They usually have the courts looking over their shoulders to check on their compliance with court orders, and they are deprived of daily, sometimes weekly, sometimes monthly contact with their children, who don't call and don't visit, often through sabotage by their mothers, who are taking revenge. These fathers see themselves as paying for childrearing of which they do not approve, often seeing the mother's child-rearing practices as neglectful, incompetent, lax, and self-serving.

These fathers miss the social contact, support, and love they used to get from their family. They are lonely and depressed. They get angry when they see their child-support money being spent on clothes, cosmetics, and entertainment for another man, which is more than they ever got when they were married to this woman. They resent paying for food that is prepared and served to some suitor. They miss the physical comfort and familiarity of their former residence and may resent that the residence is not being maintained as it once was and is deteriorating. They intensely resent court orders that keep them away from their former residence.

The fact of the matter is that divorce is hard on everyone—husbands, wives, and children. All suffer in their own ways, and all carry with them the scars as legacies of their travail. The debate as to who suffers more—men, women or children—is counterproductive. It becomes a vehicle for venting anger and hurt and pain.

Becoming Independent

A consequence of parentification for children is that it can adversely affect their ability to leave the single-parent household without considerable guilt and worry. They may have invested years in caring for their needy parent. How is that parent going to survive if the young adult leaves home to attend a college or university? Who is their mother going to confide in, rely on, lean on for support? As the following respondent illustrates, this concern for the welfare of a parent can persist even after the parent's remarriage.

> The weekends I usually spent with my mom shopping or something. When I did go out with my friends, I always had to call in and let my mom know that I was OK. I never minded because I knew that I would want her to do the same thing. I played sports and joined clubs, but I spent most of my time with my mom. She was my best friend. I would do anything for her no matter what it was or what the cost might be. I was a very shy person, never outgoing. I planned things ahead of time and I wasn't willing to take on any new challenges because I was afraid of leaving my mom. I didn't think that my mom could make it without me. She had done so much for me, but I had also done so much for her. I kept thinking to myself, what is she going to do when I leave and move out? I felt stupid for thinking this because she was an adult and she was married.

In my private family therapy practice, I have seen parentification interfere with the leaving process in a number of contexts. A child who is a good student and has been accepted into a college or university, requiring the student to leave home, suddenly begins to fail a required course for graduation from high school around April of his or her senior year in high school. Psychologists might diagnose the pattern of events as "separation anxiety," but it is more than that.

This student's academic difficulties can be interpreted as resulting from a fear that, if she left home to attend school, her single parent would not be able to cope alone. For years, this high school senior was the primary source of emotional support for the single parent. If the child failed a required course for graduation, she would not have to leave and could stay at home and care for the needy parent. It is not that this student overtly had these thoughts. Rather, what was happening existed at a less-than-conscious level.

Only when the single parent can convince the child that she can make it on her own and verbally give permission to the child to leave can the child begin to concentrate on her studies and leave home. The behavior of the child (demonstrating academic competence in the required course) had to be preceded by the parent's behavioral change, demonstrating autonomy and self-sufficiency such that the child is convinced that the parent can survive on her own. Likewise, the motivation for the parent's change is based on the parent's being convinced that the future of her daughter depends on her ability to demonstrate her own self-sufficiency.

Sometimes, if students do graduate from high school, they are so worried about how their parent is doing in life without the child that he or she cannot concentrate on college work and flunks out in his or her freshman year in order to come home and take care of the needy parent. In the following example, the student attended a college only two hours away from her mother and siblings, but she worried incessantly about her family. Although she did not flunk out, she returned to live with her family after one year of college away because she could not bear the stress and anxiety of worrying about her divorced mother and her siblings surviving on their own.

> After my parents divorced, I worried a lot about my mother, my siblings, and myself as well. I always knew that I would succeed in the things I attempted, because I wanted to

prove to the world that my parents' divorce didn't hurt me as much as it did. I buried myself in my studies while I was in high school because I wanted to go to college and prove to everyone who felt sorry for me that I could be someone terrific, without being raised in a two-parent household. I set out on a mission to prove to the world that I would not let my parents' divorce ruin me. I graduated from high school and attended college [two hours away]. I returned home after just one year because I was lonely and I felt like I needed to be home with my family, so I wouldn't worry about them all the time. I couldn't handle being so far away that I could not help my family if they needed me. I moved home after one year in college. . . .

We have previously discussed the high level of social integration that exists in a single-parent household created by divorce. One problem created by that level of social integration is the difficulty children have leaving single-parent households. It is generally more difficult for young adults to leave single-parent households than it is to leave intact nuclear family systems. One exception to this statement is when there is a troubled marriage in an intact nuclear family system. When children have spent years as parentified children protecting the fragile marriage of their parents, it is sometimes difficult for them to leave, because they fear that, if they do, their parents will divorce. They fear that, without them as mediators, the parents will never survive together.

These children have for years been communication links between mom and dad. When the parents have nothing in common, nothing to talk about between them, these children provided the parents with a common area of interest to discuss, like soccer games or baseball games or music recitals. They have spent years coaching the parents to not forget birthdays, anniversaries, or special events, sparing them conflict and disappointment. Out of fear that, if they leave the family nest, the marriage of their parents will collapse, they have difficulty leaving.

These children may sacrifice their own future to stay home and protect their parents' marriage. They need to be convinced that their parents can survive in their marriage by themselves or that it is not the child's responsibility to hold things together, giving the child permission to tend to his or her own life. The willingness to sacrifice themselves, to sacrifice their own dreams or desires for others, is a critical component in the parentification of children.

The whole issue of children being able to leave their families of origin to lead independent, autonomous, self-sufficient lives as individuals has for decades been an important theme in family therapy literature. Murray Bowen (1976, 1978) thought that an important task of functional families was to allow for the separation of young adults from the family structure. For Bowen, children had to be able to differentiate themselves from the family's ego mass to establish their own identities and individuality apart from other family members, particularly apart from their parents. This differentiation of self from one's family of origin was a crucial task that had to be completed before a successful marriage was possible, otherwise the marriage was apt to become a vehicle for resolving formerly unresolved issues from one's family of origin.

The idea that children should psychologically differentiate from their family of origin can be interpreted as the bias of a Western, Anglo-Saxon culture. It is an Anglo notion that the job of families is to produce independent, autonomous, self-sufficient adults.

Individualism, as opposed to collectivism, is largely an Anglo value. Part of individuating is developing an identity as a discreet person apart and different from one's family of origin.

Ethnic values must be considered when one discusses the importance of the differentiation process. One reason some children may have difficulty differentiating from their family of origin is that the process is not valued or expected by family members or others in an ethnic community. It is expected that identity is based on family membership, not who one is as an individual. Mexican, Italian, or Portuguese families, most Latin American and Central American families, and most Asian families would have a hard time accepting that young adults should differentiate from their family of origin. These cultures believe that children are born into a family and are members of that family forever. Many cultures value collectivity over individualism, believing that family members should always be aware of the needs of other family members and attend to their needs. Interdependence between family members is valued more than independence. The notion of filial piety in Chinese families assumes the life-long obligation of children to attend to the needs of their parents and grandparents. In most non-Anglo families, males, in particular, never leave the family of origin, even when they marry.

This belief can create conflict in a number of contexts, for example, when immigrant parents maintain the traditional values of their native culture and their children adopt Western values by virtue of their acculturation. The children may want to leave home and their parents may feel abandoned and rejected if the children do. The parents then become angry because their children have violated the parents' expectations of being supported by them.

Another context is inter-ethnic marriage, in which one spouse is Anglo and the partner is not. Their cultural differences may give each parent very different expectations relative to their young adult children leaving home. One can be tolerant of children continuing to live with their parents into their late twenties or thirties while the other parent may expect that, once the children are adults, they should live on their own and no longer be dependent on them. If the issue is not the residence of the adult child, it might be continued financial dependence on the parents, where the parents ask and differentially answer when it is appropriate for adult children to be financially supported by them and when the ties should be cut and the children left to support themselves.

The issue of financial support for adult children is often an issue for divorced parents. Should child support only extend until the child is age eighteen, when the children are cut off at the knees or should child support extend to financially support them through their college education? The laws usually require financial support of children only until the age of majority, but some parents voluntarily include in their settlement agreements support of children through a limited number of years of college. The debates over financial support of children in college relate to the question, "When are children on their own?"

Another context for conflict is that family therapists create their own professional culture, in which they are trained to believe, as part of a professional process of acculturation to family therapy thinking, that families should launch their children. When they encounter families that do not launch young adults, they pathologize this process, sometimes failing to see the process in its cultural context. The expectations of therapists may, thus, run contrary to the expectations of parents, creating conflict within the therapeutic process.

The Boomerang Syndrome

The boomerang syndrome is related to the issue of children leaving a family of origin. A boomerang is an angular object, usually made of wood. When a person throws it, the boomerang circles in the air and returns to the person who threw it. Sometimes children are like boomerangs. They leave the family of origin to marry or take a job or go away to college.

At this point, the parents may experience the empty-nest syndrome when the parents become childless again. If, when the children were present, their marital relationship centered on the children, they primarily talked to each other about the children and the activities in which the children participated. They talked about soccer games or baseball or basketball games or swim meets. They usually had the children around as conduits for communication, so a parent would speak to a child about something and the child would relay the parent's thoughts to the other parent, making it unnecessary for the parents to talk to each other. Now they have to talk to each other without the children present. They have to relearn sharing their thoughts and feelings with each other. They have to relearn how to date, go out, and enjoy each other's company. Parents who forgot how to play together, because they were so busy doing the work of parenting, have a particularly difficult time relearning how to play.

When they retire, these parents, after their children have left, have each other and the four walls. They have lost the ability to relate to each other. They have earned their time to play, it is play time, and they seek out somebody with whom they can play. Approximately 21 percent of all divorces occur in marriages of fifteen years and longer. Many of these divorces are created by the empty-nest syndrome.

If the parents divorce and a son loses his job or divorces or quits school, the son will often return to live with his divorced mother. The son gets free rent, somebody to cook and do laundry for him, someone who shows concern for his welfare, and who dotes on him. The mother gets a companion, somebody she can talk to, and somebody she can "mother," which makes her feel useful. She gets a sense of gratification and pride from the work she does for her son. The son may become parentified, becoming the emotional caretaker of his mother, providing her with entertainment or recreation, or allowing her to hang out with his friends, or he may become spousified, the Oedipal complex in spades. There is no need for either of them to find a mate of their own and these two often stagnate together for a long time.

If the parents can navigate the challenges of the empty-nest syndrome, the child who loses a job, ends a marriage, or leaves school may return to the parental home, creating considerable conflict. The parents have experienced a period of peace and quiet, of attending to their own needs rather than the needs of another. One or both of the parents may find the child's return an intrusion. Often, one parent will be tough-minded and resent the return of the child. This parent wants to throw the child out to fend for him- or herself. The other parent says, "How can we do that? I will not throw him out on the street." What to do with this child becomes a source of parental strife, stress, and worry. If there is no resolution of the conflict, one parent may present the ultimatum that it is either the child or the spouse that leaves. The boomerang syndrome can affect parental divorce. The boomerang syndrome raises the issue of caretaking for parents. When does parental caretaking end, if ever? What are the limits of parental caretaking; is a parent ever free of the obligation of caretaking their children?

CASE STUDY

When my brother was young, our mom and his dad were divorced, and, although my brother was my mom's "man of the house," he still had a pretty good childhood with few responsibilities, until I was born. When I was born, my brother took on a whole different role. My brother was six-and-a-half years older than I was so he was a good age to help mom out feeding and changing me. As we got older, my brother would have to come home and baby-sit after school while our mom was at work. I think my brother resented this because, while his friends were out playing and riding bikes, he was inside making sure I did my homework and had a snack. My brother didn't invite friends over to play because no one wanted to play with a bratty six- or seven-year-old. My brother and I were always close, but I knew that he didn't want to baby-sit me. As my brother got older, he became more distant from the family. We always knew he would be there for us, but he had his life to live. When my brother moved out, I became a parentified child. It was strange because I was the baby, but now my mom needed me. I was old enough to take care of myself, but had a sense of guilt that my mom would be lonely if I spent the night at a friend's house, and eventually, when I moved away to Hawaii, I felt the guilt of my mother's loneliness. My brother got married, had three kids, and is now going through a divorce. I have to credit my mom though. She worked very hard to make sure we had food, clothing, and shelter, and an incredible amount of love in the house. We didn't have much in the way of material things, but we always had a stable, caring family.

Questions

1. What role did the brother play once the respondent was born?
2. What was an adverse consequence for the brother of performing this role?
3. The respondent believes that her brother resented coming home after school and caring for her, yet the brother did this. What mechanisms do you believe were operating that would allow one to explain why he did something he resented doing?
4. What role did the respondent play once her brother left the household?
5. What emotion made leaving home difficult for this respondent?
6. What kind of boundary probably existed between the mother and these children?

Although the research coming out of the 1970s, 1980s, and 1990s has tended to focus on the negative consequences of divorce for children, the dawn of a new century has produced new research, the work of E. Mavis Hetherington (2002), which portrays a less pessimistic image of children of divorce. Hetherington finds that some children survive their parents' divorce relatively unscathed. Some children have a combination of personal resiliency coupled with social support systems to overcome the losses inherent in divorce. As Hetherington writes:

> I harbor no doubts about the ability of divorce to devastate. It can and does ruin lives. I've seen it happen more times than I like to think about. But that said, I also think much current writing on divorce—both popular and academic—has exaggerated its negative effects and ignored its sometimes considerable positive effects. Divorce has undoubtedly rescued many adults and children from the horror of domestic abuse, but it is not just a preventative measure. I have seen divorce provide many women and girls, in particular, with a remarkable opportunity for life-transforming personal growth. . . . (p. 5)

Hetherington describes five types of children of divorce, and two of those types have direct relevance to this book. Competent-Caring children are "socially skilled, curious, energetic, assertive, self-sufficient, flexible and had many positive coping skills . . ." (p. 153); they were heroes and heroines who were able to survive stressful situations and even grow through successfully navigating very troubled waters. Many of these children assumed significant responsibilities in caring for others. Three conditions contributed to these children surviving well. First, there was "no history of a difficult temperament, severe anxiety, depression, or antisocial behavior. Second, these children are "exposed to stress that challenges but does not overwhelm . . ." and third, these children at times of acute stress had the support of one or more caring adults. Another group of children Hetherington called Competent-at-a-Cost, experienced parentification at an earlier age than did Competent-Caring children and the siblings or parents that needed their care had more severe problems that created a challenge that could not be successfully met by these children. Such challenges might include creating sobriety in an alcoholic parent or behavioral stability in a mentally ill family member. This latter group is extremely competent, sensitive and caring, but they have internal feelings of inadequacy from their childhood experiences. They have "a sense of 'letting people down,' of not being able to do quite well enough" and exhibited "chronic low-grade depression, insecurity, and lack of self-esteem (p. 155). This group, though externally appearing to be competent, caring people are internally scarred from being overburdened and unsupported as parental and parentified children.

The research of Judith Wallerstein, which focused on the long-lasting detrimental effects of divorce for children, together with the research of Hetherington, that emphasize resilience and survival skills exhibited by children of divorce, creates what appears to be conflicting views on the effects of divorce on children.

However, both researchers can be correct. Some children carry long-lasting traumatic effects of parental divorce into their adult lives and are indelibly scarred by their experience of family dissolution. The work of Wallerstein tends to focus on these children. Other children demonstrate resiliency and survive parental divorce and lead relatively normal, happy adult lives. They take adversity and grow from it, build on it, and become stronger individuals as a consequence of the hardship and turmoil they experienced and overcame. In this chapter, most respondents exhibit a mixture of the Wallerstein and Hetherington views. They were altered by their experience of divorce;

they encountered stress and adversity, but they also saw themselves as survivors of these experiences, often being strengthened by what they faced and conquered.

In many ways, my research on parental and parentified children mirrors the work of Hetherington relative to divorce. Hetherington found a research literature that focused on the negative consequences of divorce for children just as I found a research literature that focused on the negative aspects of assuming parental and parentified roles for children. My research, like Hetherington's, illustrates that not all children are permanently scarred or damaged by their harsh childhoods. The last chapter of this book focuses on the resilience of children to overcome their experiences as parental and parentified children and make those experiences positive growth experiences.

Like the Wallerstein and Hetherington research, the synthesis of what appears to be contradictory outcomes is that some children are damaged and traumatized by what they experience in childhood and other children, having similar experiences, are able to overcome their adversity and develop into quite healthy, happy, mature, and resilient adults who have the confidence to overcome life's trials and tribulations.

Children sometimes have great strength and considerable social support to overcome adversity in their lives and they survive and live to tell the tale. Other children have less strength and less social support to endure hardship, and they may become wounded, perhaps for life. I have been struck by the high incidence of survivors in my research population and the enormous power of the human spirit to overcome adversity.

Summary

Divorce involves pain and loss for all family members. Parents grieving over their losses may exhibit a diminished capacity to parent. This ranges from their own inability to function—an inability to get out of bed and go to work—to an inability to prepare meals, procure groceries, clean the house, do laundry, supervise, and interact with children, set limits for children and sanction violations of the rules. This diminished capacity to parent creates a parenting gap that is sometimes filled by children, who either substitute for the parent, becoming a parent figure to younger brothers and sisters or become a parental figure to their needy, impaired parent. As a parentified child, the caretaker may feed the parent, be a best friend, a companion, a therapist, and a spouse substitute. Becoming a parental or parentified child can adversely affect the leaving process for some children, who may sacrifice their own hopes and dreams to attend to the needs of family members.

6

In the Absence of a Parent

The previous chapter explored how some children of divorce lose a parent. However, other children of divorce are able to maintain a continuing relationship with both parents. Some children of divorce have an unstable relationship with one parent who cycles into and out of their lives in an unpredictable way. This chapter examines three contexts in which children lose a parent temporarily or permanently. In all three contexts, there is a dramatic change in the life of a parent that affects all family members. In the first context, the death of a parent can create a family situation that is conducive to the development of parental and parentified children.

Secondly, the loss of a parent can occur in a military family when one or both parents get deployed to active duty or combat duty. When a parent has to leave the family for an unknown period, it leaves a void that often gets filled by an older child. This child moves from the role of child to the role of adult, caring for siblings, the household, sometimes extended kin like grandparents, as well as the remaining spouse. When parents are deployed to military service, this often leaves children with insecurities about the health and safety of the parent who has left. These children have no power to control the course of events, and they live with a fear that the departed parent may never return, that they will go from losing a parent temporarily to losing one permanently through death.

The third context examines what happens to children in families when one or both of their parents is imprisoned. Incarceration often occurs suddenly and the impact can be severe and frightening for children. The loss of a parent can come in the darkness of night with a knock on the front door. Suddenly, the parent is taken away by uniformed officers and the children sometimes are left without much of a support network. Often an older child rises to the occasion to become a parent figure to younger siblings as well as to the remaining spouse. This child also often maintains support of the incarcerated parent, giving that parent hope and visits, protecting that parent from worrying about what is happening at home. As a parentified child, a caretaker child assumes the task of assuring the incarcerated parent that all is well with family members, reducing the anxiety and feelings of helplessness experienced by him or her.

In all three contexts, the child is providing the family with significant adaptation to rapid change and helping to fill a void left by the loss of a parent. In doing so, the child assumes some of the adult responsibilities formerly borne by the departed parent. Children do this in a process of making indications to themselves. They recognize the existence of the loss, indicate that the loss presents a problem, and indicate that they can be helpful in reducing the problem. Some children thrive on the added responsibilities, which makes them proud of their contributions. They feel they are contributing to the family welfare in a time of crisis, which bolsters a positive image of self. Others are overburdened and overwhelmed by the work and the uncertainties in their lives.

The Death of a Parent

According to the 1990 U.S. Census, 3.4 percent of children under the age of eighteen have experienced the death of a parent. Of these children, 73 percent experienced the death of a father, 25 percent experienced the death of a mother, and 1.2 percent experienced the death of both parents. In 1994, only 36.5 percent of bereaved children were living in a single-parent household, so many bereaved children are living in blended families or are cared for by people other than their surviving parents, such as relatives. Of the bereaved children who lived in single-parent households in 1994, 85.5 percent lived with their mothers and 14.5 percent lived with their fathers; 56 percent are male children; 12.2 percent were under six, 32 percent were six to twelve years of age, and 55 percent were twelve to eighteen years old. Of these children, 56.7 percent were white non-Hispanic, 21.3 percent were Hispanic, and 21.9 percent were African American (U.S. Bureau of the Census, 1994, and reported in Lutzke et al., 1997).

Like divorce, the loss of a parent through death involves enormous loss for children. Children's responses to the loss of a parent exhibit tremendous variability so the literature tends to focus on factors that work to enhance a child's adaptation to the loss of a parent and factors that work against favorable adaptation to parental loss.

Li, Lutzke, Sandler, and Ayers (1995) discuss four central changes in children's lives following the death of a parent. First, there are changes in the children's environment. Children unknown to the children come to visit. This is one area where family bereavement tends to differ from the loss experienced by children in a divorce. On the death of a parent, there is usually a community of support that temporarily mobilizes to give comfort and help to family members. This community of support may rally too briefly, but it does mobilize. The support can come from work colleagues, church congregants, neighbors, friends, or acquaintances.

In divorce, in contrast, there tends to be a falling away of support from the family. People shy away out of fear of saying the wrong thing and having to deal with raw feelings of sadness, grief, or anger, or fear of appearing to be taking sides in a marital conflict, fear of being depended on or taken advantage of by the divorcing spouse, or fear of the awkward feelings of relating to the individual rather than relating to the couple together as they did previously. In divorce, people outside the family system tend to avoid contact as if divorce were a contagious disease.

Caretaking by Others

Another dimension of change in the children's environment is that new people, sometimes strangers, may come to care for them. Children might be exposed to new caretakers at home, from nannies or baby-sitters to extended kin, or they may be enrolled in a new after-school or preschool program. Sometimes children experience a temporary change of residence if they are asked to live with other people in another house. One of my respondents, after the death of her mother, was taken by her father to live temporarily with extended kin in Trinidad. The problem for her was that she was taken to visit her aunt, without being told by her father that she was to be left there.

> My brother and I were attending school when my father decided to send us to Trinidad, West Indies to stay with my auntie. He escorted us to Trinidad where we stayed for six months due to his diminished capacity to parent. In my opinion, this was not the best thing to do at the time because my siblings and I had just experienced the loss of one parent, and leaving us under the supervision of our auntie, we also experienced an abandonment. As children, we were not told of events unless the adults saw fit to do so. My brother and I did not know why we were being left in Trinidad.

Sometimes siblings are separated and temporarily sent to different households, adversely affecting their ability to emotionally support one another in their grief. In cases where parents are either inadequate or absent, sibling loyalty and support can be extremely important. In studies of father absence, the presence of older brothers has seemed to mitigate against some of the potentially negative consequences of paternal deprivation (Biller, 1981).

When the widowed parent starts dating, children may be cared for by the parent's lover, sometimes with disastrous results, as the following account suggests:

> After my mother's death, my father started his own truck driving business. He would have extended family members or baby-sitters or his girlfriends watching us. On one occasion his girlfriend came to live with us and baby-sat us while my father was on the road. I was 15 or 16 years old. His girlfriend was always hitting my sister. This was something my father refrained from doing. At any rate, she did not ever discipline her own children, but always found that my sister did something to warrant a smack. I told my brother that the next time she hit our sister, I would beat her up. Long story short—I beat her up, and I escaped being punished by my father after I told him what had transpired. My intentions were to protect my sister from undue reprimands. My father's girlfriend never hit my sister again . . . she is scared of me.

These children, already feeling a sense of being abandoned by the parent who died, are very sensitive to threats of abandonment by the surviving parent. They know that a parent can disappear in the bat of an eye; one has already done that. There is always the possibility that the other parent will abandon them also. This is why threats of abandonment or rejection are so frightening for children who have lost a parent to death, as the following respondent attests when her father threatens to send her away to a home.

I was not a parental child to my brother although I did look out for him. We are one year apart, and he did not regard me with much authority. Because we were so close in age, we were always fighting and arguing. As a result, my father threatened to put us into a home if we continued.

Threats of abandonment or rejection are also traumatizing to children of divorce who have experienced a parent, without warning, picking up and leaving under dark of night. These children know from experience that a parent can unexpectedly vanish from their lives, so when a parent says, "So help me, if you continue this fighting I will walk out this door and never come back!" these children become frightened because they know this just could happen and, at the moment, this is the only parent they have left.

Particularly if there is an absence of money to pay for child care, the children may be called on to assume new responsibilities themselves while the widowed parent works full-time. This is when parental children surface. An older sibling may be called on or may volunteer to care for younger siblings after the death of a parent, filling the parental vacuum. Children whose mothers die generally assume more responsibility for household chores (Silverman & Worden (1993). As one of my respondents, whose mother died, attests:

I cooked, cleaned, bought groceries, wrote checks, did laundry, ironed clothes, cared for my sister, went to my sister's school functions, and bought school clothes. I raised my sister as if she were my child. To this day, I am still a parental child to my sister. In fact, I am going out with her for Mother's Day. As a side note, I also wish my father a happy Mother's Day on the day to let him know how much I appreciate all that he has done for us as a parent. He has been a mother and a father to us.

In research by Sandler, Ramirez, and Reynolds (1986) on children who lose a parent to death, children reported hearing from the widowed parent that he or she was worried about the child's brother or sister 61 percent of the time. Such voiced concerns may be interpreted as constituting an invitation for the child who hears this to watch out for and take care of the brother or sister who is the object of the parent's concern.

Expecting Behavioral Change from Children

A second area of change for children who lose a parent to death is that people voice expectations that the children should somehow behave differently. They may be confronted with injunctions from others to "be good" or "be strong" or told, "now you help out your mother/father." Children often hear, "I guess you are the man (or woman) of the house now." This expectation implies that the child is being moved from the sibling subsystem into the parental subsystem. This expectation implies that the child should assume many of the responsibilities that were previously assumed by the deceased parent. In the research by Sandler, Ramirez, and Reynolds (1986), children were told that they now had to be responsible 40.6 percent of the time. Children are told by others that they should help to fill the vacuum created by the death of a parent.

Distraught Parents

The third change that children experience on the death of a parent is the heightened distress of the widowed surviving parent. Children see their surviving parent sad, anxious, worried, or depressed. The greater the parental distress that children perceive, the more likely it is that they will exhibit symptoms of anxiety and depression or manifest conduct-disordered behavior. In the research of Li et al., the level of parental adjustment was the most significant factor in determining the adjustment of the children.

When the surviving parent experiences a difficult adjustment to the loss of a spouse, it creates an opportunity for the child to become a parentified child, who becomes the caretaker of the grieving, needy parent. We have here a similar scenario to that described for children of divorce, who become the caretakers of needy, grieving parents.

An alternative way a child may adapt to the distraught parent is to become the parental figure for siblings, relieving the parent of responsibilities and enabling him or her to focus on the grieving process unencumbered by household obligations. The larger the family, the more burdensome parenting may be for the surviving parent and the more overwhelmed he or she may become with parental responsibilities, relying all the more on the children. Older children may become helpers to their parent by becoming parental children, sometimes in addition to caretaking the parent.

Reminders of Death

The fourth way children experience change is through encountering reminders of the parent's death. People may tell the child that the deceased parent is in heaven watching them or they say how the deceased parent was so proud of them or how the deceased parent would be so proud of them. Comments about the deceased parent can actually be helpful to children, as they counter tendencies to deny or repress the loss. The existence of death reminders in the child's life is positively related to an absence of conduct-disordered behavior in these children (Li, Lutzke, Sandler, & Ayers, 1995; Lutzke, Ayers, Sandler, & Barr, 1997).

Adaptations to the Death of a Parent

Some children are traumatized by the loss of a parent and exhibit regressed behavior. Children who had outgrown thumb sucking may resume it. Children who were previously potty-trained may start bedwetting or have more bladder control accidents. Other children may exhibit bowel control problems. Some children experience nightmares and sleep disturbances. School phobias may arise and a child will not want to go to school and only wants to stay home. Some children may become sad, withdrawn, and depressed, though the extent of time over which these symptoms persist is highly variable.

Other children adapt to the death of a parent by finishing the career of the diseased parent. This child may go into medicine to find a cure for the disease that killed the parent. Hobbies and activities of the dead parent may be taken up and become a way of continuing the life of the deceased parent. Some adaptations are very creative, such as that of

James Barrie, who began to make up stories to amuse his bereaved mother, which lead to an illustrious career as a writer (Pollock, 1978).

Children of latency age may take on certain qualities of the dead parent such as an adult attitude toward work, school, and responsibility, which is often accompanied by worry. Childhood is no longer so free of concern for these children (Samuels, 1988). These are the children who, in the chapter on alcoholism, were described as "heroes." These children seek to excel in everything they do and are often the caretakers of others. They worry about things the surviving parent worries about, adult things, like how the family will survive financially.

Worrying about how everyone in the family is doing can adversely affect the ability of these children to leave their family of origin. They worry that others will not survive without them so they stay close to insure the well-being of other family members. This difficulty with leaving was experienced by the following respondent.

> When I became of age to move out, I found it hard to launch because I did not want to leave my father to care for my sister and I worried about him in his intimate relationships. It is unbelievable how much power we had over one another. I wanted to know that he would be okay if I launched, and he always asked me my opinion on women. Even after I had left home, I did not believe that I had truly launched because I visited a lot.

Adults who discuss their relationships with children and who seek advice about those relationships from children propel those children into the role of advisors, consultants, or therapists, which are adult roles. The child is parenting the parent.

Many themes we have previously addressed in other contexts are replicated in the experience of children who lose a parent to death. Like children of divorce, these children often attempt to fill a void or vacuum created by parental loss. Their custodial parent is often paralyzed, wounded, and pained, leaving them, at least temporarily, with a diminished capacity to parent. The child may fill in by becoming a parental child, caring for siblings, or may be a physical and emotional caretaker of the needy, depressed parent. These children often function as "heroes" who caretake others. This may adversely affect their ability to leave the family nest to establish autonomous, independent adult lives.

Military Families

Throughout the decade of the nineties, at any one time there were approximately two million men and women on active duty in the combined armed forces of the United States (Black, 1993; Gordon, Ungerleider, & Smith, 1991). These military personnel had about 2.8 million spouses and dependents. The National Guard and reserve forces had about 1.6 million men and women who had about 2.2 million dependents. Thus, about 3.5 percent of the U.S. population is either on active duty, in the National Guard or reserves, or is a dependent of someone who is. About three fourths of both active duty families and about three fourths of National Guard and reserve families have children at home (Black, 1993).

People in military families have unique stressors that people in civilian life often do not experience. Life stressors faced by military families include frequent moves, the potential of being deployed into culturally diverse, and sometimes hostile, environments, frequent periods of family separation, geographical isolation from family support systems, low pay, and being young compared to the general civilian population. Military families must also confront the threat that their loved ones may be killed or wounded in combat or in military accidents. If any of these stressors occurred in isolation, the family would likely cope and move on. But these stressors usually exist as an aggregate, making it likely that military families will experience crisis.

Deployment

People associated with the military learn that their lives can be suddenly disrupted as occurred in 1990, during the Persian Gulf War and, more recently, as a result of the deployment of troops to Afghanistan. Children of military personnel know that there is someone more powerful than their own parents, the military. Against the wishes of all family members, the military can deploy a parent for active duty anywhere in the world. Particularly for people in the Navy or Marines, duty assignments can remove a parent for six months or more at a time. Navy submarine duty is a particularly long-term deployment. Under the stress of repeated and extended separations, submarine wives experience headaches, back aches, occasional insomnia, temporary loss of muscle power, periodic depression, short temper, minor weight changes, edginess, and tension (Bey & Lange, 1974; Pearlman, 1970).

When a parent leaves the family through deployment, the family must adapt and that parent's responsibilities must be assumed by other family members. Particularly the spouses of active-duty enlisted personnel are often very young and recently married, compared to spouses of active duty officers and national guard or reservist officers, who are generally over age 30 (Black, 1993).

I used to supervise the premarital counseling of minors and was frequently surprised by the young women who were about to marry a military enlistee. When asked why they were getting married now and so young, they would often respond that they were escaping what they saw as tyrannical parents. What they failed to envision was that they would soon have the most tyrannical parent imaginable, the bureaucracy that would tell this wife and her husband where they would live and where they would work, and that they had no choice but to conform to the wishes of this bureaucracy, whether they liked it or not.

It is most likely the husband who is deployed. His young wife may be faced with having to file income taxes, balance checkbooks, and pay bills, activities in which she often has little or no experience. Common complaints of wives dealing with military separations include loneliness, lack of companionship, and adequate social outlets, problems making decisions alone, disciplining children, and handling finances, and feeling that the military is unconcerned about their well-being (Black, 1993; Garrett, Parker, Day, VanMeter, & Cosby, 1978).

Black (1993) depicts the process of grieving experienced by spouses left at home after deployment, which follows the stages of grieving of loss established by Kubler-Ross (1969). Spouses experience shock and denial about two weeks before the separation. As the departure date nears, many feel anger about being left alone. Some then feel guilty about their feelings of anger; after all, military families are expected to be tough in managing adversity. After the departure, a period of depression and loneliness sets in, resulting in increased tension, crying, irritability, and insomnia. About six weeks after separation, the spouse either accommodates to the separation and revels in the independence, autonomy, and resilience or goes into deep despair and withdrawal (Bermudes, 1977). This latter response results in a diminished capacity to parent, much like a parent left by a spouse in the marital separation preceding divorce.

If there are sons in the family, the sons are often told, "you will be the man of the house now," which propels them from the sibling subsystem into the parental subsystem to function as adults with adult responsibilities. Responsibilities may involve protecting the now-single mother, providing emotional support and companionship for her, escorting the mother to social functions, or doing home repairs or car maintenance when needed. These adolescents generally do whatever they can to replace their father, assuming as many duties as they are capable of assuming that the father performed when he was home (West, Mercer, & Altheimer, 1993). If he sees that the mother is highly stressed or depressed by the temporary loss of her partner, he becomes a parentified child and provides as much emotional support for his mother as he can. He takes on the responsibility of making the mother content and helping her emotionally survive her loss.

Daughters, seeing their mothers stressed and anxious about the deployment, adapt by making special efforts to assist their mothers and reduce the mother's load of household responsibilities. This sometimes involves additional supervision of younger siblings, creating an opportunity to, at least temporarily, become parental children. The daughters also provide emotional support and companionship for their mothers in an attempt to protect and care for her. In this way, they became parentified children caring for their overburdened parent.

Increasingly, military families may be single-parent households rather than intact nuclear family units. When the single parent is deployed, the children may be sent to a grandparent, aunt, or uncle or some other relative. But sometimes there is no kin who can be used as a resource. At times, neighbors care for the children of deployed single parents. If there are no adults available, the children are sometimes left to care for themselves, in which case older children function as parents to their younger siblings. These children often have no idea how long it will be before their parent returns.

The military often create "corporate towns" around major military bases. These towns provide off-base housing for military personnel. The children of military families attend local schools in these towns, and local businesses cater to military consumers for groceries, hardware, auto repair and maintenance, banking, and a host of other goods and services.

In 1990, the United States fought Iraq in the Persian Gulf War. This brief but intense war involved more than 475,000 American troops in the Middle East, their immediate families, extended families, and friends (Miller, Martin, & Jay, 1993). Both active duty and reservists were deployed. This was particularly difficult for the reservists, who saw their military involvement as a second job that would occupy them one weekend per month and a few weeks over a summer. Most did not expect to ever be activated.

The deployment of troops for the Persian Gulf War not only disrupted the families of the troops but also the civilian families living in the towns that serviced military bases. The "corporate towns" that served the military became ghost towns. Schools were emptied as children were sent to distant relatives. Nonmilitary spouses left to live with relatives who could provide support to the family system. Stores closed for lack of business, many going bankrupt. Sometimes these townsfolk were called on to take in the children of deployed single parents until they returned.

When military children of deployed parents are asked to live in a new household, the children tend to band together into a cohesive unit, and the oldest siblings become parental children whose job it is to care for their younger siblings both physically and emotionally. This can be a huge responsibility, because the younger children are often stressed and anxious at the loss of their parent, the major source of security. There is grieving over the loss, sometimes resulting in anger and acting-out behavior with which the older sibling has to contend.

The children starting in a new household want to pose as little intrusion as possible to their new caretakers, and it becomes the responsibility of the older children to keep the younger ones in line, obeying rules and being as self-sufficient as possible. The consequence of creating too great a disturbance is to be sent elsewhere, which causes more anxiety and the prospect of yet another move.

The emotional support of younger children is difficult because all the children are in fear of their parent dying in combat. And their fears were well founded. Death could come from missiles, bullets, poison gas, disease, accidents or friendly fire, or several species of poisonous desert snakes (Galloway, 1990).

Return of the Parent

When the deployed parent returns to the family, the child is expected to relinquish the adult roles and return to being a child. The returning parent expects to resume his or her responsibilities as if he or she had never left. The military family is, thus, called on to continuously adapt and readapt to the individual's exits and returns into the family system and this adjustment is sometimes made with considerable difficulty. With enhanced responsibilities often comes increased power in the family system. When the absent parent returns, he or she resists the enhanced power of the child, power the child wants to maintain, resulting in parent–child conflict.

The spouse, the one who was left behind, is likely to have experienced a new independence that enhanced his or her self-confidence. If a wife, she came to realize that she could do it all and survive, an experience likely to create a new balance in the marital relationship when the spouse returns. If a husband, he might have come to appreciate the efforts of his wife, realizing what it took to balance home and work, as he gained a new appreciation for the stresses and strains, time, and energy it takes to maintain a household and raise and care for children.

For families whose member returned from the Persian Gulf, the adaptation was particularly difficult. Those returning from military service had faced many stressors in the Middle East that scarred them. The ever-present threats of SCUD missile attacks and the potential of horrific death from chemical and biological weapons caused some soldiers to experience prolonged tension and anxiety. Experiencing scenes of death, destruction, torture, and deprivation left vivid images in the minds of soldiers that were not easily erased.

It was distressing to encounter Iraqi soldiers, many of whom were dead, and to observe the miles and miles of Iraqi soldiers, many of whom were wounded and suffering.

Soldiers of ethnic minorities, which represented 40 to 60 percent of our troops in the Persian Gulf (Scurfield & Tice, 1991), reported racial stereotyping, inequitable treatment and discriminatory assignments. Reservists also complained of discriminatory treatment, saying they were treated with disdain, as second-class citizens by regular active-duty personnel, who sometimes left areas of combat earlier than the reservists, who were left to "clean up the mess."

More than 35,000 female soldiers served in the Persian Gulf War, somewhere between 11 and 15 percent of the total number of troops (West, Mercer, & Altheimer, 1993). Eleven women were killed and two were taken prisoner by Iraqi troops. Women soldiers faced special stressors, such as sexual harassment by male officers, having to sleep in quarters and use latrines and showers with men, being discounted by male soldiers as not being "real" soldiers, and experiencing cultural shock, such as not being allowed to drive vehicles or go to some "male only" restaurants, not being allowed to speak to men on the streets, or being required to wear long black dresses in public.

The diverse experiences of these war veterans left many exhibiting the symptoms of post-traumatic stress disorder (PTSD) when they returned home to their families. These veterans had trouble sleeping, often experiencing nightmares or flashbacks. They experienced guilt over a host of actions in which they engaged or did not engage, as well as survivor's guilt because they lived through the war when friends did not. They experienced irritability, moodiness, and depression. Their irritability was sometimes associated with "lashing out" behavior that resulted in domestic violence toward their spouse or children. Some used alcohol or drugs to deaden the pain they felt.

But it was not only the veterans who experienced the symptoms of post-traumatic stress disorder. The spouses who remained at home also experienced symptoms of PTSD either as a function of the stress they endured while parenting alone or as a function of the readaptation stress incurred by the return of their psychologically wounded spouse (Figley, 1993).

When the military spouse returned, there were probably one, and perhaps two, pained and wounded parents, creating an opportunity structure for the development of parental or parentified children. If it was only the returning veteran who exhibited symptoms of stress, then the situation was much the same as a chronically physically or mental ill parent. The nonmilitary spouses may well have turned their attention to caring for their partner, creating a parenting gap filled by an elder child. This parental child freed a parent from parenting responsibilities enabling him or her to nurture the military partner. Children may also assist a parent in caring for the military spouse, which creates a parentified child, both as caretaker of the military spouse and as nurturer and supporter of the supportive caretaker spouse.

If both parents are stressed and partially paralyzed in their parenting, children may fill the parenting vacuum by being both parental and parentified. The literature on military families is devoid of research on the role of children in enabling families to survive separation either from deployment or moving. This is an area of research that is much needed because children are critical in helping their families adapt, enabling both parents to cope with enormous stress and anxiety. Much of the literature on military family adaptation to stress is written by social workers, who emphasize the importance of external support groups for parents. Such groups were of great value to the families of military service personnel who fought in the Persian Gulf War, but these authors tend to ignore the internal family support network of children. There are only vague allusions to children as instruments of support to their parents.

Watanabe (1985) found that adolescents in military families had higher self-images than their nonmilitary counterparts, despite the frequent moves and adaptations they experienced. He further found that military adolescents had greater impulse control than did their nonmilitary counterparts, which he attributed to the military's attitude toward discipline. He found military adolescents having higher vocational and educational goals than nonmilitary adolescents, which he attributed to the fact that, in the military, career advancement is largely based upon education and training.

Higher self-esteem among military adolescents might be enhanced by their successfully assuming adult roles in their families as a function of deployment and frequent moves. These children have successfully aided their parents in surviving the rigors of military life by, at times, playing parental and parentified roles. When they are successful at performing these roles, they acquire skills that lead to self-sufficiency and autonomy. They have experienced their competence as the caretakers of siblings and parents, which gives them a sense of fulfillment, pride in their accomplishment, and a sense of belonging to a family in which everyone's contributions are critical to survival. Successful performance of parental and parentified roles contributes to high self-esteem.

Moving

On average, a military family moves once every three years. About one third of both active-duty and enlisted officer families have been at their current location less than one year. More than 60 percent of all active-duty families have spent less than two years at their current location (Black, 1993). This illustrates the lack of power that families have in the military; they move whether they want to or not. Although the child in a military family has parents who have power over them, parental power is negligible compared to the power the military has over its personnel and their families.

The frequency of moves for families in the military means that most families are torn away from relatives, which means that these families lack an important external support network, and places great pressure on parents with children because they have less support. The frequent moves do not allow them sufficient time to develop peer support network among friends. The military family is apt to experience social isolation because of its mobility. They may be surrounded by people, but they are not people they know very well.

Moving is probably most difficult for adolescents. At a time when peer relationships are more important to them than family relationships, moves mean being torn away from peers at school. At a time when adolescents are distancing themselves from parents, moves sometimes bond them to parents, particularly before the adolescent can generate a peer support network at a new school. Often placed in an environment that is neither familiar nor comfortable, the adolescent must rely on parents as a source of stability and comfort at a time of acute stress and anxiety.

If both parents work and cannot be home much, or if a single parent's military obligations remove the parent from the home, then the younger siblings will rely on an older sibling for that stability and emotional support. This creates an opportunity structure for the development of a parental child.

Sometimes adolescents who are juniors or seniors in high school are so resistant to being moved in these two years that they convince a parent to pass up a voluntary assignment that requires a family move. If a military officer has no choice but to move the family, another option that is sometimes chosen is to move the family except for the rebellious adolescent, who will live with the family of a friend so that he or she can stay in the same school and graduate with his or her classmates. This separates the adolescent from the family and prevents this adolescent from becoming a parental or parentified child in his or her family of origin.

Because of frequent moves, parents are torn away from other sources of support, their peers. Moves uproot adults from friends, neighbors, clergy, congregants, and co-workers who constitute the adult's emotional support network. The move necessitates establishing a new network from strangers, which may not be accomplished speedily or easily. In such situations, it is tempting to use adolescent children as confidantes, friends, and therapists because they know the parent better than anyone else; the children represent stability in the parent's life, transcending the transitory nature of geographical location. Feelings of loneliness and social isolation engendered by frequent moves create a scenario in the family system that facilitates the creation of parentified children, who become the caretakers of their parents.

These parents are socialized to put on a "can do" demeanor to the outside world, This is a theatrical performance. While playing out this performance, inside they feel vulnerable because they have no power over where they will live and they have no idea when the next move will come. They are vulnerable because each move reduces their support network, at least temporarily. Who is readily available as a source of support and encouragement? One's children are, and these parents sometimes turn to their children for comfort from feelings of powerlessness, anxiety, depression, sadness over the losses incurred by the move.

There are many sources for anxiety among these parents. Often the military does not fully compensate a military family for the expenses incurred in moving, so moves can financially distress a family. If one parent is in the military but the other is not, the non-military spouse has to find a new job if the family is to maintain a stable standard of living. New child-care arrangements may have to be made, new friends, congregations, groups and activities have to be found, and a long process of adaptation to one's new environment has to be navigated.

Children also face the anxieties of enrolling in new schools, finding new friends, and accommodating to a new environment. For some children, these challenges may seem overwhelming and they may internalize their feelings by exhibiting behavior that is withdrawn, lethargic, and regressed, or they can externalize their feelings by becoming aggressive, defiant, resistive, or destructive. These behaviors in younger siblings may mobilize older siblings to become caretakers of these distressed brothers or sisters, trying to protect them, comfort them, be with them, talk with them, parent them. They do this because the parent has lost control of the stressed child, has become ineffectual in dealing with this child, and the adolescent sees that the parents (and the child) need help.

There is also an element in the military that judges the competence of the military serviceperson on the basis of how his or her spouse and children behave. If the person does not have the competence to control members of the family and produce people who are a credit to the military, this can impact promotions or quality assignments. As a result, all family members feel an obligation to pitch in and do what they can to make the serviceperson look competent. The serviceperson's status in the military affects all family members, so all family members are invested in promoting the serviceperson's career to the best of their ability. It is in the whole family's interest to have children who are model citizens, who handle adversity and change with dignity and grace. If parents need help getting this accomplished, then adolescent children help their parents out by joining the parental system in controlling the other children.

Friendships for military children are hard enough to maintain as a result of frequent moves, but parental and parentified children have additional barriers to maintaining friendships when younger siblings and household responsibilities dominate their after-school time. This is reflected in the account of the following respondent, who writes about one of her friends who lived on a military base:

> It wasn't uncommon for Mike to miss out on a group outing with friends. Many times his excuse was 'my mom needs me to help out with house chores' or 'I'm going to the store with my mom for groceries.' For the most part, it seemed as though he had a good relationship with his mom, but still some of the things he said he had to do pointed directly to him being a parentified child. It was as if Mike was now the man of the house in the absence of his father. As far as Mike was concerned, I know firsthand some of his friendships ended solely because there was hardly any interaction. He was always rushing home to do something for his mom.

This respondent describes another friend who seemed to have a childhood similar to Mike's.

> Ken was always on his way somewhere other than with his friends after class was over. Ken had two younger sisters both in elementary school. From what I remember, Ken was not only responsible for picking them up from school, but he walked them to school everyday until he was able to drive. Even after he was able to drive, though, he continued to pick them up and take them to school. Ken was very responsible. Both of his parents were in the military. On occasion, Ken would invite a few of his friends over including myself to his house after school for homework. Not only did he complete his homework, but he also helped his two sisters out as well. He would also find time to clean out their backpacks and lunch boxes, fix dinner, and give them baths before putting them to bed. From the outside it appeared he had a normal life, but Ken was taking care of his two siblings as if they were his own children while maintaining his own personal life. Ken was the man of the house. Yes, his father was present in the household, but it was Ken who saw to it that his little sisters did well with their schoolwork, had a decent lunch in their backpacks each day, and a warm cooked meal each night. It was Ken who also on occasion when his mother was unable to on the weekends, would complete the grocery shopping and other odds and ends

that were not completed by his parents. The relationship he had with his parents was neither strained nor the best. In fact, Ken hardly spoke of them. I don't believe he was bitter towards them, instead, he just saw the relationship and duties he followed through on as an everyday part of his life. Most likely, Ken knew nothing else and had grown used to his role.

In part because of their social isolation, these parental children have limited opportunity to compare their lives in their families with the lives of other children. They have difficulty understanding what a "nonparental" childhood is like or how many of their peers live such a life.

Overlapping Issues

Many contexts that we have previously discussed pertain to military families. There is a high incidence of alcohol abuse in military families, sometimes by a serviceperson, sometimes by the spouse of a serviceperson. When there is alcoholism in a military family, it creates a context for the development of parental and parentified children, as was discussed in Chapter 3.

Although most servicepeople in today's military are technicians and bureaucrats, in basic training they are initially trained to be killing machines. This training for aggressive behavior is conducive to domestic violence in families. Nobody knows for sure how much domestic violence there actually is because it is likely that family members will be secretive about violent behavior, inasmuch as it can adversely affect the career of the serviceperson, which, in turn, will adversely affect the quality of life for all members of the family. I have previously pointed out that, when domestic violence occurs in families, children take on the role of parentified child when they attempt to protect the victim parent from the abusive parent. They do this through distracting behavior, or by overtly attempting to stop the violence.

Domestic violence often occurs in the presence of children. Whether this is because the abusive parent needs an audience or whether it is because the presence of the children serves to moderate the violence so that nobody gets killed is not completely understood by social scientists. The presence of the children often serves as a controlling mechanism as the children yell, cajole, or plead for the violence to stop.

When older children protect younger siblings from witnessing the violence or when they take children away so the children will not be hurt themselves, they are functioning as parental children. In the role of parental child, they are protecting their siblings as parents protect children from harm, whether that harm is physical or psychological.

Increasingly, military personnel are single parents. When they are at work, an older child is frequently functioning as a parental figure to younger siblings in the absence of the parent. Because pay in the military is low, there are usually insufficient financial resources to provide paid child care for children. This means that they must often provide their own child care. Children also serve as companions, confidantes, and support for the single parent, who attempts to provide for both the physical and emotional needs of family members alone. These children support their parent by cleaning the house, cooking meals, doing laundry, and "being good" so as to avoid adding to the burden the single parent already shoulders.

When there is an intact nuclear family system, it is likely that both parents will be gainfully employed, in an attempt to supplement the meager military salary. With both parents working, there will likely be a parenting gap at home, which often comes to be filled by children.

Should a parent die, the military family will experience a huge loss and children often attempt to make up for that loss by performing tasks formerly performed by the deceased adult. Because training in the military is physically strenuous, training may result in physical injury of a serviceperson, such that he or she may be incapable of performing normal household tasks. Children often compensate for this loss by taking over the jobs that the parent temporarily cannot execute.

In the next section of this chapter, I will discuss another context in which families experience the loss of a parent, when a parent is incarcerated by the criminal justice system. In this context, we will again find many overlapping issues that have already been discussed.

The family may be a single-parent household with an overburdened parent who becomes partially paralyzed by the responsibilities. Children might help through gainful employment or by illegal activities to supplement the family income. These families are often poor and cannot afford paid child care, so child care is provided by the children themselves. The family could also have one or both parents who are chemically dependent or one or both parents who are chronically physically or mentally ill. Incarceration is then an additional situation to which the children must adapt.

Incarceration of a Parent

In the United States, the number of children with at least one parent in a state or federal prison rose by more than 500,000 between 1991 and 2001, with the current figure being 1,498,800 (Temin, 2001). While many of these children live with their mother while their fathers are serving time, increasingly it is the mother who is incarcerated. In 1998, there were 80,000 women in state and federal prisons and, of these, 80 percent were mothers, with the average mother having two or three children under the age of eighteen (U.S. Department of Justice, 1998).

When a mother is imprisoned, the effect for children is usually that their primary caregiver disappears from their daily lives. When mothers are incarcerated, children often grieve as if the mother had died. These children experience fear, anxiety, sadness, and grief, and they sometimes display verbal and physical aggression, social isolation, withdrawal, hypervigilance, regressed behavior, or sexualized behavior (Bush-Baskette, 2000). A child whose mother is incarcerated has a greater chance of being involved in the juvenile justice system, becoming a substance abuser, or joining a gang. Children who have had either parent incarcerated are five times more likely to be sentenced to prison as adults than are children who have not had a parent who served time in prison (Bush-Baskette, 2000).

According to Young and Smith (2000), 71.7 percent of children with mothers in prison lived with their mother before she went to prison while only 52.9 percent of children lived with their father before he was incarcerated. It is much more likely that children whose father is incarcerated will live with their mother than it is that children whose mother is incarcerated will live with their father. During the incarceration of a father, 89 percent of the children will live with their mothers. During the incarceration of a mother, 25.4 percent of children will live with their father; 50.6 percent will live with their grandparents, 20.3 percent live with other relatives, 8.6 percent live in foster homes, 4.1 percent live with friends, 2.1 percent live in an agency or institution, and 2 percent live alone (Young & Smith, 2000).

It is difficult for children to maintain a relationship with an incarcerated parent. There are more prisons for men than for women, which means that prisons for women are geographically dispersed, making visiting a mother involve lengthy travel and, perhaps, the expense of overnight accommodations. There are more parent–child visitation programs, overnight and telecommunication programs for mothers and children facilitated by women's prisons than there are for fathers in men's prisons (Bartlett, 2000; Kauffman, 2001). It is likely that, when a father is incarcerated, his ties with his children will be severed.

When one looks at the development of parental and parentified children as a function of the incarceration of a parent, one has to consider the situation of the family prior to incarceration, as these roles often existed within the family well before the parental incarceration. The likelihood of incarceration is inversely related to social class. The poor constitute the primary "clients" of the criminal justice system.

Many poor families are not intact nuclear family units but, rather, are single-parent households, either as a function of a nonmarital birth, as a function of divorce, or as a function of desertion of a father from the family. The desertion of a father may not just be a function of irresponsibility. Some fathers leave because it is painful for them to observe the pain and suffering endured by family members because the father's perceived failure to financially support the family. Fathers tend to see their role as to provide for the physical needs of family members, providing food, clothing, and shelter. If they are not able to do this, they often feel guilty. They realize that it may be easier for the family to receive welfare assistance if there is no able-bodied male living in the household, so they leave to enable family members to qualify for welfare assistance. As the research of Liebow finds, these males may come in and out of the family, depending on their ability to financially provide for family members. As Bill Clinton once asserted, "It's jobs, stupid," implying that adult male involvement in family structures is a function of their ability to find and maintain gainful employment.

In the absence of an adult male, the single female head of household attempts to perform the instrumental function in the family through her work, often at multiple low-paying jobs. This leaves a parenting gap in the home, which is frequently filled by an adolescent girl who supervises younger siblings and whose job it is to protect the health, safety, and welfare of her brothers and sisters, creating a parental child. Because the family has such limited finances, professional child care is not a realistic option, so their own children or extended kin must be used as child-care providers, using available, free resources from within the family rather than going outside the family.

If the family was an intact nuclear family prior to the incarceration of the father, the mother is left to fulfill all the responsibilities that were assumed by her husband. She will likely work full-time in at least one job, taking her out of the household for long periods of time. She will be in charge of maintaining the home and meeting the emotional needs of her children (Coulturier, 1995). She will need help from her children to survive, and this creates an opportunity structure for the development of parental and/or parentified children. In the following account, a fifteen-year-old boy assumes parental and parentified roles because his father is in jail and his mother has to work full-time to support the family. This boy cares for his younger brothers and gives emotional support to his stressed and exhausted mother.

> Because their father was imprisoned for attempting to murder his family, the eldest son, who is now 15 years old has taken the role of parental and parentified child. The reason that the eldest child has taken both roles is that his mother is serving the instrumental function in the family. She works nights as a registered nurse and often works extra hours when needed. Since the mother is rarely home, the eldest son does most of the cooking for his younger brothers. He provides his mother the emotional support she needs because she feels fatigued from being the only one managing the household. Because she is so fatigued, the mother has found no time to search for a new mate.

In part because poverty creates great stress, pain, and suffering for family members, and in part because illegal drugs are readily available in poor neighborhoods (in the absence of legitimate avenues for obtaining money, an available avenue is the "business" of illegal drug sales), it is tempting to use drugs as a form of medication to relieve the pain and stress. The possession, use, or sale of illegal drugs is linked to many parental incarcerations among the poor. Most female inmates are arrested for nonviolent crimes (Henriques, 1982) and 70 to 80 percent of these inmates have a history of drug abuse (Swann, 1992).

If a single head of household was using alcohol or drugs prior to the arrest, it is likely that this usage led to impaired parenting, resulting in an adolescent filling the parenting vacuum by caring for younger siblings as well as caring for the parent who was incapacitated, fragile, vulnerable, and in need of special care. A child was present and came at no cost and so that child assumed the role of parental and parentified child.

In the following account, one of my respondents interviewed a male prisoner who was a facing his "third strike" in California. His third strike consisted of failing to notify a parole officer of a change of address, for which he faced five to ten years of prison time, which would have separated him from his three children for a significant portion of their childhood. Regarding the children,

> they all experienced some kind of anger when they found out their father had been sent to jail. The way they expressed it was very different; two held it in and one lashed out right away as a result of their frustration. 'My children have a hard time dealing with it. It is hard because their mother is a crazy [drug] addict, and their father is in prison. My daughter seems to think that she needs to be the mother to the other two, since their mother has always been using drugs and has never really expressed any care or concern for their welfare. She never had a mother around to nurture her, so as the oldest child, she felt it was her

responsibility to take care of the two younger children and become their mother so they do not grow up without a mother too. I have tried to be a good father and make sure that they are safe, but I know my daughter is angry with me because deep down she doesn't think anyone cares about her or her well-being. The aunt [my sister] is very understanding about the whole thing, and I am lucky she is willing to look after my children.'

Children of incarcerated parents often wind up living with a relative if one is available (Hungerford, 1996). These relatives sometimes are burdened with keeping a secret as to why the children are living with them because the incarcerated parent does not want the children to know that he or she has been incarcerated and asks the relative to make up a fictitious tale as to why the parent is absent. Sometimes the tale is that the parent has fallen ill and is in the hospital, which only worries the children that their parent might die. Sometimes one or more older children are told the truth but are told to fabricate a story to their younger siblings as to why the parent has disappeared. This burdens the older child to maintain a secret. This is parentification of the older child, who is called on to protect the parent from embarrassment or to protect the image of the incarcerated parent in the eyes of the younger children.

Lies and fictional tales are often a part of the incarceration process. When asked if they have children, the incarcerated parent often tells authorities that they do not have children, for fear that their children will be taken away from them. Seventy-five to eighty percent of incarcerated women in U.S. prisons have children that they are leaving behind (Shaw, 1998). If undiscovered, the children are left to fend for themselves. If the children are discovered by child protective service authorities, they will be taken to a shelter and may eventually be put in foster care, but, as the following account illustrates, the children may be divided into different foster care families so that they cannot maintain their protective and supportive sibling network.

This account comes from a respondent who worked in a residential care facility for at-risk children (a group home). She describes one of the young women who lived in that home.

Her father was in and out of her life; he was often incarcerated. She was always in charge of taking care of her brother and sister when her mother was at work; she was in charge of making the nightly meals for the family, and the grocery shopping for the household. Although her mother had a job, she was heavily into drugs and left her children alone most of the time. The young girl told me stories of taking her siblings shopping for school clothes, and walking with them to church on Sunday morning to make sure they made it to Sunday school safely. She had become their primary caregiver despite the fact that she was only a child herself. Then at the age of 15, this young lady lost her mother to the criminal justice system as well; her mother was convicted of drug possession. She and her siblings were taken to live with a relative. The relative was less than thrilled to have the children in her care. This young lady tried to take care of her brother and sister in order to keep her family together. She got a job baby-sitting so that she could bring in money to help pay for her siblings' care. Nonetheless, her efforts were in vain as the relative realized that it was no longer feasible to shoulder the responsibility of raising three young children. The young lady's family was quickly split up and shipped off to Social Services.

Now, almost 18, she is working and saving money to take care of her brother and sister. Although the siblings were separated for some time, the young lady still exemplifies the signs of a child that was parental for some time. Her mother was released from prison, but has only visitation rights with her children, who are still all separately in residential care facilities. The young lady told me something that has stuck with me and continuously enters my thoughts: 'I did not choose to have the life that I had. It was a result of my parents' actions. However, I have to do what I have to do to preserve my family and take care of my siblings. I do not wish for history to repeat itself in my family. I have to be a parent to my siblings so that they know that someone loves them.'

A theme in the two former accounts is that a child becomes parental to siblings to provide siblings with things they themselves never got from parents—care, attention, affection, time, energy, nurturance, or love. These children want to break the family cycle of parental neglect and impairment and the only way to do that is to become a parental figure themselves to provide to their siblings what they know they needed in their lives but never got.

When Wallerstein (2000) studied children of divorce, she found that most of these children had no warning of or preparation for a marital separation. They woke up one morning to discover that one parent, while they were asleep, had left the household. Children who have a parent incarcerated often have a similar experience inasmuch as the parent is arrested suddenly; the children have no warning of or preparation for the loss of that parent (Gabel & Johnston, 1995). The arrest of the parent is often frightening for the child as the child is likely to be present at the time of the arrest. They often have to watch their parent being taken away. They sometimes have to accompany the parent when he or she is booked, and some are even locked in a holding cell with the parent until someone can be found to care for them.

During the period of parental incarceration, older children sometimes get jobs to enable all the children to survive. The children assume the household responsibilities that were performed by the parent before incarceration. These children have to grow up fast. They assume adult responsibilities and have little opportunity to experience a carefree, play-filled childhood.

Over time, as adults, these children will feel overly responsible for others. They will have a hard time saying "no" to others and setting limits where they cannot be called on for help by others. They will fear dependence on others. They will have difficulty with intimate relationships because they will not be able to relate to others as equals, as peers, but will seek to enter into relationships in which they are the caretakers of others. They create skewed relationships in which they are one-up caretakers partnering with one-down people who are dependent on them. They are so busy caretaking others that they have difficulty getting their own needs met, and may even have difficulty recognizing what their own needs are. They are focused on others outside themselves and so have difficulty with introspection or focusing on themselves (Swann, 1992). Schneller (1976), a criminologist, wrote:

> It seems strange that society fails to give any thought whatsoever to the prisoner's family when he (she) is summarily locked up. His (her) dependents are the real sufferers. It is likewise strange that so little research has been done concerning this group and their status.

Those words are equally applicable today. There has been relatively little research, particularly longitudinal research, done on the children of incarcerated parents.

Measures to maintain the incarcerated parent's role in the family system, which might reduce the destructive parentification of children in these families, might include frequent family visits, either allowing the children to come to the parent or allowing the parent to have home leaves periodically (remember, most of these parents are nonviolent offenders).

Summary

In this chapter we have explored three contexts in which children lose a parent, either permanently as in the case of death, or temporarily, as in military families. The absence of a parent leaves a parenting gap that is often filled by a child, who assumes the adult responsibilities formerly assumed by the parent. When children care for younger siblings as a parent, they take the role of parental children. When they are caretakers of the remaining parent, who is functioning as a single parent, they function as parentified children.

In the case of military and incarcerated parents, the return of the parent to the family forces an adaptation of the family that sometimes creates conflict. The children are often asked to return to their role as children, requiring them to relinquish the considerable power they gained to offset their increased responsibilities. They may not be so willing to relinquish that power, exacerbating parent–child conflict.

With frequent deployments or incarcerations, the family is called on to continuously adapt and readapt to a parent's leaving and reentering the family system. This adaptation requires family members to take on the responsibilities of the departed parent and then give those responsibilities back to the parent when he or she returns. The child is treated like a yo-yo, sometimes performing up as an adult in the family, and sometimes performing down as a child.

Part III

Consequences for Parental and Parentified Children

Having reviewed the diverse contexts in which one is apt to find the development of parental and parentified children, it is appropriate to analyze the consequences of playing these roles in the adult lives of these children. What legacies do parental and parentified children carry and how do these legacies affect their ability to develop intimate relationships as adults? How does being a parental or parentified child affect the kinds of people to whom they are attracted as adults? How does being a parental or parentified child affect the kinds of professions to which they are attracted, for which they train, and into which they enter? How does being a caregiver child establish a life script for caretaking in one's adult life?

Part III analyzes how respondents defined and interpreted their childhood. Most respondents seem to identify the roles they assumed in their families as what Jurkovic would label "adaptive parentification." Respondents often defined themselves as survivors, not victims, of their caretaking experiences. They defined their experiences as having strengthened them and matured them, making them more independent, autonomous, competent, and empathic adults. These respondents demonstrated resilience in overcoming the adversities of their childhoods.

The book closes with a look at how politicians are likely to view the pervasive position of children as parental and parentified children. Politics affects social policy and the role of government in effecting changes in family life. The book ends with a modest, cost-free proposal that parents can use to reduce the negative impact of children being caregivers in their families.

7

Conclusions

A popular, "common sense" way of conceptualizing caregiving in families is that parents are the caregivers to children; parents nurture, support, and protect children. One conclusion of this book is that caregiving in families is not unidirectional, not just given by those of an older generation to members of a younger generation, but, rather, caregiving is reciprocal and interactive in families. Children are often caregivers to their parents as well as their brothers and sisters, nurturing, supporting and protecting them. Children are not helpless but make constructive, sometimes critical contributions that enable family members to survive.

In Chapters 3, 4, 5, and 6, I explored the many contexts that create an "opportunity structure" for the development of parental or parentified children. An opportunity structure for the creation of these roles features situations in which there is a parenting gap or vacuum created by parents who are overwhelmed by their financial and/or caretaking responsibilities. A parenting vacuum can be created by physical or mental illness, by substance abuse, by poverty or large families with many children, by a single parent being overwhelmed by having to be gainfully employed full-time and also being the exclusive or primary caretaker of children and maintainer of a household. A parenting vacuum can also exist in intact nuclear family units, if both parents are so exhausted by full-time employment that they have little energy left for the children when they get home.

Another kind of opportunity structure for the creation of parental and parentified children features the loss of a parent, such as exists when a parent dies, is incarcerated, or is deployed by the military. This creates a void in the parental subsystem, a vacuum that gets filled by a child in an adaptive process whereby the child assumes the tasks that used to be performed by the departed adult. In doing this, the child acts less and less like a carefree, playful child and more and more like a responsible, working adult.

Just because a family has a parenting vacuum is no guarantee that the vacuum will be filled by a child. The structure only creates an opportunity for the child to fill the void. The void could be filled by relatives or by neighbors and friends. The void could be filled by adults such as coaches, day-care workers, nannies, baby-sitters, music and dance teachers, or community recreation directors, many of whom become surrogate relatives for the

family, serving a role that used to be served by aunts and uncles, in supervising, protecting, teaching, and emotionally supporting the children. As a society, we are socially constructing "extended kin" beyond people who are related to the child through blood or
marriage. Middle-class families, in particular, are outsourcing labor to support households
through the hiring of gardeners, housecleaners, launderers, caterers, and dog-walkers.
They are also extending out into the community for adults who perform the same functions that are performed by relatives and parents; families are using these resources as if
they were extended kin.

However, children often do fill the parenting vacuum created by adults who are either away from the home working or at home but not fully functioning as competent parents for one reason or another. There are different ways children are parentified. In poor
families, some children may caretake their parents by becoming gainfully employed as
adolescents, as stock boys, janitorial or landscaping assistants, distributing newspapers or
getting baby- or pet-sitting jobs to help their parents financially and ease their parents'
worries over money. While some may work, others may supervise and care for younger
siblings at home while their parents work.

Middle-class children may be parentified through extracurricular activities such as
sports activities, music or dance lessons, religious instruction, or lessons on language or
culture, and their performances provide the parents with recreation and entertainment and
an arena for socially interacting with other parents who have children in these activities.
These children provide the parents with a sense of pride and a, sometimes, delusional idea
that they are great parents. After all, how can anything but a great parent produce such a
competent, wonderful child?

Given all the contexts in which parental and parentified children exist, it is this
author's contention that these roles are not statistically pathological, not statistically on the
fringes of a bell curve, but are, rather, *normative roles in the lives of children living in a
postindustrial society.* I believe that the majority of children in a postindustrial world experience playing the role of either a parental or parentified child before they reach adulthood. This may be short-term, as when a parent undergoes surgery and a child takes over
some of the parent's responsibilities during the parent's recuperation period. For some
children it is long-term caretaking of others. Generally, the longer children play these
roles, the more likely the roles will leave adverse legacies for them in adulthood.

Children are caregivers in families as part of a process of role succession, whereby
children have partially replaced women as caretakers of children and households. As part
of the post-World War II experience, when postindustrial societies began to exist, women
who were mothers of children became gainfully employed, entering the job market in
great numbers. When women were homemakers, they were flooding into therapists' offices because they found their considerable work to be unappreciated and unrecognized by
other family members. Children, as inheritors of a domestic caregiver role, often experience the reality that their considerable efforts are unrecognized or appreciated by other
family members, which is apt to increase the negative effects of performing these roles.
The fact that they are taken for granted in their families undermines their self-esteem and
diminishes their sense of self-worth when their labor is not valued by others. Some will
spend a lifetime working and caretaking others in the hope that somebody will see that
they are worthy of praise and being appreciated or loved.

In the United States, young adults are marrying at later ages than they have married in the past. The median age of first marriage now nears twenty-seven for men and twenty-five for women. Some scholars have largely attributed this delayed age at first marriage to economics. Young couples cannot afford to marry until they can accumulate wealth to build a nest for themselves, to purchase a house or make the first month's rent and security deposit on an apartment.

Other scholars have attributed delayed age at first marriage to young peoples' skepticism about marriage. They are skeptical about the advantages of marriage over singlehood. They are skeptical about marriages lasting very long amidst the frenzy, fatigue, and distractions of a postindustrial world. Divorce rates soared in the United States during the decades of the 1960s and 1970s. Many young adults who are now of marrying age experienced the divorce of their own parents. That experience has them scared to death of marriage. They do not want to experience what they saw their parents experiencing. They do not want to put children through what they went through themselves.

What one does not find in the literature on delayed marriage is that some measure of delayed marriage is a function of the parentification of children in families of origin. When young adults leave their family of origin, they may have spent a considerable number of years caretaking siblings and parents and they are tired of caretaking others. They want time out from caretaking. They want time for themselves, time to play and experience an absence of caretaking responsibilities that they have shouldered for so long.

Some young adults see marriage as the renewed assumption of caretaking responsibilities. Marriage involves meeting the needs of spouses and, eventually, children. Many children who have been parental or parentified children want to delay returning to these caretaking roles, hence their motivation to delay getting married. They want time to play and only be responsible for taking care of themselves, of meeting their own needs rather than having to meet the needs of another.

Personality

The discipline of sociology has a long and distinguished literature relating roles people play in the social structure of a system to the development of personality characteristics for the people who play those roles. An example of this relationship between social structure and personality is the effect bureaucratic social structures have on the development of personality in adults who work in those bureaucracies.

Max Weber, the German sociologist, writing at the turn of the twentieth century, saw bureaucracies as hierarchically structured organizations that coordinate a specialized division of labor in which each person performs a specialized function in the social structure. People are governed by norms that mandate conformity and stifle creativity. People who work in bureaucracies come to need order and structure and have difficulty making decisions on their own. People who work in bureaucracies have trouble being masterful and taking control in unstructured situations. There develops what Thorsten Veblen (1928) called a "trained incapacity" to be flexible and accommodate to unstructured situations.

The roles people play in bureaucracies lead to the development of passive personalities for people who work in those bureaucracies eight hours a day, five days a week for fifty weeks a year. These employees tend to become conformists who have difficulty establishing their identities outside of the groups in which they are integrated. Weber wrote:

> Imagine the consequences of that comprehensive bureaucratization and rationalization which already today we see approaching. Already now, throughout private enterprise in wholesale manufacture, as well as in all other economic enterprises run on modern lines, Rechenhaftigkeit, rational calculation, is manifest at every stage. By it, the performance of each individual worker is mathematically measured, each man becomes a little cog in the machine and, aware of this, his one preoccupation is whether he can become a bigger cog. . . . This passion for bureaucracy, as we have heard it expressed here, is enough to drive one to despair. It is as if in politics the spectre of timidity . . . were to stand alone at the helm; as if we were deliberately to become men who need "order" and nothing but order, who become nervous and cowardly if for one moment this order wavers, and helpless if they are torn away from their total incorporation in it. That we should know no men but these: it is in such an evolution that we are already caught up, and the great question is therefore not how we can promote and hasten it, but what can we oppose to this machinery in order to keep a portion of mankind free from this parceling-out of the soul, from this supreme mastery of the bureaucratic way of life (Weber, 1956, pp. 126–127).

Merton (1957) echoed Weber's concern. He saw the effects of working full-time in a bureaucratic social structure as wearing on the ability of people to script their own lives, to be their own playwrights in the drama of life. Bureaucracies diminish a person's ability to think for themselves and to be creative or innovative or to have any sense of personal efficacy. Bureaucrats came to be very good at executing orders given by others, and very inept at creating structure themselves. The theme of people overly conforming to the norms of a social structure and losing their individuality in the process became a repetitive theme in the writings of sociologists in the 1950s and early 1960s in books such as *A Nation of Sheep* (Lederer, 1961) and *The Oversocialized Man* (Wrong, 1961).

The literature that exists on parental and parentified children indicates that playing these roles can affect the development of personality characteristics for these children. Playing these roles over extended periods of time affects the ways in which these children act as adults. Jones and Wells (1996) identify three different personality characteristics that can be linked with the parentification of children: masochistic or self-defeating behavior, overt narcissisitic behavior, and compulsive behavior. Masochistic behavior is induced when children are expected to care for parents' physical and emotional needs, such as by being a good listener or friend, suppressing autonomous strivings by being "mother's little helper" or the "little man of the family." These are children who link their sense of self to meeting parental needs. The narcissisistic personality is created when the success of children as musicians, athletes, or students serves parental needs. Compulsive features arise from shame over past experiences when they were not able to exercise any control over a parent's drinking or unpredictable behavior, such as anger or violence. Compulsive features include the desire to be perfect and, as a result of basic insecurity, to be able to control one's external environment and the people in that environment. One mechanism by which people achieve control over others is by caretaking them.

In general, adults who were parental or parentified children tend to be very serious, responsible, dependable, competent adults. They are often compulsive perfectionists, who are very embarrassed by making mistakes and are very critical of themselves whenever they feel they have not done something perfectly. This need to be perfect coexists with a basic insecurity that they are never doing well enough, resulting in a ritualized striving for control through "compulsive caretaking" (West & Keller, 1991).

The Need for Control

Teyber (2001) claims that problems that arise from excessive caregiving in childhood usually become manifest during late adolescence and early adulthood. As a consequence of not having their emotional needs met, children grow to resent their parents for depriving them of a normal childhood. According to Teyber, these children tend to feel exceedingly responsible for other people. They have difficulty setting limits, establishing boundaries, and saying "no." They often feel guilty over meeting their own needs. They are apprehensive about asking for help from others or being dependent on others because they interpret this as giving up control over their own lives, and they do not want to relinquish that control.

There are many contexts in which children grow up feeling an absence of control. Children who grow up in families where there is parental substance abuse experience unpredictability in their lives. They never know when a parent is going to arrive home inebriated. They never know whether inebriation will result in an abusive episode, and they cannot predict what chaos or destruction or injury such an episode will produce. They never know when a parent who is attempting rehabilitation will relapse.

In a family where there is chronic physical or mental illness, there is unpredictability for the child. Will the family member have a good or a bad day? What new crisis lies around the corner? In a military family, there is unpredictability regarding when a parent is going to be deployed, and, if deployed, for how long? When will the next move come and to where?

Parental children often feel an absence of control when younger siblings refuse to comply with the parental child's wishes or directives. Sibling conflict is common when there are parental children in a family because the child fails to recognize the authority of the parental child, after all, the parental child is not a parent. According to Haley (1976) parental children are often given responsibilities by a parent without being given the authority by the parent to successfully execute those responsibilities. To protect the health, safety, and welfare of their siblings, the parental child must have parental support such that the parents tell the younger children that the parental child is in charge and they are to do what their older sister tells them to do. Parental children need parental reinforcement, which they often do not get. As Haley writes:

> The position of this parental child is often quite difficult because he has the responsibility for the younger children but not the power. Therefore, he is caught in the middle between misbehaving children and a mother who does not delegate full power to him. What typically happens is that the mother sides with the children against the parental child when there is trouble. She insists that parental child be in charge while not giving sufficient autonomy to deal with the situation (p. 113).

In the absence of authority, in the absence of legitimized power or power with the consent of the governed, parental children sometimes feel they have to resort to coercion to get younger siblings to do what they want them to do. This attempt to exercise control can result in extreme measures, such as is cited by Wholey (1988) who quotes a respondent who reported, "My brother and I were extremely aggressive toward each other. He'd hit me over the head with a hammer, and I'd knock him off of his bicycle and break his arm" (p. 50). Swan and Houston (1985) quote a respondent who told them, "When they won't listen, I get my father's gun out, that really scares them" (p. 129).

One of my respondents reports of having difficulty controlling younger siblings until her mother verbally supported her, enhancing her authority in the household.

> I made sure my sister did her homework, and, when it was late, I made sure she came in from playing before it got dark. I even made her breakfast sometimes. It wasn't long before my sister began to resent the power I was establishing within the household. She soon became defiant and uncooperative. My mother explained to her that she needed my help in keeping things around the house going well and even though my sister didn't like it, she became slightly easier to handle.

The level of control parental children have over younger siblings is sometimes fragile and precarious. To lose control is to risk angering and disappointing the parents, to risk being a failure at executing the responsibilities that they have been assigned. Failing to control the behavior of others further risks endangering the well-being of those others.

Children who experience consistent chaos and unpredictability as children seek control as adults whereby they can create some sense of order and structure and predictability in their lives. One way of creating this order and structure is to engage in the caretaking of others. This has been called the "caretaking syndrome" (Peek & Trezona, 1984; Valleau, Bergner, & Horton, 1995).

According to Bowlby (1977), compulsive caregiving behavior in adults has its roots in patterns of affectional bonding in their family of origin. According to Bowlby, who seems to reflect the tendency to blame mothers for everything wrong with their children (a tendency common for his time): "The typical childhood experience of such people is to have a mother who, due to depression or some other disability, was unable to care for the child but, instead, welcomed being cared for and perhaps also demanded help in caring for younger siblings" (p. 207). The parent's conditions for attaching with the child is that the child caretake the parent and be a support for the parent. This is conditional love. It is given based on the behavior of the child rather than acceptance of the child for who the child is. In an effort to bond with the parent, such children renounce their own need for care, attention, or affection and, instead, give it to the parent. This process gets generalized in adults as a pattern for attachment with others (West & Keller, 1991). They come to believe that they can only attach to others if they are taking care of those others. As Jones & Wells (1996) put it, "parentification in childhood may lead to an adult relationship pattern characterized by compulsive caregiving . . ." (p. 146). This follows from the work of West and Keller (1991) who wrote that, "the structure of the person's interaction with the parent is carried forward into adulthood and serves as a template for negotiating current relationships" (p. 246).

Problems with Establishing Intimacy

Compulsive caretaking of parents by children may affect the kind of romantic relationships in which they engage as adults. As adults, caretaker children may only be attracted to people they can caretake. This is apt to be dependent, needy people. It may be people who have their competency impaired by physical or emotional disabilities. It may be people who are pained or wounded by past experiences. By caretaking these others, the caretaker creates indebtedness in the person who is cared for, creating a one-up, one-down relationship in which the caretaker has some measure of power and control.

People who manifest the caretaker syndrome have great difficult maintaining egalitarian relationships. They have difficulty with relationships based on interdependence and mutuality. They are more comfortable in relationships based on reciprocal roles, such as giver and taker or caretaker and dependent.

Career Choice

The caretaker syndrome extends to the kinds of careers to which caretakers are attracted. They find jobs attractive where they can care for others who need care. Such career options include jobs in the medical field, such as physicians and nurses or medical counselors, where they physically and emotionally care for people. Caretakers are tempted to train for jobs as psychotherapists or social workers. Lackie (1983) found that social workers were frequently caretakers, parental and parentified children, in their families of origin. Caretakers might also be attracted to teaching, preschool child care, or geriatrics.

The literature on children in families of alcoholics indicates that the roles of parental and parentified children can have consequences for personality development for these children. Children who play the role of "hero" will often develop personalities as adults that manifest serious, responsible, dependable, competent adult behavior. These adults often have trouble being light, spontaneous, or fun-loving. They tend to be compulsive perfectionists and have difficulty with failure or incompetence in any context.

Heroes are thought to become codependents or enablers in their adult lives and in their families of procreation. The label "codependent" tends to be popularly accepted but is widely criticized in academic literature. One debate that exists around codependency is a gendered controversy. Some women argue that males are more prone to perceive codependency as pathology with these males taking a "tough-minded" position that one should not assume the problems of others, that personal boundaries need to be protected, and people should leave the problems of others to those others. The tough-minded person takes the position "that is your problem, don't make it mine." However, this position lacks empathy and compassion and some would argue that codependency is cooperation, caring about others, and that helping others who need assistance makes this a better world where people care for and help one another.

Wells, et al. (1999) do not discuss this debate and assume that codependency is a form of pathology, where "codependent individuals are prone to feelings of both low self-esteem and shame. Hence, these individuals not only may feel unsuccessful or of low worth but also typically experience themselves as inherently flawed or inadequate"

(p. 68). Caretaking may function to compensate for these feelings of inadequacy. Wells, et al. (1999) also link codependency to parentification inasmuch as "individuals who present as 'codependent' are likely to come from families in which they were parentified, and they may continue to demonstrate parentified behaviors in their current relationships. Many individuals who are parentified as children remain bound to the original family in a caretaking role . . ." (p. 68).

Children who play the role of rebel or scapegoat in families where there is substance abuse often become irresponsible adults who resist conformity to norms. They may be charming and likable, but they exhibit characteristics that resemble "the Peter Pan Syndrome": they have difficulty "growing up" and being responsible, dependable, competent, serious adults, but they play well and hard. Children who play parentified roles as deviants, who distract parents from their own issues and problems through their own deviance, are apt to continue their defiant, nonconforming behavior into adulthood. Parentification through deviance, however, is less common as a caretaking style than is parentification through competence, the hero's style.

Children as Victims

Literature on parental and parentified children is primarily written by psychologists and therapists. Therapists tend to see the worst victims of destructive parentification, those who are so overburdened by these roles that they exhibit impaired functioning in their lives. These clients worry about those they are supposed to care for. This worry often has distracted them from their schoolwork, and they may have difficulty concentrating because their thoughts are elsewhere.

These clients may exhibit anxiety disorders, where they experience abnormally high levels of anxiety. This anxiety is over successfully completing all the household jobs they have or meeting the considerable demands of others. These demands exist because they are the most competent family member—efficient, energetic, and responsible, so others depend on them. This anxiety may be triggered by responsibilities they have taken on that are impossible to achieve, such as preventing a parent from consuming alcohol or preventing one parent from being physically or verbally abusive to other family members. This high level of anxiety can lead to sleep disorders in these children. These children also experience a great deal of stress.

If there are insufficient outlets from this stress, such as exercise or recreation, the stress can be manifest in psychosomatic illnesses in these children. Often the burdens they shoulder do not permit them time to exercise and have fun, so psychosomatic illnesses develop, including frequent headaches, nausea or upset stomach, bladder or bowel control problems (a metaphor for other things or people in their lives being out of their control), rashes and skin problems, or chronic fatigue. These illnesses permit the children to get some "time out" from their responsibilities in a way that is tolerated by others. They permit the caretaker child to be nurtured and cared for by others occasionally, perhaps the only time that they hear expressions of concern or love from others.

Because it is the children who are wounded by destructive parentification that these therapists tend to see on a weekly basis, the perception of many therapists is distorted by what they see. As a family therapist, I also see children who are wounded by excessive parentification. As a university professor, however, I also observe and interact with a nonclinical population of young adults who also grew up experiencing parentification in their families of origin. Most of these young adults seem to have survived their experience relatively unscathed. They are not seeing therapists, and they report that, though their experiences as parental and parentified children were painful and difficult, they are thankful for those experiences, which they feel made them stronger, more independent, self-sufficient adults. These students had the resilience to survive their experiences rather than be victimized by them.

Survivors

Particularly when one reviews the literature that deals with "destructive parentification" of children, one finds that these children are often described as victims of parental incompetence and abuse.

> parentification in the family entails a functional and/or emotional role reversal in which the child sacrifices his or her own needs for attention, comfort, and guidance in order to accommodate and care for logistical or emotional needs of the parent. Because children need their parents, children learn readily to respond to what their parents need. Responsiveness to parental need is not inherently problematic, and in fact, in a healthy sense, it helps the child develop sensitivities and reciprocity with others. In its worst sense, however, exacting such "responsiveness" from one's children may be gravely exploitative of them. In extreme cases when a parent's dependency is too great and when the parent abdicates parental responsibility for structuring and protecting the child from "doing too much" or "carrying the load," the parentified child may learn in this process that her needs are of less importance than those of others, or may actually become depleted of energy and time for pursuing school, friendships, childhood activities, and, at later stages, exploration of career and relationship possibilities (Chase, 1999, pp. 5–6).

The victimization of the child involves a loss of childhood. In assuming adult responsibilities for the parent, the child loses a play-filled, carefree childhood. The loss of childhood means that the child cannot attend to his or her own needs, instead attending to the needs of other family members, whether it is parents or siblings. The following respondent speaks with the voice of a victim who bemoans her life as a child because she had to assume too many adult responsibilities.

> Eventually you need to let go and let the children that you raised be children. I know that I am very responsible and most single-parent children are, they have to be, but I wish that somewhere we could all learn that a child is a child and a parent is a parent. Children will have their time to take care of mom and dad later in life. Also, single parents need to pay attention to the little ones sometimes so that they don't forget who the parent is in the household. All things happen for a reason and they say that somewhere in time you will find out what it all means. Maybe there is a plan for the children that take on so much in their daily lives, and we will all learn what it means to have been a parent at a time when we should have been able to live our lives as children.

Parentification is abusive inasmuch as the child is never acknowledged or thanked or appreciated for his or her efforts in helping out or caretaking parents. The child is taken for granted. This is not only unfair to the child, but it is abusive in its exploitation of the child.

One can dwell on one's abuse; one can live an entire adult life bemoaning one's childhood. However, seeing oneself as a victim of the behavior of others is paralyzing. People who see themselves as the victims of others usually employ external attributions whereby they see themselves as powerless against forces external to themselves, whether those forces are God, fate, chance, or luck. The external forces that govern one's life can be governmental agents such as police, probation officers, or social workers. The external forces over which the children have no control can also be parents who have expectations for them that are not age-appropriate, expectations that burden the children with responsibilities that they have difficulty accomplishing successfully. One may get sympathy from others by playing the victim role, but that role is very difficult to leave over time.

Most respondents in this study did not define themselves as victims of their childhood. Most saw their caretaking responsibilities as beneficial to them and believed that their caretaking responsibilities made them more independent, self-sufficient, competent, stronger people. They saw their experiences as parental or parentified children as helping them be resilient in times of crisis. They saw their caretaking as strengthening bonds between themselves and other family members, whether that was the siblings for whom they cared or the parent whom they helped. They saw their caretaking of brothers and sisters as helping in bonding with them. They saw their role as coparent as a means of bonding with their parent in a shared struggle for survival. They became soulmates to their parent in teaming with him or her to overcome adversity.

> My mother, on the other hand, would tell me her problems and this led me to feel stressed out and I had to grow up fast. My maturity I think helped me out because I would give her advice like if I was a married woman with children who was just real experienced. She would always tell me that I was so intelligent, and she would let me know that she did not know what she would do without me.

My group of respondents, largely working-class young adults, who did not constitute a clinical sample, perceived their experiences as parental or parentified children as helpful to them in their adult lives. In symbolic interactionist terms, they defined their situation as painful and difficult at the time (particularly because the roles created social isolation from peers) but they interpreted these roles as ultimately constructive. Most respondents saw themselves not as victims but as survivors.

> I am who I am today because I have taken my life experiences and used them for the best. I hope that all children can do the same.

> I am grateful for this uphill battle, as I am sure my mom is, because it equipped us with necessary people skills that made my life a little easier. Life is not fair, but if you are a good person inside and out, people will recognize that and be drawn toward you.

> As a former latch-key kid myself, I can say that there are some advantages to self/sibling care. I do feel that this situation fosters maturity and can be a positive experience as long

as the child is mature enough to handle it in the first place. It is nice to be trusted and know that you are competent. I see it more as a logical step towards independence when a child is ready.

There was a period of time when I was responsible for my younger sister and brother daily for about a year. My sister attended private school and my little brother had just started kindergarten. I was responsible for driving to the next city to pick my sister up as well as my little brother after school. After, we would go home and I made sure that they had an after-school snack before making sure my sister completed her homework. I would also straighten up the bathroom and do the morning dishes before starting a dinner my mom would complete if she got home in time. Nine times out of ten I was lucky enough to have one phone call with a friend and start my homework that same night. I'm not bitter towards my parents for putting me in this situation. Instead I believe this allowed me a better way of understanding what it must be like to be a parent.

My findings are similar to the findings of Lillian Rubin (1994) in her research on children who were abused or neglected. Despite horrible experiences, these children exhibited a resilience, an ability to transcend their childhoods and move on to productive lives as adults.

The past, of course, leaves scars that, when picked, can bleed. But the transcendent child long ago learned to live with the pain. In fact, it often seems like a familiar if difficult friend who, for all the anguish, has played a positive role in the development of a life. The tolerance for pain—the ability to recognize it, to live with it, to accept it, to understand its source, and to master it—breeds the strength necessary for transcendence (Rubin, 1994, p. 12).

Rubin (1994) carries this theme of transcendence to parental and parentified children when she writes:

Both parental and parentified children are cheated in their lives. They both are cheated out of a pleasant childhood, parents who love them and the all-around stability and structure that every family should have. But let's not condemn these children, because in many cases growing up this way has made them stronger individuals. Many know they can get through anything, if they survived their troubled childhood. Witnessing the kinds of lives their parents have led has many times convinced them to do things differently with their own lives. As for myself, I see a very bright future for myself as well as for my children to come. I now know what I don't want to do in raising my children, and the things I may want to focus on more, such as love, attention, compassion, time, the things that were not given to me as a child. The experiences of all these individuals have shaped them all into better people, people who know what it's like to be abused and hurt, but who also know how to jump back and start fresh with a family of their own.

But those who transcend their pasts soon become adept at finding and engaging alternative sources of support. Almost always a surrogate, a mentor, a model, a friend plays an important role in the life of the child—assuaging the loneliness, presenting the possibility of another life, of a different way of being.

Sometimes it's a real person—a teacher, a relative, a neighbor, a friend; sometimes one who lives in imagination alone—a stuffed animal that's anthropomorphized, a fantasy playmate, or an imaginary 'good' parent to whom that child turns for comfort and consolation (Rubin, 1994, pp. 8–9).

One can experience destructive parentification and overcome it as a function of inner strength, an internal resilience that is part of the person. But one can also overcome destructive parentification through the use of support systems. Wolin (1995) reports that resilient children can often identify at least one person in their childhood who was a positive, supportive figure and instrumental in giving them the strength to survive and overcome their challenges . . . a teacher, a grandparent or other relative, a neighbor. Of course, it is difficult for parental and parentified children to reach out to external others because their involvement at home has socially isolated them. But some overcome this and do get support from others.

The majority of my respondents report what Jurkovic would call "adaptive parentification," which was difficult for them, which at some time in their life overburdened them, but which they do not see as creating for them lifelong adverse effects. In fact, they interpret their experiences as toughening them, maturing them, and generally making them better people in the long run.

My findings, consistent with Rubin's (1994) and Hetherington's (2002), are congruent with Teyber's (2001) contention that, if tasks given to children are not excessively demanding, the responsibilities that parental and parentified children assume can produce children who are resilient, more compassionate for others, and more competent than are other children their age.

Benedek (1995) has listed guidelines of household duties that are suitable for children at different ages. She insists that household chores must be age-appropriate for the child. A child between the ages of six and eight can be expected to pack a school lunch, straighten up the bathroom and kitchen after using them, sweep the garage, and place dirty dishes in the dishwasher. She believes that children younger than ten years old should not be left alone at home unsupervised and children younger than twelve should not baby-sit their siblings. She believes that household chores should not interfere with schoolwork, the sleep of the caretaker, or the caretaker spending time with their friends. Many of my respondents' parents violated Benedek's recommendations; many found caretaking responsibilities interfering with time spent with their friends, for instance.

Reciprocal Caretaking in Families

Much of the literature on parental and parentified children seems to reflect a view of family life that reflects a Western cultural bias. That bias views family life as consisting of a caretaking parental generation that nurtures and cares for children. It is an image of children that was portrayed by the legislators of the Progressive Era—as somewhat passive recipients of adult action.

The Western view of family life that is often portrayed is that parents and children have complementary roles in which parents give and children take. Parents give love, attention, affection, food, shelter, clothing, money, medical treatment when needed, and discipline. Parents give knowledge, wisdom, and they teach children what they need to know to be competent adult members of society through a process of socialization. They give children instruction in learning how to talk, walk, feed themselves, dress themselves, read, write, and understand and obey social norms or rules. Parents bestow on their children socioeconomic status and the resources children have available to them is a consequence of the economic resources of their parents. Children are the recipients of what their parents give them.

Parentification of children makes sense in this context because parentification involves a role reversal. Parentified children give their parents love, attention, affection, food, sometimes money, sometimes medical treatment when needed, companionship, advice, or nurturance and support. This constitutes deviance from norms and expectations. It constitutes a reversal of the hierarchy in which children are in charge of the welfare of their parents rather than the reverse.

One of the factors that makes parentification destructive for these children is the absence of acknowledgment or appreciation for their caretaking efforts. The caretaking actions of the children are largely taken for granted both by members of the nuclear family and by extended kin.

This raises the question of whether parental and parentified children exist in non-Western families and, if so, to what extent do they exist? Anderson (1999) maintains that he could find no reference to the parentification of children in the literature on African American families. Truong (2001) also finds no reference to the parentification of children in the literature on immigrant Vietnamese families. Why?

African American, Mexican, and Vietnamese families all have cultural traditions that value collectivism and family interdependence. All have traditions of an agrarian-based society in which families tend to be large because children are valued as resources to their family; their labor is important to family survival. Life is hard, a struggle for survival, and in that struggle everyone in the family is expected to participate and contribute to the family welfare. Protection is an important theme of family life in all three cultures. Parents are expected to protect children and older children are expected to protect, nurture, and care for younger siblings. Parental children do not, thus, represent deviance from a norm but are congruent with cultural norms.

Furthermore, in all three cultures, families are immersed in a broad network of extended kin and community structures, such as churches. Unlike Western families, the nuclear family is not isolated from an external support network but, rather, exists within a larger network of support. Children in these cultures exist within a broad social context where they can be acknowledged and appreciated for their caretaking activities. If they are taken for granted by a parent, they can be acknowledged for their efforts by extended kin, friends of the family, congregants in a church, or neighbors. The broader social networks function to ameliorate the tendency for caretaker children to be ignored and taken for granted by others. Others notice and comment on the contributions of these children.

What exists in African American, Mexican American, and Vietnamese American families is a systemic approach to caretaking in which all family members provide nurturance and support when it is needed and, in turn, receive nurturance and support from others. There is no expectation of unidirectional caretaking, that it only be given by parents to children. It is reciprocal caretaking: children sometimes take care of their siblings, sometimes assist and support their parents and even grandparents. Furthermore, this reciprocity of caretaking is culturally encouraged and expected. This means that children caring for their parents is not deviance; it is congruent with normative expectations of the culture. Further, the caretaking is not really a reversal of a hierarchy because, though children may care for parents, parents are still regarded with deference and respect and maintain their dominance over children.

Likewise, the caretaking of younger siblings by older siblings is congruent with cultural norms. These caretaking children are critical in protecting the health, safety, and welfare of their brothers and sisters. The caretaking function enables parents to go to work responsibly, having delegated parental responsibilities to adolescents. These adolescents are contributing members of the family, part of a social system in which everyone contributes to the welfare of the family. The family certainly does not perceive this caretaking as deviance or pathology. If the family does not perceive the caretaking as deviance or pathology, is it? From a symbolic interactionist perspective, reality is perceived, and that subjective reality is the only reality that organizes the behavior of people.

Are the roles of parental and parentified children as pathology a definition imposed on families by therapists who form their own culture, with its own biases and predispositions that influence their definitions, interpretations, and labels? Are these interpretations ethnocentric as well as professionally biased, and how culturally sensitive are they? There is very little literature on parental and parentified children from a diverse cultural perspective, using different cultural standards to interpret and analyze interpersonal relationships in families. Is the expectation that one leaves one's family of origin an Anglo expectation? How culturally universal is such a concept of independence for adults? In many cultures, one is born into one's family and is expected to be an active, participating, and contributing member of the family for the rest of one's life. The concept of leaving is foreign and, in fact, violates cultural expectations.

Much of the literature on parental and parentified children mentions that the caretaking of these roles adversely affects the ability of children to physically and psychologically leave their family of origin. But in many cultures of the world, if there is no expectation of children leaving, then staying in the family is not seen as problematic. If it is not problematic within the family, why should it be problematic for therapists who are analyzing the family? It is only problematic for the therapists inasmuch as what they see violates their expectations of what ought to happen in families, expectations that are instilled in their graduate school and professional conferences.

Questions

When scholars study a phenomenon, the research often leads to more questions than answers. The study of parental and parentified children is an example of this phenomenon. This country exhibits great diversity in how its citizens define and treat children. The perception of children by parents affects the expectations parents have of children. Expectations placed on children to care for others or to work in a family is a function of the age and gender of the child, the ethnicity of the family, the social class of the family, and the size of the family.

The older the child, the more likely it is that the child will be expected to care for others, whether those others be siblings or the parent. Adult children are often expected to care for elderly parents. Adolescents are expected to care for younger siblings. Girls, more than boys, are expected to be the caretakers of siblings, but adolescent boys may be expected to help the family financially.

White Europeans, particularly middle-class Anglos, are more likely to see children as dependents to be cared for and nurtured by parents. They are more likely to see a linear relationship between parents and children, perceiving parents as givers and children as receivers of love, money, attention, affection, and time. African American, Mexican American, and Chinese American families are more likely to see families systemically, focusing on interdependence among family members; all are expected to give to their family to the best of their abilities. Children are expected to both give and receive from parents; children are expected to be workers contributing to the family as a whole. The integration of children in the family division of labor is seen as critical for survival.

In upper-class families, children tend to be bound out, socialized by professionals in boarding schools so they do not generally live with their parents for much of the year. Labor is outsourced in these families and children are generally not expected to participate in domestic labor. Middle-class children are less likely to be parental children than are working-class or poor children because the family has resources to provide for child care in the parents' absence. They often become parentified children by caring for their parents emotionally by engaging in extracurricular activities through sports, music or dance lessons, language or cultural education, and excelling in these activities. As stars, they provide their parents with entertainment, social interaction with other adults, pride, and a vehicle for showing the outside world what wonderful parents they are.

The style in which middle-class, working-class, and poor children exhibit parentification is different. Middle-class children tend to manifest expressive management for the parents while working-class and poor children tend to manifest instrumental caretaking: helping a parent out financially by contributing money to the household. Instrumental parentification can also involve helping a parent with household chores such as cleaning, doing laundry, cooking, grocery shopping, or child care.

The larger the family, the more likely it will be that older children are enlisted to help parents with caretaking younger children. Family size is linked to social class; the larger the family, the more likely it will have limited financial resources, limited access to health-care services and information, such as access to contraceptive information and technology. The more limited a family's financial resources, the more critical the labor of older children becomes because this is free labor and the family usually does not have the resources to pay for professional child care. Working-class and poor families are likely to use relatives to care for children and, if adult relatives, such as grandparents, aunts, or uncles are not available, the labor of children becomes critical for family survival. If the parents are gainfully employed, the assistance of children at home becomes an important adaptive strategy to deal with parental absence.

If working-class and poor families are most likely to enlist the assistance of children as workers, and if one is interested in reducing the number of overburdened parental children or parentified children in a society, then there are a number of social policy suggestions for assisting financially impaired families. These suggestions include the need for more affordable child care for working parents and after-school child-care programs that allow the daytime schedule of the child to be congruent with the daytime schedule of the parents. Corporations and businesses can be helpful to employees who are parents by providing free on-site child-care facilities for preschool children as an employee benefit. Parents could benefit from an increase of flexible work hours and job-sharing opportunities that would not deprive job-share employees of health benefits and paid family leave policies, which could give parents a given number of paid hours per month for family emergencies. Opponents to these corporate suggestions cite increased costs to businesses, but these costs would be offset by increased employee loyalty, productivity, and stability.

Given this diversity in the roles children play in families in this society, one is led to ask at what point is caretaking by children in families excessive or exploitive? What should the role of children be in families? Is the role of the parental or parentified child deviant or normative in this society? Is destructive parentification a label for a violation of European expectations of the role of children in families? The expectations that are imposed on children for how much caretaking or work they should perform in a family, what their tasks should be, are a function of how children are defined in any given family, and those definitions are diverse.

It is the nature of a post-industrial society to celebrate diversity and accept the fact that people define objects, people, and events in different ways. Do any of us have the right to impose our views on others and be critical of how others view children or what they expect of children? Social service agencies, child protective agencies, and dependency courts answer this question affirmatively. They impose standards on families of how children are to be treated and violations of these standards constitute parental abuse, neglect, or exploitation. Parents can be imprisoned for violating these standards, parental rights can be removed by courts, and children can be involuntarily removed from parents for violating agency standards. A standard for prosecution in most jurisdictions is whether or not a prosecution will result in a conviction. Unfortunately, often, the poorer the family, the more likely it is that authorities will prosecute because poor parents do not have the legal resources with which to competently defend themselves.

Negotiating Social Order

Anselm Strauss (1978) argues that all social organization comes to exist through a process of interpersonal negotiation. He writes that, "a given social order, even the most repressive, would be inconceivable without some forms of negotiation" (p. 235). Strauss examines how social order is constructed through negotiations in a variety of social contexts, from clan intermarriage and dowry or bride-wealth negotiations to labor negotiations in work settings, from legal negotiations such as plea bargaining to international bargaining to resolve crises such as in the Middle East, the Balkans, or in negotiating international alliances. Strauss's work, when applied to the study of parental and parentified children, raises some questions that suggest interesting lines for future research. Negotiation is a process that creates and recreates social structure (how people organize themselves) as a continually changing phenomenon.

Strauss suggests a variety of questions that need to be asked and answered by social scientists who research the process of negotiation. It is important to know how many people are negotiating, formally or informally, and whose interests those negotiators are representing. This is a complex issue because negotiators have different levels of visibility, some negotiators being quite overt and others negotiating in a more covert way, having little visibility as negotiators. What is the style by which negotiations proceed? Are the negotiations one-shot or repeated, sequential, serial, or multiple? Related to this is the question of what options are perceived as available to the negotiators for avoiding or discontinuing negotiation, or escalating the stakes of the negotiations. Related to this last point is the question of the stakes in the negotiation and how those stakes change over time. Lastly, one might ask what is the relative balance of power exhibited by the parties participating in a negotiation and how does this change over time?

If one were researching parental children, one might ask how they can negotiate with a parent to get time out for themselves so that they can go to school events, spend time with friends, or engage in activities other than caretaking their siblings. How do parental or parentified children negotiate reprieves for themselves, times when they can extricate themselves from the role, even for a few hours? Do they enlist the help of siblings for support? Do they rehearse scripts used to negotiate with parents? What do they perceive as useful and potentially productive strategies that might get them what they want and what do they define as unsuccessful strategies in the process of negotiation? Are their attempts one-shot attempts or do they persist in the negotiation after an initial failure? How do parental and parentified children get their own needs met in the face of expectations that they exist to meet the needs of others? What strategies do they employ to successfully negotiate for themselves?

How do siblings subtly negotiate the process whereby one of them becomes parentified and is delegated the task of being the primary caregiver to one or both parents? The styles of negotiation will be diverse, making theory-building difficult. The questions alone present methodological challenges, for the process of researching negotiation styles, knowing what to look for and what questions to ask, makes for complex social research.

What is the process of negotiating social structure in a family that has recently immigrated to the United States? How does the family negotiate which children will help the parents with specific tasks? How do the children negotiate with the parents when and how they will help? How do parents and children negotiate assistance so that the parents can retain high status within the family despite the fact that the children have superior skills, abilities, or knowledge in some areas. The process of negotiation will have unique properties for each family studied, but there may also be general trends or tendencies when a significant number of families have been studied. Can generalizations be made for families of a given ethnic group or a cluster of ethnic groups from a specific region of the world? How do families of one ethnic group differ from families of another ethnic group in the way they negotiate the creation of parental or parentified children?

What is the process of negotiating social structure in a family that has a chronically physically or mentally ill individual? How do members negotiate which children will become caretakers and how they will caretake? Will the caregivers care for the ill member or focus on caregiving the family member who is the primary caretaker of the ill person? How is this decided?

What is the subtle process of negotiating which adult child will care for elderly parents? Do all the children, except for one, unilaterally move away from the parents, leaving one child to reside near the parents and how is that caretaker child selected in the sibling system? Does a parent select the caretaker child by moving themselves to the city or town of their chosen child? How does the caretaker child negotiate help from their siblings, either financial help or "time-out assistance" from caretaking ("Why don't you invite mom to come visit you this summer?")? What is the process of negotiation between parent and siblings when a parent has to be placed, against their will, perhaps, into an assisted living or skilled nursing facility, that is, what is the process of negotiation by which critical decisions are made relative to the elderly parent?

A researcher can take any of the contexts discussed in this book and examine how a family negotiates caregiving. Who will be the caregivers and to whom will the care be given? How will be the care be given, for it has to be given in a way that preserves the dignity of and is acceptable to the recipient. The answers to these questions may change over time, depending on the context in which caregiving occurs, so the process of caregiving is constantly being negotiated and renegotiated. The process of caregiving in a family is always in flux.

Likewise, the political process that legislates caregiving in a society is constantly being negotiated at a national level. It is to the negotiation of caregiving at the level of social policy that I turn next.

Social Policy Issues

For societal authorities to adopt a laissez-faire or libertarian position that parents have the freedom to impose their own expectations on their children, that the role of government is not to tell parents what to do, what is acceptable or unacceptable treatment of children is problematic, because it exposes children to the tyranny or abuse of parents and offers them no community protection. We live in one of the most permissive societies in the world, where people are given a wide range of choices from which to construct their own behavior. In such a society, we find great diversity, and we tend to celebrate that diversity, including the broad spectrum of how children are children.

When people are critical of others, they may be accused of disrespecting those others, of being intolerant, or of not understanding the environment or the culture or the circumstances in which others find themselves. Concepts such as destructive parentification carry with them a critical aura, an insinuation that it is not OK, that it violates the rights and developmental needs of children, as well as, perhaps, cultural norms and expectations. The challenge facing society, and its representatives—courts, therapists, social-service agencies, and families—is to determine to what extent the government can or should impose a societal standard of what children should experience in their lives and to what extent this should be left to parents and families to determine, based on situational contingencies such as how parents define their children, what they need from their children to survive, what their children offer of themselves, what financial and cultural resources they have, and what competencies and impairments exist within the family.

The study of parental and parentified children sheds light on the broad spectrum that exists within our society regarding how children experience their childhood. We have seen that, in many contexts, children are the caretakers of others and that this is how children have lived through most of the history of this country. Caretaking for most children involves a constructive adaptation to the needs of family members. It is when one finds destructive parentification or overburdened parental children that the question arises, What should society do about them? This is a question about which there is intense debate.

Political conservatives generally support the libertarian view that government should not intrude on the private lives of its citizenry. The conservative view is that government is already too big, too intrusive, and too expensive: the cost of government, the number of people in government, and the restrictions of government on businesses and families should be reduced. Conservatives will likely not see the issue of parental and parentified children as being of government concern.

Political liberals see government as an important instrument of protection, protection of civil liberties through legislation and enforcement, protection of the poor through social legislation, protection of children by legislation and enforcement as well as through federal funding of education (like Head Start) and health enhancement programs (like federally supported universal immunization programs and universal health care for children).

The politically liberal position would be that if parental and parentified children are harmed by poverty, and if these roles have long-term destructive effects, then one must seek to eliminate or significantly reduce poverty in this country. If parental children are created from an absence of available and affordable child care for families in this country, government must create incentives or subsidies to improve the availability and affordability of child care. If parental children are created through the lack of after-school programs in their schools, then government should create incentives or provide subsidies to increase the availability and affordability of after-school child-care programs. If parental children are created because parents are so impoverished that they cannot afford to hire child-care services, then government should increase the minimum wage to make the money available to families.

If children are parentified as a result of the poor health of parents who cannot afford preventive medicine, then government needs to provide its citizens with more affordable preventive health-care services. If children are parentified through parental substance abuse that is pervasive throughout our society, then government should subsidize more substance-abuse treatment and rehabilitation programs. If immigrant children are parentified because their parents have limited English proficiency, then government should support more English as a Second Language instruction for its citizenry.

The problem with the liberal agenda is that it takes money to implement the many programs that meet the diverse needs of families. From a conservative perspective, these programs take too much money and require too much government.

A Modest Proposal

While liberals and conservatives debate the issues of money and government, there is one way of reducing destructive parentification that is not related to government and that does not take any money. It is something that can be done in families, and that is for all parents to take a long, hard look at the contributions their children are making to the survival and efficiency of family life. What chores are the children doing? Who are the children protecting and how are they doing this? How are the children supporting the parents and how are they supporting each other? It involves recognizing the contributions of the children, acknowledging those contributions, and thanking the children for those contributions so that they know that somebody has noticed and appreciated what they are doing to make the family work.

John Gottman (1995, 2000) has done research on what makes interpersonal relationships rewarding and healthy and developed the 5 to 1 principle. Rewarding, healthy relationships contain five times more compliments, statements of appreciation, and thank yous than they have complaints, criticisms, or rebuffs. This is true for partners and couples as well as for parents and children. Parents too often look at how their children are messing up (people generally find what they are looking for) and are oblivious to times when their children are doing what they are supposed to be doing and behaving themselves. When children are contributing and behaving, they are taken for granted because they pose no problem. Nothing is said to them. What should be said is, "I noticed you did the dishes. Thank you." "I noticed you emptied the dishwasher. Thank you." " I noticed you started a load of wash. Thank you." "I noticed you helped your brother with his homework. Thank you." This is a very small step, but we all have to start someplace.

Glossary

Adaptive parentification: A concept developed by Gregory Jurkovic signifying the process of giving children caregiving responsibilities that are are a response to some change in a family, such as divorce, the deployment of a military parent, the sudden illness of a parent, the death of a parent, or the incarceration of a parent. Children are able to cope with their responsibilities because they are appreciated and complimented by others for their contributions, they receive external support from others, or they get breaks from their adult responsibilities.

Alcoholism: A condition where the consumption of alcohol, regardless of frequency or amount of consumption, adversely affects an individual's relationship with others, such as family members, friends, or coworkers.

Assimilation: Socially integrating into a group or society.

Authority: Legitimized power, power with the consent of the governed.

Boomerang syndrome: When a child leaves the family of origin to become an independent adult and later returns to live with the parents. These adult children can usually enjoy a higher standard of living in the residence of their parents than they can have living on their own.

Boundaries: A physical barrier or mental construct that enables one to identify who is "inside" and who is "outside" a group or society. Boundaries become problematic when they become either rigid or diffuse, when they become excessively closed or open.

Caretaker syndrome: When children who were caretakers of others maintain their caretaking in their adult lives. Parental and parentified children may be drawn to occupations in which they care for others and in their intimate relationships may be attracted to people they can care for.

Chemical dependency: Having an addiction or need for alcohol or some other drug. This adversely affects relationships the dependent has with others, such as family members, friends, or coworkers.

Clear boundaries: What family therapists see as ideal. These are mental constructs that allow people to distinguish who is inside and outside a generation or a family but the boundaries can be transcended such that people outside can come in to provide resources to family members and family members can go outside the family system to get their needs met. One had control over that transcendance, however, such that people can say no to outsiders at times when they want privacy or they can say no to employers when they want family time or play time and they can say no to family members when, for instance, a parent wants a child to stay home rather than going out to play with friends.

Closed boundaries: Also known as rigid boundaries, like walls of a prison, closed boundaries exist as norms that do not permit family members to go outside the family to get their needs met and the outside world is not allowed inside the family to serve as resources to family members. Closed boundaries often exist in families with secrets, such as families with alcoholism or domestic violence. Children are not allowed to bring friends home for fear that the family secret will be discovered.

Clown: A role played by a person, often a child, in an alcoholic family in which the person provides comic relief, is usually immature, cute, and funny. This person is rarely taken seriously. This person distracts family members from serious problems.

Codependent: A role, also called an enabler, played by someone who is usually nice, sympathetic, understanding and highly competent and who blocks another from realizing negative consequences of their behavior, thus reinforcing or maintaining the behavior, even if that behavior, such as drinking, is problematic.

Dependent: The name of the role played by the person who is chemically dependent, someone who is an alcoholic or is addicted to some other drug.

Destructive parentification: A concept developed by Gregory Jurkovic signifying the process of giving children caregiving responsibilities that overburden the child, that are beyond their ability to successfully accomplish, thus psychologically damaging the child in some way, such as giving the child, throughout their life, a sense of powerless, the sense that they are failures, leading to low self esteem.

Differentiation of self: A concept created by family therapist Murray Bowen, whereby an individual distinguishes him or her self from the family as a collectivity, where a person individuates, becomes a person in their own right apart from his or her family of origin.

Diffuse boundaries: Like having no boundaries at all, leading to enmeshment or overinvolvement between people such that two people often function as one, are inextricably tangled together like strands of spaghetti. In families, a parent may become so involved in the problems of a child that it creates fusion between the parent and child such that both have the problem.

Diminished capacity to parent: Used by Judith Wallerstein to describe impaired parenting exhibited by a wounded, pained parent who is either recently separated or divorced. The diminished capacity to parent creates an opportunity structure for the development of parental and parentified children.

Disengagement: People are disengaged when they are emotionally and cognitively unaffected by the behavior of others around them.

Divorce: The legal termination of a valid marriage contract.

Dramaturgical approach in sociology: An orientation in sociology linked to Erving Goffman such that people are seen as actors, playing out a theatrical performance for an audience, managing or constructing an image for others of who they are and what they are like.

Dual worker household: A household in which two adults, usually parents, are gainfully employed.

Enabler: A role, also called a codependent, played by someone who is usually nice, sympathetic, understanding and highly competent and who blocks another from realizing negative consequences of their behavior, thus reinforcing or maintaining the behavior, even if that behavior, such as drinking, is problematic.

Enmeshment: A concept developed by family therapist Salvador Minuchin meaning overinvolvement with another. Enmeshment arises from the existence of diffuse boundaries.

Ethical norms: Rules or "shoulds" that prescribe appropriate behavior. When people exhibit behavior that is congruent with ethical norms, this is called conformity.

Expressive role: Managing the emotional states of others so that they are happy, not depressed or bored, not worried or sad.

Filial piety: An expectation, usually associated with Chinese culture, that younger people respect and care for older, particularly elderly people. Adult children in families are expected to respect and care for their parents.

First-generation immigrant: A person who was born in or raised in one country and comes to a different society. First generation immigrants usually speak the language of their former country, cook the foods of that country, identify with that country, and often communicate with friends and relatives in that country.

Fragmented parental system: Where parents sabotage each other because they have different parenting styles or philosophies, where the parents do not present a united front, supporting one another. Fragmented parental systems can lead to out of control children where the child has more power than either parent and neither parent can get the child to do what they want the child to do because the child has more power than either parent.

Grandparent system: Grandmother and grandfather constitute what is usually the oldest system in a three generation family.

Healthy nonparentification: A concept developed by Gregory Jurkovic where children are assigned responsibilities in their families that are age appropriate for them. Work is mixed with the ability of children to play.

Hero: Usually the role played by the oldest child in a family, a person who is highly competent, mature, responsible and dependable, gets good grades in school, is well liked by peers, is a superb athlete or musician or dancer, and who unwittingly contributes to the denial of an alcoholic parent who asks "if there was a problem in the family, how could we produce such a wonderful child?"

I: In the work of symbolic interactionist George Herbert Mead, this is a part of the "self" that constructs spontaneous, non-meaningful behavior that is reflexive and not preceeded by making indications to oneself in the mind.

Industrialized society: An urbanized society where people work primarily manufacturing products, converting raw materials to manufactured goods. Middle class families in the United States during the 1950's often had a wage earning husband and homemaker wife who cared for and nurtured children.

Infantilization: A concept developed by Gregory Jurkovic where children are egocentric, underfunctioning and dependent; they have virtually no responsibilities or commitment imposed on them by parents.

Instrumental function: Contributing to the family financially through work or in completing tasks that are necessary for survival such as grocery shopping, cooking, cleaning, and supervising children to insure their health and safety.

Intimacy: Sharing one's thoughts, feelings, and experiences with another. Intimacy requires self-disclosure to show another who you are.

Latch-key children: Children who are told to go home after school and stay at home until one of their parents returns home from work. This role is often socially isolating.

Looking-glass self: A concept created by Charles Horton Cooley conveying that our image of self is a mirror image of the appraisals we hear about ourselves from others, that we internalize what we hear about ourselves from others, soaking up those appraisals much as sponges soak up water.

Lost child: A child, often found in families where one or more people are alcoholics. This is a child who stays out of the way, spends much time socially isolated in their room, stays out of trouble and is generally inconspicuous.

Mascot: A role, sometimes called "the clown," played by a person, often a child, in an alcoholic family in which the person provides comic relief, is usually immature, cute, and funny. This person is rarely taken seriously. This person distracts family members from serious problems.

Me: The thinking part of the self.

Meaningful behavior: Behavior that is constructed in the mind as a consequences of defining situations and people in those situations, considering alternatives of action relative to the situation, and anticipating consequences of those alternatives.

Mind: The ability of people to make indications to themselves, to think, to construct behavior through defining situations and people in those situations, considering alternatives of action relative to the situation, and anticipating consequences of those alternatives.

Non-meaningful behavior: Behavior that is not preceeded by a process of rational thought, that is spontaneous or reflexive behavior.

Norms: What sociologists call rules that govern behavior.

Open boundaries: Physical or psychological barriers that distinguish people who are within a social structure from people who are outside that structure. Open boundaries allow family members to leave the family system to get their needs met and allow people in the outside world into the family to serve as a resource to family members.

Opportunity structures: A concept created by Peter Blau where the organization of a social system creates a situation that is conducive for some event or phenomenon to occur. The diverse types of families, discussed in Part II of this book all create opportunity structures for the development of parental or parentified children.

Parental child: A child who leaves the sibling system to become a parental figure to brothers or sisters.

Parental subsystem: Adults in the social structure of a family who occupy the roles of a mother or a father to children. Parental children are children who act as though they were part of the parental system.

Parentified child: A child who leaves the sibling system to become a parental figure to their own parents.

Post-industrial society: A highly urbanized society where people work in service-related occupations. The U.S., Japan, Great Britain, and Germany are examples of post-industrial societies, where there is diversity in the population and significant freedom of choice and tolerance of diverse behavioral patterns.

Power: The ability to get others to do what you want them to do. There are two main types of power: authority, which is legitimized power, power with the consent of the governed, and coercion, power derived from force or threat of force.

Pre-industrial society: A society that features little industrialization or urbanization, where people are gainfully employed primarily harvesting raw materials, such as in mining, lumbering, fishing, and agriculture.

Progressive Age: A historical period in the U.S. from 1880–1920 which generated legislation designed to protect children from parents (vis à vis physical or sexual abuse) and employers (vis à vis labor abuses). Children were defined as different kinds of people from adults, people who had special needs and required special protection. Legislation from this age included child labor laws and compulsory schooling for children.

Rebel: Also called a scapegoat, this is a role played by a child in a family where a member is alcoholic. These children are in trouble in school or with the law; they engage in deviant behavior that calls attention to themselves and away from others. Children who play this role can be seen as protecting someone else, such as unifying parents in their concern, thus protecting an otherwise devitalized marriage from divorce, or protecting a parent from depression or boredom.

Reciprocal roles: Patterns of behavior that people take relative to another that involve complementarity such that one cannot play one role without another person playing the complementary role; givers cannot exist without takers, caregivers cannot exist without someone who is cared for.

Revolving slate: A concept developed by Ivan Boszormenyi-Nagy referring to interactional patterns that recur within families generation after generation.

Rigid boundaries: The equivalent of closed boundaries where people within a family cannot go outside the family to get their needs met and people in the "outside world" cannot provide resources to family members.

Scapegoat: Also called a rebel, this is a role played by children in a family where a member is alcoholic. These children are in trouble in school or with the law; they engage in deviant behavior that calls attention to themselves and away from unifying parents in their concern, thus protecting an otherwise devitalized marriage from divorce, or protecting a parent from depression or boredom.

Second-generation immigrants: The children of first generation immigrants who generally seek to assimilate into a peer group at school. This assimilation is perceived as requiring that they do not act, dress, speak, or look any different from their peers. They seek to be "100% American," often rejecting the culture of their parents.

Second shift: A concept central to a book by sociologist Arlie Hochschild indicating that when women are gainfully employed, they often come home to put in a "second shift," that is, they often are expected to perform domestic tasks as though they were not gainfully employed at all; they work harder and longer at home than do their husbands.

Self: The ability of people to perceive themselves, define themselves, and act toward themselves as they would any object in their external environment.

Sibling subsystem: Children in the social structure of a family who occupy the roles of brother or sister to one another.

Single-parent household: Where there are children living in a household with one parent. These households are usually created by divorce or marital separation, widowhood, or a non-marital birth.

Social role: A pattern of behavior that assumes a meaning relative to others. Caregivers constitute a social role inasmuch as their behavior attends to the physical or emotional needs of others.

Social structure: The organization of a group or society. When one describes social structure, one must identify the parts of a system and the way those parts are organized. Sociologists sometimes focus on one element that defines the way a society is organized, so feminists see gender as being the central basis by which society is organized while social stratification theorists see social class (wealth, power, and prestige) as being the central characteristic by which society is organized. Salvador Minuchin saw the central organizational factor in families to be age where families are organized into generations.

Socialization: A life-long process in which people learn what they need to know to be a competent adult member of a society. In childhood this involves learning how to walk and talk, controlling bladder and bowels, reading and writing. One learns norms for behavior and the values that are shared by a culture; one learns how to perform many roles.

Split-shift household: Found in a dual-worker household where the parents work different shifts (one a day shift, the other a swing shift) to maximize the likelihood that one parent will be available to serve the needs of the children.

Statistical norms: What most people usually do, the way most people usually behave.

Stigma: As used by sociologist Erving Goffman, a fact about us that has the potential of damaging our identity in the eyes of others. Stigmas could be that we or our parents are alcoholics or that we or our parents have a prison record or that we were previously married or that we have some chronic physical or mental illness or that we failed the fifth grade.

Symbolic interactionism: A theoretical framework in sociology that focuses on the ability of people to construct their own behavior in their minds. This framework views people, groups, or behavior as capable of assuming multiple meanings; how one defines and interprets a situation and those within that situation influences how one will act toward that situation. Children, throughout history, have been defined and interpreted in different ways.

Taking the role of the other: The ability of people to step in another's shoes, to see the world as they see it, to define and interpret reality as they define it, to understand- to cognitively and emotionally grasp—what it is like to be that person and to live their life.

Third-generation immigrants: The children of second generation immigrants and grandchildren of first generation immigrants. These children find that to be "100% American" is to give them no sense of cultural identity, so they seek to return to their cultural roots, thus allying with their grandparents. They often seek to speak the language and cook the food of their grandparents as well as visit the homeland of their grandparents.

References

Ackerman, R. J. (1987). *Children of alcoholics.* New York: Learning.

Adams, J. (1965). Inequity in social exchange. In L. Berkowitz (Ed.), *Advances in experimental social psychology,* (Vol. 2, pp. 8–62). New York: Academic Press.

Ahrons, C. (1994). *The good divorce.* New York: Harper/Collins.

Alston, L. (1992). Children as chattel. In E. West & P. Petrick (Eds.), *Small worlds* (pp. 208–231). Lawrence, KS: University Press of Kansas.

Amato, P. R. (1993). Children's adjustment to divorce: Theories, hypotheses, and empirical support. *Journal of Marriage and the Family, 55,* 23–38.

Amato, P. R. (1995). Single parent households as settings for children's development, well-being, and attainment: A social network / Resources perspective. *Sociological Studies of Children, 7,* 19–47.

Amato, P. R., & Keith, B. (1991). Consequences of parental divorce for the well-being of children: A meta-analysis. *Psychological Bulletin, 110,* 26–46.

Amato, P. R., Rezac, S. J., & Booth, A. (1995). Helping between parents and young adult offspring: The role of parental marital quality, divorce, and remarriage. *Journal of Marriage and the Family, 57,* 363–374.

Anderson, L. P. (1998). Parentification in the context of the African American family. In N. D. Chase (Ed.), *Burdened Children: Theory, Research, and Treatment of Parentification,* (pp. 154–170). Thousand Oaks, CA: Sage.

Arbetter, S. (1990). Children of alcoholics don't talk, don't trust, don't feel. *Current health,* 14–17.

Aries, P. (1962). *Centuries of childhood.* New York: Vintage.

Assman, J. S. U. (1981). The overloaded parent: results and reasons in family size effect on parenting. In *Family structure and process in socialization of children,* B. C. Rollins (Ed.). Provo, UT: Brigham Young University Press.

Avenevoli, S., Sessa, F. M., & Steinberg, L. (1999). Family structure, parenting practices, and adolescent adjustment: An ecological examination. In E. M. Hetherington, (Ed.), *Coping with divorce, single parenting and remarriage.* Mahwah, NJ: Lawrence Erlbaum.

Bartlett, R. (2000). Helping inmate moms keep in touch: Prison programs encourage ties with children. *Corrections Today, 62*(7), 102–104.

Bartow, J. (1961). Family size as related to child-rearing practices. *Dissertation Abstracts International, 22,* 55–81.

Beiser, H. R. (1988). Support systems. In S. Altschul, (Ed.), *Childhood bereavement and its aftermath.* Madison, WI: International Universities Press.

Belle, D. (1999). *The after-school lives of children: Alone and with others while parents work.* Mahwah, NJ: Lawrence Erlbaum.

Benedek, E. P. (1995). *How to help your child overcome your divorce.* New York: Newmarket.

Berg-Weger, M. (1996). *The elderly in America.* New York: Garland.

Berlinshy, E. B., & Biller, H. B. (1982). *Parental death and psychological development.* Lexington, MA: Lexington Books.

Berman, C. (1997) *Caring for yourself while caring for your aging parents: How to help, how to survive.* New York: Henry Holt.

Bermudes, R. W. (1977). Separation: Its effects and adaptations. *Chaplain, 34,* 18–34.

Bey, D. R., & Lange, J. (1974). Wailing wives, women under stress. *American Journal of Psychiatry, 131,* 283–286.

Bierstedt, R. (1957). *The social order: an introduction to sociology.* New York: McGraw-Hill.

Biller, H. (1981). Father absence, divorce, and personality development. In M. E. Lamb, (Ed.), *The role of the father in child development,* (2nd ed., pp. 319–358). New York: John Wiley.

Black, C. (1981). *It will never happen to me.* New York: Ballantine.

Black, C. (1990). *Double duty.* New York: Ballantine.

Black, W. G., Jr. (1993). Military-induced family separation: A stress reduction intervention. *Social Work, 38* (3), 273–280.

Blankenhorn, D. (1995). *Fatherless America: Confronting our most urgent social problem.* New York: Basic Books.

Blau, P. M. (1994). *Structural contexts of opportunities.* Chicago: University of Chicago Press.

Blau, P. M. (1964). *Exchange and power in social life.* New York: John Wiley.

Bloch, M., Beoku-Betts, J. A., & Tabachnick, B. R. (1998). *Women and education in sub-Saharan Africa: Power, opportunities, and constraints.* Boulder, CO: Lynne Rienner.

Blumer, H. G. (1969). *Symbolic interactionism: Perspective and method.* Englewood Cliffs, NJ: Prentice-Hall.

Boszormenyi-Nagy, I., & Spark, G. M. (1973). *Invisible loyalties: Reciprocity in intergenerational family therapy.* New York: Harper & Row.

Boszormenyi-Nagy, I., & Ulrich, D. (1981). Contextual family therapy. In A. S. Gurman & D.P. Kniskern (Eds.), *Handbook of family therapy* (pp. 159–186). New York: Brunner/Mazel.

Bourdieu, P. (1977). *Outline of a theory of practice.* (Trans., R. Nice). Cambridge, England: University Press.

Bourdieu, P., & Passeron, J-C. (1977). Reproduction in *education, society, culture.* Beverly Hills, CA: Sage.

Bowen, M. (1976). Theory in the practice of psychotherapy. In P. J. Guerin, (Ed.), *Family therapy: theory and practice* (pp. 42–90). New York: Gardner Press.

Bowen, M. (1978). *Family therapy in clinical practice.* New York: Jason Aronson.

Bowlby, J. (1977). The making and breaking of affectional bonds. *British Journal of Psychiatry, 130,* 201–210.

Bravo, E. (1995). *A 9 to 5 guide: The job/family challenge.* New York: John Wiley.

Briggs, R. (1998). *Caregiving daughters: Accepting the role of caregiver for elderly parents.* New York: Publishing.

Brown, E. M. (1989). *My parent's keeper: Adult children of the emotionally disturbed.* Oakland, CA: Harbinger.

Brown, S. (1985). *Treating the alcoholic: A developmental model of recovery.* New York: John Wiley.

Brown, S., Beletsis, S., & Cermak, T. (1989). *Adult children of alcoholics in treatment.* Deerfield Beach, FL: Health Communications.

Burt, A. (1986). *Generational boundaries in the families of alcoholics.* Unpublished master's thesis, Georgia State University.

Bush-Baskette, S. (2000). The war on drugs and the incarceration of mothers. *Journal of Drug Issues, 30*(4), 919–928.

Casper, L. M. (1997). My daddy takes care of me! Fathers as care providers. *Current Population Reports.* Washington, DC: United States Census Bureau (P70-59).

Chase, N. D., (Ed.). (1999). *Burdened children: Theory, research and treatment of parentification.* Thousand Oaks, CA: Sage.

Chase, N. D., Deming, M. P., & Wells, M. (1998). Parentification, parental alcoholism, and academic status among young adults. *American Journal of Family Therapy, 26*(2), 105–114.

Cohen, I. A. (1995). *Addiction: The high-low trap.* Pompano Beach, FL: Health Press.

Collins, R. (1975). *Conflict sociology: Toward an explanatory science.* New York: Academic Press.

Conley, J. J. (1978). Ordinal position, personality and alcoholism. *Dissertation Abstracts International.* Microfilm No. 7907050, 168.

Corsaro, W. A. (1997). *The sociology of childhood.* Thousand Oaks, CA: Pine Forge Press.

Coontz, S. (1992). *The way we never were: American families and the nostalgia trap.* New York: Basic Books.

Coser, L. A. (1956). *The functions of social conflict.* Glencoe, IL: Free Press.

Cott, N. (1972). *Root of bitterness: Documents in the social history of American women.* New York: Dutton.

Couturier, L. (1995). Inmates benefit from family services programs. *Corrections Today, 57,* 100–105.

Crawford, C. (1978). *Mommie dearest.* New York: William Morrow.

Crespi, T. D. (1990). *Becoming an adult child of an alcoholic.* Springfield, IL: Charles C. Thomas.

Crespi, T. D., & Sabatelli, R. M. (1997). Children of alcoholics and adolescents: Individuation, development, and family systems. *Adolescence, 32,* 407–418.

Cuijpers, P., Langendoen, Y., & Bijl, R. V. (1999). Psychiatric disorders in adult children of problem drinkers: prevalence, first onset, and comparison with other risk factors. *Addiction, 94,* 1489–1498.

Deater-Deckard, K., & Dunn, J. (1999). Multiple risks and adjustment in young children growing up in different family settings: A British community study of stepparent, single mother, and nondivorced families. In E. M. Hetherington, (Ed.), *Coping with divorce, single parenting and remarriage* (pp. 47–64). Mahwah, NJ: Lawrence Erlbaum.

DeGenova, M. K. (1997). *Families in cultural context: Strengths and challenges in diversity.* Mountain View, CA: Mayfield.

Demos, J. (1986). *Past, present and personal: The family and life course in American history.* New York: Oxford University Press.

Despert, J. L. (1962). *Children of divorce.* New York: Doubleday.

Dolan, J. M. (1992). *How to care for your aging parents and still have a life of your own.* Studio City, CA: Mulholland Pacific.

Door, R. C. (1924). *A woman of fifty.* New York: Funk & Wagnalls.

Duncan, G. J., & Hoffman, S. D. (1985). A reconsideration of the economic consequences of marital disruption. *Demography, 22,* 485–489.

Earle, A. M. (1898). *Home life in colonial days.* New York: Macmillan.

Ebaugh, H. R., & Curry, M. (2000). Fictive kin as a social capital in new immigrant communities. *Sociological Perspectives, 43,* 189–210.

Ehrenreich, B. (1989). *Fear of falling: The inner life of the middle class.* New York: Pantheon.

Ekstrand, L. H. (1979). Replacing the critical period and optimum age theories of second language acquisition with a theory of ontogenetic development beyond puberty. *Educational and Psychological Interactions, 69,* (School of Education, Malmö).

Elster, J. (1999). *Addictions: Entries & exits.* New York: Russell Sage.

Feldman, R. S. (1997). *Development across the lifespan.* Englewood Cliffs, NJ: Prentice-Hall.

Feldstein, A. L., Harburg, E., & Hauenstein, L. (1980). Parity and blood pressure among four race-stress groups of families in Detroit. *American Journal of Epidemiology, 111,* 356–366.

Figley, C. R. (1993). Coping with stressors on the home front. *Journal of Social Issues, 49,* 51–71.

Freud, S. (1961). *Civilization and its discontents.* New York: W. W. Norton.

Furstenberg, F. F. (1990). Coming of age in a changing family system. In S. S. Feldman & G. R. Elliot (Eds.), *At the threshold: The developing adolescent* (pp. 147–170). Cambridge, MA: Harvard University Press.

Gabel, K., & Johnston, D. (1995). *Children of incarcerated parents.* New York: Lexington Books.

Galloway, J. L. (1990, December 24). Life on the front lines. *U.S. News and World Report, 109,* 18–35.

Garrett, G. R., Parker, B., Day, S., Van Meter, J. J., & Cosby, W. (1978). Drinking with the military wife: A study of married women in overseas base communities. In E. J. Hunter & D. S. Nice (Eds.), *Military families: Adaptation to change* (pp. 222–237). New York: Praeger.

Glick, P. C., & Lin, S. (1986). Recent changes in divorce and remarriage. *Journal of Marriage and the Family, 48,* 737–739.

Goffman, E. (1963). *Stigma: Notes on the management of spoiled identity.* Englewood Cliffs, NJ: Prentice-Hall.

Goglia, L. R. (1982). *An exploration of the long-term effects of parentification.* Unpublished Master's thesis, Georgia State University.

Goglia, L. R. (1986). *Personality characteristics of adult children of alcoholics.* Doctoral dissertation, Georgia State University.

Goglia, L. R., Jurkovic, G. J., Burt, A. M., & Burge-Callaway, K. G. (1992). Generational boundary distortions by adult children of alcoholics: child-as parent and child-as-mate. *American Journal of Family Therapy, 20,* 291–299.

Gordon, M. (Ed.). (1983). *The American family in social-historical perspective* (3rd ed.). New York: St. Martin's Press.

Gordon, S., Ungerleider, A., & Smith, G. L. (Eds.). (1991). *1991 uniformed services almanac* (33rd ed). Falls Church, VA: Uniformed Services Almanac.

Gottman, J. M. (1995). *Why marriages succeed or fail, and how you can make yours last.* New York: Fireside Press.

Gottman, J. M., & Dedaire, J. (2001). *The relationship cure: A five-step guide for building better connections with family, friends, and lovers.* New York: Crown.

Gottman, J. M., & Silver, N. (2000). *The seven principles for making marriage work.* Three Rivers, MI: Three Rivers Press.

Gouldner, A. W. (1960). The norm of reciprocity: A preliminary statement. *American Sociological Review, 25,* 161–178.

Greenleaf, B. K. (1978). *Children through the ages: A history of childhood.* New York: McGraw-Hill.

Grollman, E. A., & Sweder, G. L. (1986). *The working parent dilemma: How to balance the responsibilities of children and careers.* Boston: Beacon Press.

Grych, J., & Fincham, F. (1990). Marital conflict and children's adjujstment: A cognitive contextual framework. *Psychological Bulletin, 108,* 267–290.

Hairston, C. (1998). The forgotten parent: Understanding the forces that influence incarcerated fathers' relationships with their children. *Child Welfare, 77,* 617–639.

Haley, J. (1976). *Problem-solving therapy* (2nd ed). San Francisco: Jossey-Bass.

Hansson, R. O. (1994). *Relationships in old age: Coping with the challenge of transition.* New York: Columbia Press.

Hareven, T. (1989). Historical changes in children's networks in the family and community. In D. Belle (Ed.), *Children's social networks and social supports* (pp. 15–36). New York: Wiley.

Hart, A. D. (1997). *Helping children survive divorce: What to expect, how to help.* Dallas, TX: Word Publishing.

Haymon, S. W. (1996). *My turn: Caring for aging parents and other elderly loved ones: A daughter's perspective.* Tallahassee, FL: Magnolia Productions.

Henriques, Z. W. (1982). *Imprisoned mothers and their children.* Washington, DC: University Press of America.

Hertz, R. (1986). *More than equals: Women and men in dual-career marriages.* Berkeley, CA: University of California Press.

Hetherington, E. M. (1989). Coping with family transitions: Winners, losers, and survivors. *Child Development, 60,* 1–14.

Hetherington, E. M. (Ed.). (1999). *Coping with divorce, single parenting, and remarriage: A risk and resiliency perspective.* Mahwah, NJ: Lawrence Erlbaum.

Hetherington, E. M., & Clingempeel, G. (1992). Coping with marital transitions: A family systems perspective. *Monographs of the Society for Research in Child Development, 57,* (2–3, Serial No. 227).

Hetherington, E. M., Cox, M., & Cox, R. (1982). Effects of divorce on parents and children. In M. Lamb (Ed.), *Nontraditional families* (pp. 223–285). Hillsdale, NJ: Lawrence Erlbaum.

Hetherington, E. M., & Kelly, J. (2002). *For better or for worse: Divorce reconsidered.* New York: W. W. Norton.

Hetherington, E. M., Stanley-Hagan, M., & Anderson, E. R. (1989). Marital transitions: A child's perspective. *American Psychologist, 44,* 303–312.

Hewlett, S. A., & West, C. (1998). *The war against parents: What we can do for America's beleaguered moms and dads.* Boston: Houghton Mifflin.

Hobe, P. (1990). *Lovebound: Recovering from an alcoholic family.* New York: Penguin.

Hochschild, A. (1989). *The second shift: Working parents and the revolution at home.* New York: Viking/Penguiin.

Hoffman, L. W., & Nye, F. I. (1974). *Working mothers.* San Francisco: Jossey-Bass.

Homans, G. C. (1958). Social behavior as exchange. *American Journal of Sociology, 63,* 597–600.

Homans, G. C. (1961). *Social behavior: Its elementary forms.* New York: Harcourt Brace.

Homans, G. C. (1964). Bringing men back in. *American Sociological Review, 29,* 809–818.

Houser, B. B., Berkman, S. L., & Bardsley, P. A. (1985). Sex and birth order differences in filial behavior. *Sex Roles, 13,* 641–651.

Hungerford, G. (1996). Caregivers of children whose mothers are incarcerated: A study of kinship placement. *Children Today, 24,* 23.

Inciardi, J. A., Lockwood, D., & Pottinger, A. E. (1993). *Women and crack-cocaine.* New York: Macmillan.

Jensen, L., & Chitose, Y. (1994). Today's second generation: Evidence from the 1990 U.S. Census. *International Migration Review, 28,* 714–735.

Johnson, P. L., & O'Leary, K. D. (1987). Parental behavior patterns and conduct disorders in girls. *Journal of Abnormal Child Psychology, 15,* 573–581.

Johnston, J. R., Gonzalez, R., & Campbell, L. E. (1987). Ongoing post-divorce conflict and child disturbance. *Journal of Abnormal Child Psychology, 15,* 497–509.

Jones, M. B., Offord, D. R., & Abrams, N. (1980). Brothers, sisters and antisocial behavior. *British Journal of Psychiatry, 136,* 139–145.

Jones, R. A., & Wells, M. (1996). An empirical study of parentification and personality. *American Journal of Family Therapy, 24,* 145–151.

Jurkovic, G. J. (1997). *Lost childhoods: The plight of the parentified child.* New York: Brunner/Mazel.

Jurkovic, G. J. (1998). Destructive parentification in families: Causes and consequences.In L. L'Abate (Ed.), *Family psychopathology.* New York: Guilford Press.

Jurkovic, G. J., Jessee, E. D., & Goglia, L. R. (1991). Treatment of parental children and their families: Conceptual and technical issues. *American Journal of Family Therapy, 19,* 302–314.

Kamo, Y. (2000). Racial and ethnic differences in extended family households. *Sociological Perspectives, 43,* 211–230.

Karpel, M. A. (1976). Intrapsychic and interpersonal processes in the parentification of children. Doctoral dissertation, University of Massachusetts, 1976. *Dissertation Abstracts International, 38* (University Microfilms No. 77–15, 090).

Kaslow, F. W. (Ed.). (1993). *The military family in peace and war.* New York: Springer.

Kaslow, F. W., & Ridenour, R. I. (1984). *The military family: Dynamics and treatment.* New York: Guilford Press.

Kauffman, K. (2001). Mothers in prison. *Corrections Today, 63,* 62–65.

Kenkel, W. F. (1977). *The family in perspective.* Santa Monica, CA: Goodyear.

Kerbo, H. R. (1996). *Social stratification and inequality.* Boston, MA: WCB/McGraw-Hill.

Komarovsky, M. (1962). *Blue-collar marriage.* New Haven: Vintage.

Kritsberg, W. (1985). *The adult children of alcoholics syndrome.* Deerfield Beach, FL: Health Communications.

Kubler-Ross, E. (1969). *On death and dying.* New York: Macmillan.

Lackie, B. (1983). The families of origin of social workers. *Clinical Social Work Journal, 11,* 309–322.

Landale, N. S. (1996). Immigration and the family: An overview. In A. Booth, A. C. Crouter, & N. S. Landale (Eds.), *Immigration and the family: Research and policy on U.S. immigrants.* Hillsdale, NJ: Lawrence Erlbaum.

Lasch, C. (1995). *Haven in a heartless world: The family beseiged.* New York: W. W. Norton.

Lederer, W. J. (1961). *A nation of sheep.* New York: W. W. Norton.

Li, S., Lutzke, J., Sandler, I., & Ayers, T. S. (1995, June). Structure and specificity of negative life event catregories for bereaved children. Poster presented at the Biennial Conference of the Society for Commmunity Research and Action, Chicago, IL.

Lisansky, E. (1958). The woman alcoholic. *Annals of the American Academy of Political and Social Sciences, 315,* 73–82.

Lloyd, C. B. (1994). Investing in the next generation: The implications of high fertility at the level of the family. *Reseach division working papers No. 63.* New York: Population Council.

Lollock, L. (2000). The foreign born population in the United States: Population characteristics. *Current Population Reports,* P20–534. Washington, DC: U.S. Census Bureau.

Long, P. (1986). Growing up military: separation, moves, new beginnings—that's the norm for military brats. *Psychology Today, 20,* 30.

Lutzke, J. R., Ayers, T. S., Sandler, I. N., & Barr, A. (1997). Risks and interventions for the parentally bereaved child. In S. A. Walchik & I. N. Sandler (Eds.), *Handbook of children's coping: Linking theory and intervention* (pp. 215–243). New York: Plenum Press.

Maccoby, E. E., & Mnookin, R. H. (1992). *Dividing the child: Social and legal dilemmas of custody.* Cambridge, MA: Harvard University Press.

Madanes, C. (1980). Protection, paradox and pretending. *Family Process, 19,* 457–470.

Madanes, C. (1981). *Strategic family therapy*. San Francisco: Jossey-Bass.

Marsh, D. T. (1992). *Families and mental illness*. New York: Praeger.

Marsh, D. T. (1998) *Serious mental illness and the family*. New York: John Wiley.

Marsh, D. T., & Dickens, R. M. (1997). *Troubled journey: Coming to terms with the mental illness of a sibling or parent*. New York: Tarcher/Putnam.

Martin, J. I. (1995). Intimacy, loneliness, and openness to feelings in adult children of alcoholics. *Health and Social Work, 20,* 52–59.

Marx, K. (1906). *Capital: A critique of political economy*. New York: Random House.

Matthews, S. H. (1995). Gender and the division of filial responsibility between lone sisters and their brothers. *Journal of Gerontology: Social Sciences*, 50B: 5) S312–S319.

Matuk, L. C. (1996). Alcohol use by newcomers. *American Journal of Health Behavior, 20,* 42–49.

Mayers, R. S., Kail, B. L., & Watts, T. D. (1993). *Hispanic substance abuse*. Springfield, IL: Charles C. Thomas.

McDonough, P. M. (1994). Buying and selling higher education: The social construction of the college applicant. *Journal of Higher Education, 65,* 427–446,

McDonough, P. M. (1997) *Choosing colleges: How social class and schools structure opportunity*. Albany: State University of New York Press.

McGoldrick, M., Pearce, J. K., & Giordano, J. (1982). *Ethnicity and family therapy*. New York: Guilford.

McLanahan, S. (1999). Father absence and the welfare of children. In E. M. Hetherington (Ed.), *Coping with divorce, single parenting and remarriage*. Mahwah, NJ: Lawrence Erlbaum.

Mead, G. (1934). *Mind, self and society*. Chicago: University of Chicago Press.

Medrich, E., Roizen, J., Rubin, V., & Buckley, S. (1982). *The serious business of growing up: A study of children's lives outside school*. Berkeley: University of California Press.

Merton, R. (1957). Bureaucratic structure and personality. In R. K. Merton (Ed.), *Social theory and social structure* (pp. 195–206). Glencoe, IL: Free Press.

Miller, T. W., Martin, W., & Jay, L. L. (1991). Clinical issues in readaptation for Persian Gulf veterans. *Psychiatric Annals, 21,* 684–686.

Mindel, C. H., Habenstein, R. W., & Wright, R., Jr. (1998). *Ethnic families in America: Patterns and variations* (4th ed.). Upper Saddle River, NJ: Prentice-Hall.

Mintz, S., & Kellogg, S. (1988). *Domestic revolutions: A social history of American family life*. New York: Free Press.

Minuchin, S. (1974). *Families and family therapy*. Cambridge: MA: Harvard University Press.

Minuchin, S., Montalvo, B., Guerney, B. G., Jr., Rosman, B. L., & Schumer, F. (1967). *Families of the slums*. New York: Basic Books.

Minuchin, S., Rosman, B. L., & Baker, L. (1978). *Psychosomatic families: Anorexia nervosa in context*. Cambridge, MA: Harvard University Press.

Nasaw, D. (1985). *Children of the city: At work and at play*. New York: Doubleday.

Newcomb, M. D., Stollman, G. D., & Vargas, J. (1995). Adult children of alcoholics in and out of psychotherapy: Issues of intimacy and interpersonal relationships. *Journal of Applied Social Psychology, 25,* 279–296.

Newman, K. S. (1989). *Falling from grace: The experience of downward mobility in the American middle class.* New York: Vintage.

Nielson, L. (1999). College age students with divorced parents: Facts and fiction. *College Student Journal, 33,* 543–572.

Nye, F., Carlson, J., & Garrett, G. (1970) Family size, interaction, affect and stress. *Journal of Marriage and the Family, 32,* 216–226.

Parsons, T., & Bales, R. F. (1955). *Family, socialization and interaction process.* Glencoe, IL: Free Press.

Pearlman, C. A., Jr. (1970). Separation reactions of married women. *American Journal of Psychiatry, 126,* 946–950.

Peek, C. J., & Trezona, P. (1984). The caretaker syndrome: A matter of status and eligibility. Paper presented at the sixth annual conference of the Society for Descriptive Psychology, Boulder, CO.

Pollock, G. H. (1978). On siblings, childhood sibling loss, and creativity. *The Annual of Psychoanalysis, 6,* 423–436. New York: International Universities Press.

Pollock, L. (1983). *Forgotten children.* New York: Cambridge University Press.

Popenoe, D. (1988). *Disturbing the nest: Family change and decline in modern societies.* New York: deGruyter.

Popenoe, D. (1996). *Life without father.* New York: Free Press.

Portes, A., & Rumbaut, R. G. (1996). *Immigrant America.* Berkeley, CA: University of California Press.

Prinz, R., & West, M. O. (1987). Paraental alcoholism and childhood psychopathology. *Psychological Bulletin, 102,* 204–254.

Ray, V. (1989). *Design for growth.* New York: Harper & Row.

Rossi, A. S. (1972). Family development in a changing world. *American Journal of Psychiatry, 128,* 108.

Rousseau, J. J. (1993). *Emile* (originally published in 1762). Trans. Barbara Foxley. London: Everyman.

Rumbaut, R. G. (1994). The crucible within: Ethnic identity, self-esteem, and segmented assimilation among children of immigrants. *International Migration Review 28,* 748–794.

Rubin, L. B. (1992). *Worlds of pain: Life in the working class.* New York: Basic Books.

Rubin. L. B. (1994). *The transcendent child: Tales of triumph over the past.* New York: HarperCollins.

Rubin, L. B. (1995). *Families on the fault line: America's working class speaks about the family, the economy, race, and ethnicity.* New York: Harperperennial Library.

Ryan, W. (1976). *Blaming the victim.* New York: Vintage.

Ryff, C. D. (1996). *The parental experience of midlife.* Chicago: University of Chicago Press.

Samuels, A. (1988). Parental death in childhood. In S. Altschul (Ed.), *Childhood bereavement and its aftermath.* Madison, WI: International Universities Press.

Sandler, I. N., Rameriz, R., & Reynolds, K. D. (1986, August). *Life stress for children of divorce, bereaved and asthmatic children.* Poster presented at the American Psychological Association Convention, Washington, DC.

Schneller, D. (1976). *The prisoner's family: A study of the effects of imprisonment on the families of the prisoners.* San Francisco: R & E Research.

Scurfield, R. M., & Tice, S. (1991, April). Acute psycho-social intervention strategies with medical and psychiatric evacuees of "Operation Desert Storm" and their families. *Operation Desert Storm Clinical Packet (ODS-CP).* Written and compiled by The National Center for Post-Traumatic Stress Disorder. Washington, DC.

Seelbach, W. C. (1997). Gender differences in expectations for filial responsibility. *The Gerontologist, 17,* 421–425.

Segrin, C., & Menees, M. M. (1996). The impact of coping styles and family communication on the social skills of children of alcoholics. *Journal of Studies on Alcohol, 57,* 29–33.

Seixas, J. S., & Youcha, G. (1985). *Children of alcoholism.* New York: Harper & Row.

Sessions, M. W., & Jurkovic, G. J. (1986). *The Parentification Questionnaire.* (Available from Gregory J. Jurkovic, Department of Psychology, Georgia State University, University Plaza, Atlanta, GA 30303.)

Shaw, R. (1998). *Prisoners' children: What are the issues?* New York: Routledge.

Sher, K. (1997). Psychological characteristics of children of alcoholics. *Alcohol Health and Research World, 21,* 247–254.

Silverman, P., & Worden, W. (1993). Children's reactions to the death of a parent. In M. Stroebe, W. Stroebe, & R. Hansson, (Eds.), *Handbook of bereavement: Theory, research and intervention* (pp. 300–316). New York: Cambridge University Press.

Silverstein, M. P., Parrott, T. M., & Bengtson, V. L. (1995). Factors that predispose middle-aged sons and daughters to provide social support to older parents. *Journal of Marriage and the Family, 57,* 465–475.

Skolnick. A. (1991). *Embattled paradise: The American family in an age of uncertainty.* New York: Basic Books.

Smith, K. (2000). Who's minding the kids? Child care arrangements. Current Population Reports. Washington, DC: United States Census Bureau (P70–70).

Sorrentino, C. (1990). The changing family in international perspective. *Monthly labor review, 113,* 41–58.

Sroufe, L. A., & Ward, J. J. (1980). Seductive behavior of mothers of toddlers: Occurrence, correlates, and family origins. *Child Development, 51,* 1222–1229.

Stacey, J. (1993). Good riddance to "the family": A response to David Popenoe. *Journal of Marriage and the Family, 55,* 545–547.

Stack, C. B. (1974). *All our kin: strategies for survival in the black community.* New York: Harper and Row.

Stanton, M. D., & Todd, T. C. (1982). *Family therapy of drug abuse and addiction.* New York: Guilford Press.

Stierlin, H. (1974). *Separating parents and adolescents: A perspective on running away, schizophrenia, and waywardness.* New York: Quadrangle.

Strauss, A. (1978). *Negotiations: Varieties, contexts, processes and social order.* San Francisco: Jossey-Bass.

Stromquist, N. P. (1989). Determinants of educational participation and achievement of women in the third world: A review of the evidence and a theoretical critique. *Review of Educational Research, 59,* 143–183.

Sugar, M. H. (1994). *When mothers work, who pays?* Westport, CT: Bergin & Garvey.

Swan, H. H., & Houston, V. (1995). *Alone after school: A self-care guide for latchkey children and their parents.* Englewood Cliffs, NJ: Prentice-Hall.

Swann, L. A. (1992). *Families of black prisoners.* New York: McGraw-Hill.

Teachman, J., & Paasch, K. (1994). Financial impact of divorce on children and their families. *The Future of Children, 4,* 63–83.

Temin, C. (2001). Let us consider the children. *Corrections Today, 63,* 66–68.

Teyber, E. (2001). *Helping children cope with divorce.* San Francisco, CA: Jossey-Bass.

Thibaut, J. W., & Kelley, H. H.(1959). *The social psychology of groups.* New York: John Wiley.

Thomas, W. I., & Thomas, D. S. (1928). *The child in America.* New York: Knopf.

Thomas, W. I., & Znanecki, F. (1958). *The Polish peasant in Europe and America* (Vols. 1 and 2). New York: Dover.

Toffler, A. (1970). *Future shock.* New York: Bantam.

Toffler, A. (1984). *The third wave.* New York: Bantam.

Truong, A. T. (2001). *Exploring parentification of children in the context of Vietnamese families.* Unpublished master's thesis, San Jose State University.

U.S. Census Bureau (2000). *Statistical Abstract of the United States: The National Data Book.* Washington, DC: U.S. Government Printing Office.

U.S. Department of Justice (1998). *Bureau of Justice statistics sourcebook of criminal justice statistics.* Washington, DC: U.S. Government Printing Office.

Valenzuela, A. (1999). Gender roles and settlement activities among children and their immigrant families. *American Behavioral Scientist, 42,* 720–742.

Valleau, M. P., Bergner, R. M., & Horton, C. B. (1995). Parentification and caretaker syndrome: An empirical investigation. *Family Therapy, 22,* 157–163.

Van Kleeck, M. (1913). *Artificial flower makers.* New York: Survey Association. Cited in R. Baxandall, L. Gordon, & S. Reverby (Eds.), *America's working women: A documentary.* (1976). New York: Vintage.

Veblen, T. (1928). *The theory of the leisure class.* New York: Vanguard.

Vinovskis, M. (1988). *An "epidemic" of adolescent pregnancy?: Some historical and policy considerations.* New York: Oxford University Press.

Wagner, M. E., Schubert, H. J. P., & Schubert, D. S. P. (1979). Sibship-constellation effects on psychosocial development, creativity, and health. In H. W. Reese & L. P. Libsitt (Eds.), *Advances in child development and behavior* (pp. 58–155). New York: Academic Press.

Wagner, M. E., Schubert, H. J. P., & Schubert, D. S. P. (1985). Family size effects: A review. *Journal of Genetic Psychology, 146,* 65–78.

Waite, L., Bachrach, C., Hindin, M., Thomson, E., & Thornton, A. (2000). *Ties that bind: Perspectives on marriage and cohabitation.* New York: Aldine de Gruyter.

Waller, M. B. (1993). *Crack affected children.* Thousand Oaks, CA: Sage.

Wallerstein, J. S. (1985). The overburdened child: Some long-term consequences of divorce. *Social Work, 30,* 116–123.

Wallerstein, J. S., & Blakeslee, S. (1989). *Second chances: Men, women and children a decade after divorce.* New York: Ticknor & Fields.

Wallerstein, J. S., & Kelly, J. B. (1980). *Surviving the breakup: How children and parents cope with divorce.* New York: Basic Books.

Wallerstein, J. S., Lewis, J. M., & Blakeslee, S. (2000). *The unexpected legacy of divorce.* New York: Hyperion.

Walster, E., Walster, G. W., & Traupmann, J. (1978). *Equity: Theory and research.* Boston: Allyn & Bacon.

Warshak, R. A. (1986). Father-custody and child development: A review and analysis of psychological research. *Behavioral Sciences and the Law, 4,* 2–17.

Wasow, M. (1995). *The skipping stone: Ripple effects of mental illness on the family.* Palo Alto, CA: Science & Behavior Books.

Watanabe, H. K. (1985). A survey of adolescent military family members' self-image. *Journal of Youth and Adolescence, 14,* 99–107.

Weber, M. (1956). *Gesammelte Augsaetze zur Soziologie and Sozialpolitik,* pp. 412ff. English translation in Mayer, J. P., *Max Weber and German Politics,* 2nd ed. (pp. 126–128). London: Faber and Faber.

Wegscheider, S. (1981). *Another chance: Hope and health for the alcoholic family.* Palo Alto, CA: Science and Behavior Books.

Wegscheider-Cruse, S. (1985). *Choicemaking for co-dependents, adult children and spirituality seekers.* Pompano Beach, FL: Health Communications.

Weiss, R. S. (1979). Growing up a little faster: The experience of growing up in a single parent household. *Journal of Social Issues, 35,* 97–111.

Weiss, R. S. (1981). *Going it alone: The family life and social situation of the single parent.* New York: Basic Books.

Weitzman, L. (1985). *The divorce revolution: The unexpected social and economic consequences for women and children in America.* New York: Free Press.

Wellman, B. (1988). Structural analysis: From method and metaphor to theory and substance. In B. Wellman & S. D. Berkowitz (Eds.), *Social structures* (pp. 19–61). Cambridge: Cambridge University Press.

Wells, M., Glickauf-Hughes, C., & Jones, R. (1999). Codependency: A grassroots construct's relationship to shame-proneness, low self-esteem, and childhood parentification. *American Journal of Family Therapy, 27,* 63–71.

West, E., & Petrik, P. (1992). *Small world: Children and adolescents in America, 1850–1950.* Lawrence, KS: University Press of Kansas.

West, L., Mercer, S. O., & Altheimer, E. (1993). Operation Desert Storm: The response of a social work outreach team. *Social Work in Health Care, 19,* 81–98.

West, M. L., & Keller, A. E. (1991). Parentification of the child: A case study of Bowlby's compulsive care-giving attachment pattern. *American Journal of Psychotherapy, 45,* 425–431.

Whitehead, B. (1993, April). Dan Quayle was right. *Atlantic Monthly, 271,* 47–84.

Whitfield, C. I. (1987). *Healing the child within.* Pompano Beach, FL: Health Communications.

Wholey, D. (1988). *Becoming your own parent.* New York: Doubleday.

Wiggins, D. (1985). The play of slave children in the plantation communities of the old South, 1820–60. In N. Hiner & J. Hawes (Eds.), *Growing up in America: Children in historical perspective* (pp. 173–192). Urbana, IL: University of Illinois Press.

Wilson, W. J. (1987). *The truly disadvantaged.* Chicago: University of Chicago Press.

Winton, C. (1995). *Frameworks for studying families.* Guilford, CT: Dushkin.

Woititz, J. G. (1983). *Adult children of alcoholics.* Pompano Beach, FL: Health Communications.

Wolin, S. J., & Wolin, S. (1994). *The resilient self: How survivors of troubled families rise above adversity.* New York: Villard.

Wolkin, J. R. (1984). Childhood parentification: An exploration of longterm effects. *Dissertation Abstracts International, 45,* 2707 (University Microfilms No. 84-24601). Unpublished doctoral dissertation, Georgia State University, Atlanta, GA.

Wrong, D. (1961). The oversocialized conception of man in modern sociology. *American Sociological Review, 26,* 184–193.

Young, D., & Smith, C. (2000). When moms are incarcerated: The needs of children, mothers, and caregivers. *Families in Society, 81,* 130–141.

Zhou, M. (1997). Growing up American: The challenge confronting immigrant children and children of immigrants. *Annual Review of Sociology, 23,* 63–95.

Index